JUSTICE AND CRIME

The Right Honourable The Lord Emslie,
M.B.E., P.C., L.L.D., F.R.S.E.

JUSTICE AND CRIME

Essays in Honour of The Right Honourable The Lord Emslie,
M.B.E., P.C., L.L.D., F.R.S.E.

Edited by

Robert F. Hunter., LL. B., Advocate

T&T CLARK
EDINBURGH

T&T CLARK
59 GEORGE STREET
EDINBURGH EH2 2LQ
SCOTLAND

First Published 1993

ISBN 0 567 0 9644 0

British Library Cataloguing in Publication Data
A catalogue record for this book
is available from the British Library

Typeset by Trinity Typesetting, Edinburgh
Printed and bound in Great Britain by
Biddles Ltd, Guildford and King's Lynn

CONTENTS

FOREWORD

The Rt. Hon. Lord Hope

I have had the privilege of observing George Emslie's career at close quarters for over a quarter of a century. So it gives me a particular pleasure to be able to contribute a foreword to this volume of essays which have been written in recognition of his contribution to the law of Scotland over so many years. Not only can I join with all the other contributors in this expression of admiration and respect. It enables me also to reminisce and to recall the deep impression which he has made on me at various stages in my own career.

By a lucky chance I had the opportunity of appearing with him as counsel within only a few months after being admitted to the Faculty. By then he was, of course, already at the height of his powers as an advocate and was within a few months of being elected Dean of Faculty. The case was, as all cases are, important to the client, although it was not of sufficient importance to be reported in any of the recognised Law Reports. I still have a cutting from the next day's Scotsman which reminds me that it was all about books from the Newbattle Collection which had been put into the care of the National Library of Scotland by the Marquess of Lothian's Trustees. A dispute arose when the Trustees wanted the books to be returned to them. The case had come out on the Procedure Roll before Lord Avonside, and at very short notice I was instructed to appear for the Trustees. I found myself in distinguished company, although there was scarcely room for all of us ranged along the Bar in Court No. 8. The National Library were represented by the

Honourable H.S. Keith QC and by J.J. Clyde, Advocate, as they then were. On my side were G.C. Emslie QC and J.P.H. Mackay QC. Fortunately for all involved my only function was to 'cover' these two Silks, because in those days the rule was that no Silk could appear without a junior. It was to John Speirs, Advocates Clerk, in whose stable we three all were that I owed the experience of being able to observe George Emslie's skills as an advocate for the first time in my own practice at the Bar. His argument, according to the Scotsman, was the simple one that the Library's claim failed on a point of relevancy. My cutting tells me that at the end of the debate Lord Avonside made avizandum, and I have no record or recollection of the result. That does not matter now. What was of lasting value to me was to observe the precision and courtesy with which the debate was conducted, and to appreciate for the first time a point which was to come back to me again and again over the years that the secret of fine presentation in court is careful preparation in advance.

A few months later George Emslie was elected Dean of Faculty, unopposed, with A. M. Johnston QC (later Lord Dunpark), as one of his sponsors. There then began what I think for him was the most demanding period of his life at the Bar. He was very frequently in court, instructed regularly by the National Coal Board as the leader of a team comprising himself and James Mackay as the Seniors and Malcolm Morison and James Clyde as the Juniors. There were of course many other cases in which he was involved as well, and he had a monument of opinion work since the opinion of the Dean of Faculty has always been, by tradition, the ultimate authority short of – perhaps even beyond – an opinion of the court. I found myself appearing in coal mining cases with increasing frequency, at first on the other side on the instructions of Evan Weir WS for the National Union of Mineworkers and then, when Malcolm Morison took Silk and there was a vacancy at the junior end of the team, on behalf of the Coal Board. It is hard to decide which was the more demanding role – to appear with him or against him. On either side there was no room for the second best, and the problem about being on his side was that one's inadequacies were the more likely to be found out.

The abiding memory of those days is of George Emslie's approach to written pleadings. Of course his mastery of the art of cross-examination and of the equally difficult art of taking evidence-in-chief in a case for the defence was a pleasure to watch. The first question was whether to lead evidence at all. The next question was, if there was to be evidence, how to restrict it to only what was needed for success. Usually it was the medical witness who was called. Only if we were in real trouble would he risk calling the manager of the mine, and if he did the technique was to exude through the words of the witness supreme confidence that all steps required by the statute and regulations had been taken. But the cases were as often as not won on the pleadings. The skill was to spot the defect in the relevancy of the opponent's case, which in those days was almost always a point worth taking. Then one had to be careful to aver as little as possible for the defence. These tactics were put into effect by a careful use of language, and since the practice was for every adjustment by Junior Counsel to be approved by Senior Counsel before it was intimated by the Coal Board there was a constant course of tuition for me in how to develop this skill. I still have the form of words which he prepared for use in all cases brought under section 48(1) of the Mines and Quarries Act 1954, marked by me with the words 'Dean's adjustment', to meet the developing case law about what was to be expected in evidence from the manager. There were many other examples of his skill as a leader which set the standard for his generation at the Bar. The great lesson was that every step in written pleading was to be taken with care and precision if a sound foundation was to be laid for the case.

The sense of loss when he was appointed to the Bench in 1970 was very great, but it was already clear that his time in the Outer House would be short and that he would succeed Lord Clyde as Lord President. That is indeed what happened, and at the beginning of the summer term in 1972 he took his seat in the First

Division Court Room where he was to remain as President for seventeen years. Almost at once he set about the major task of modernising the administration of the Court of Session and the High Court of Justiciary. He also began to review the provisions of the Rules of Court, which were failing to meet with what was required to keep pace with an increasing volume of work. The merging of the posts of Principal Clerk of Session and Principal Clerk of Justiciary was one of the reforms for which he was responsible. This reflected a reform some 150 years earlier by which the then separate office of Lord Justice General was thereafter to be held by the Lord President. In this case, however, the reform went very much deeper, since the entire machinery of the system of administration was thoroughly reviewed and brought up to date.

One of the earliest changes to the Rules of Court was the introduction of a new rule about the time for lodging of the appendix in causes awaiting hearing in the Inner House. This was Rule of Court 294A introduced by Act of Sederunt on 19th December 1972. Its aim was in part to weed out of the Court's programme surplus appeals which were not to be persisted in, and in part to speed up and improve the presentation of those cases which were to be argued. The rule was exacting in its requirements, and it was a breach of it which brought together again in the First Division the team which had worked for so long for the National Coal Board – only this time George Emslie was on the Bench. James Mackay was my Senior, and his motion that the Board should be excused from the consequences of its failure to lodge the appendix caused great anxiety, not only to us but also to the clerk in the Board's Legal Department who had made the mistake. The motion was not opposed, but the Rule had been applied rigorously to good effect over the short period since it had been introduced. It was far from certain that the relief which was sought would be granted. This case, reported as *Comrie* v. *National Coal Board* 1974 SC 237, was a challenge to Lord Emslie's impartiality as a judge. No one had been more careful than he had to insist upon high standards and adherence to the rules. Yet the clerk whose mistake had created the difficulty had, to his knowledge, given loyal and exemplary service to the Board for many years. It would be a personal tragedy for him if the case were to be lost purely because of his mistake. The argument which was presented was listened to with great care and complete detachment, and the result remained in doubt until the end of the debate. The granting of the motion came as a huge relief. But even more memorable was the generosity of the remark by the Lord President in his opinion that this had been 'a genuine mistake or oversight on the part of a competent and experienced clerk, whose record in the matter of compliance with the Rules of Court has been without blemish'. This was a point James Mackay had not risked making, in these terms, in the debate. Thus Lord President Emslie was able with great skill to reconcile the standards which he expected from everybody with his understanding of the realities of the case.

There were, of course, many more appearances in the First Division yet to come, both in the Single Bills and in the Summar Roll, and usually at the end of each term there were petitions for the variation of trust purposes. Trust variations never seemed to summon up much enthusiasm. There was none of the sense of adventure which one encountered in the days of Lord President Clyde, by whom the system had been set up. But Single Bills were always a challenge because no one knew the Rules of Court from end to end as well as George Emslie.

And there were many memorable debates of great intensity on the Summar Roll. George Emslie's claim was that he never asked a question to which he did not already know the answer. His questions were restrained, so that, as with a good referee, play could run on with advantage. But they were never put out of idle curiosity, and frequently with one question he could change the entire atmosphere of the debate. All the great cases over which he presided are in the Reports, and they can speak for themselves about the care which he gave to each opinion and the wise and lasting influence they have had on the development of our law. Some of the lesser cases are in the Reports as well, especially in the criminal field. It was one of his few complaints that too many cases from the Criminal Appeal Court were reported. There were of course more opinions there because, unlike his predecessor, he insisted on delivering extempore judgments in almost every case which he did not take to avizandum. This was a practice which modern conditions expected of that Court, and he was not slow to adopt it or to adjust himself to the detailed preparation which is so essential if such judgments are to be given effectively without delay. I learned later for myself as an Advocate-Depute how demanding a week in the Criminal Appeal Court could be, and I also learned that there was on his part a total dedication to these demands. He gave up long hours to preparation for each week's business in that Court, and at the end of the case his mastery, whether of road traffic law or of criminal practice or of the rules of evidence, shone through the judgment which he delivered.

For a while after I had left the Crown Office I saw very little of him in Court because, like his sons Nigel and Derek, both now members of the Senior Bar, I was engaged for a year and a half in a long-running cause in another Court. When I returned from that exile it was an immense pleasure to experience again the atmosphere of the First Division under his chairmanship. But in the later years I saw more of him in private as Dean of Faculty than I did of him in Court. His insistence that the elected office of Dean was the finest compliment that the Profession could bestow was borne in on me time and time again as we met and talked together about matters of mutual concern to the Faculty and to the Court. And there were occasional moments of crisis when his sound knowledge and experience, and his understanding, were of great importance to me and through me to the Faculty. His influence for good in the Profession, by his own steady example and eye for detail, was of immense practical importance at a time of unprecedented activity in all areas of the law.

Now that he has retired and we can all reflect on what he has achieved and upon the legacy which is ours to continue, it is right that these Essays should be presented to him as a mark of admiration and respect. There is no common theme here except that of justice, which has been his central concern throughout his nineteen years on the Bench and which he has done so much to uphold. All kinds of writers are represented here, and not all that has been written need be accepted as accurate or be believed. But each essay has been written in honour of a Judge of immense skill and dignity, and it is to be hoped that the reader will share in the sense of admiration and friendship which has been their inspiration.

PREFACE

It is with great pleasure that I, on behalf of all the contributors, present this book of essays to and in honour of Lord Emslie, formerly Lord President of the Court of Session and Lord Justice-General for Scotland. It is a mark of the esteem with which Lord Emslie is regarded that there was no shortage of willing participants in this venture. Hopefully, the end result is a book that has something for everyone, from the legal historian, to the academic, student and practitioner.

George Carlyle Emslie was born on 6th December 1919. Educated at Glasgow High School and the University of Glasgow, his contemporary was another luminary in Scottish legal circles, David M. Walker. During the Second World War he was commissioned in the Argyll and Sutherland Highlanders, serving with distinction and was awarded the M.B.E. in 1946. He passed advocate in 1948 and quickly established a practice, especially in reparation cases. In 1965 the Faculty of Advocates voted him to be their leader and he remained as Dean of Faculty until his elevation to the Bench in 1970, on the death of Lord Guthrie. His tenure in the Outer House was only for two years when, on Lord Clyde's resignation, he was promoted into the Inner House as head of the First Division, there to remain until his own resignation in 1989.

The only theme running throughout this book is that of justice, a matter in which Lord Emslie has not lost interest for, whilst there was disappointment in Parliament House that his Lordship intended to resign at a relatively early age, it is heartening that, having been elevated to the peerage in 1980, Lord Emslie has not been slow to travel to London and hear causes coming before the House of

Lords. Indeed, in *D.P.P.* v. *P.* [1991] 2 A.C. 447, his Lordship was one of the majority of three Scottish Law Lords who heard an English criminal appeal, a stark contrast to the normal position of the majority of judges hearing Scottish appeals being English.

Areas covered in this volume have been the subject of recent discussion. The more important points to be borne in mind are: (1) that, *Meredith* v. *Lees* 1992 S.C.C.R. 459 was reported too late for detailed discussion to be made by Sheriff Gordon in his contribution on Corroboration; (2) that the *Lord Advocate's Reference (No. 1 of 1992)* (judgment of the High Court of Justiciary, 24th June 1992, unreported) made a new exception to the rule against hearsay in respect of computer records and thus supplements Sheriff Wilkinson's contribution on the subject – see also: Ferguson, "Computer evidence and the rule against hearsay" (1992) 37 J.L.S.S. 321; and (3) that, on war crimes, interested parties should supplement their reading of Poustie and Upton's contribution by considering the defamation case of *Gecas* v. *Scottish Television plc* (judgment of Lord Milligan, 17th July 1992, O.H., unreported) and, on the War Crimes Act 1991, an article by A.T. Richardson and one by Gabriele Ganz found respectively at (1992) 55 M.L.R. 73 and 87.

The contributors and I are especially pleased to note our thanks to Lord Emslie's successor, Lord Hope for writing the Foreword and to Lord Grieve, a lifelong friend of Lord Emslie's and companion on the Bench, for writing a short personal appreciation. The publishers have been, as ever, of great assistance in the preparation of this book.

Parliament House   R.F.H.
EDINBURGH
18th August 1992

TABLE OF CASES

TABLE OF SELECTED STATUTES

SELECTED BIBLIOGRAPHY

Alison, A. J., *Principles and Practice of the Criminal Law of Scotland* (2 vols., Edinburgh, 1832, 1833).

Anderson, *The Criminal Law of Scotland* (2nd edn., Edinburgh, 1904).

Archbold: Pleading, Evidence and Practice in Criminal Cases (43rd edn., London 1988).

Balfour, Sir James, *Practicks* (1754).

Bell, G. J., *Principles of the Law of Scotland* (10th edn. by W. Guthrie, Edinburgh, 1899).

Birks, P. and McLeod, G., *Justinian's Institutes* (London, 1987).

Blackstone, W., *Commentaries on the Laws of England* (4 vols. 1st edn., Oxford, 1705-69).

Burnett, J., *A Treatise on Various Branches of the Criminal Law of Scotland* (Edinburgh, 1811).

Clive, E. M., *The Law of Husband and Wife in Scotland* (2nd edn., Edinburgh, 1982).

Craig, T., *Jus Feudale* (Edinburgh, 1732).

Erskine, J., *An Institute of the Law of Scotland* (8th edn. by J. B. Nicholson, Edinburgh, 1870).

Gane, C. H. W., and Stoddart, C. N., *A Casebook on Scottish Criminal Law* (2nd edn., Edinburgh, 1988).

Glanville Williams, *Textbook of Criminal Law: The General Part* (2nd edn., London, 1961).

Gordon, G. H., *The Criminal Law of Scotland* (2nd edn., Edinburgh, 1978 with Supplement, 1984).

Hale, M., *Historia Placitorum Coronae: The History of the Pleas of the Crown* (2 vols., London, 1736).

Hume, D., *Commentaries on the Law of Scotland respecting Crimes* (4th edn. by B. R. Bell, Edinburgh, 1844).

Macdonald, J. H. A., *A Practical Treatise on the Criminal Law of Scotland* (5th edn., Edinburgh, 1948).

Mackenzie, Sir G., *The Laws and Customs of Scotland in Matters Criminal* (Edinburgh 1716, 1722).

Maxwell, *The Interpretation of Statutes* (12th edn., London, 1969).

Renton, R. W. and Brown, H. H., *Criminal Procedure according to the Law of Scotland* (5th edn., Edinburgh, 1983, looseleaf).

Skene, J., *Regiam Majestatem. The Auld Lawes and Constitutions of Scotland* (Edinburgh, 1609).

Smith, T. B., *A Short Commentary on the Law of Scotland* (Edinburgh, 1962).

Smith, J. C. and Hogan, B., *Criminal Law* (6th edn., London, 1988).

Stair, *The Institutions of the Law of Scotland* (5th edn. by J. S. More, Edinburgh, 1832).

Wilkinson, A. B., *The Scottish Law of Evidence* (Edinburgh, 1986).

1

STEALING FISH

The Rt. Hon the Lord Rodger of Earlsferry

Some distance to the east of Selkirk lies a stretch of water which was formerly the Lindean Reservoir but is now just a haunt of bird-watchers and anglers. Even the most dedicated local angler, however, would hesitate to describe the former reservoir as a 'fishpond'. Yet in *Pollok* v. *M'Cabe*[1] Lord Ardwall who was 'an indefatigable angler'[2] in effect decided that the reservoir was a fishpond. A study of this somewhat neglected and surprising corner of our criminal law is offered to Lord Emslie who has done so much to bring order and clarity to the system.

In 1904[3] the county council constructed the Lindean Reservoir on land purchased from a Mr Scott Plummer. The land had formerly been marshy in summer and a large pool in winter. Mr Scott Plummer reserved the shooting and fishing rights and proceeded to stock the reservoir with trout. Once in the reservoir the trout could not escape because of wire netting or grating placed across the outlet pipe. At about 3 o'clock one morning in July 1909 Mr Francis and Mr Nicholas M'Cabe were caught taking five trout by rod and line from the reservoir.

The procurator fiscal's complaint against the M'Cabes contained alternative charges of theft of the fish and of a breach of what

---

[1] (1909) 6 Adam 139; 1910 S.C.(J.) 23.
[2] J. Buchan, *Andrew Jameson Lord Ardwall* (Edinburgh and London, 1913), p. 129.
[3] Information on a board at the former reservoir.

is now the Theft Act 1607.[4] That Act makes it an offence to steal 'fisches in propir stankis and loches'. At the hearing the procurator fiscal dropped the common law theft charge and proceeded with the statutory charge alone.[5] The honorary sheriff-substitute, the future Lord Carmont,[6] dismissed the case on the ground that 'the "stank" or loch in question, from which the trout were taken, is a reservoir, the main purpose of which is to supply a district with drinking water' and that this 'reservoir or pond is not a "stank" or loch within the meaning of the act of 1607.'[7] The procurator fiscal appealed, the question for the High Court being whether the reservoir or pond was a 'stank' or loch within the meaning of the Act. The High Court said that it was and allowed the appeal.

In 1909 the statute provided:

> 'Oure Souerane Lord and Estaittis of this present parliament Considering how woddis parkis and all sorte of planting and hanyng decayes within this realme And how dowcattis ar brokin bees stollin mennis propir lochis and stankis heryit To the great hurte and prejudice of the countray and decay of policie THAIRFOIR Ratefeis and appreves all actis of parliament maid of befoir for conseruatioun of planting and policie and aganis brakeris of dowcattis steiling of beis and of fisches furth of mennis stankis and propir Lochis In the haill pointis articlis and clauses thairof And ordinis the samin to be put to executioun aganis the Controveneris thairof And forder the saidis Estaittis Statutis and Ordinis that quhasoeuir shall be fundin heireftir To brak doun his nichbouris woddis and park dyikis fenses stankis or closouris to pasture within the saidis fenses Cutte treis browme or schear grasse within the same or yit brakis

---

[4]Act 1607, c. 3; A.P.S. III, 373, c. 6. The Act was given its present title by The Statute Law Revision (Scotland) Act 1964 (c. 80), s. 2 and Sched. 2.

[5]6 Adam, at p. 140; 1910 S.C.(J.), at p. 24.

[6]The case marks Lord Carmont's début in the Law Reports. His last reported decision was given almost 56 years later in July 1965.

[7]6 Adam, at pp. 140 et seq.; 1910 S.C.(J.), at p. 24.

dowcattis Steillis Beis and fisches in propir stankis and loches Shall be callit and convenit thairfoir as a braker of the Law ather befoir the privie counsall or ony vther ordinar magistrat within this realme at the optioun of the pairtie complenar And the penaltie to be Imposit and takin of the Controvenaris befoir the saidis ordinar Inferiour Judges Aucht nocht to exceid the sowme of fourtie pundis of this Realme And the secrete counsaill to Impose sic penalteis aganis the controvenaris of this present act as eftir tryell tane in the cause they sall find the offendar to merite and deserue But preiudice alwayes of putting of all former actis maid anent the premises to executioun eftir the forme and tennour thairof.'

Since the issue in the case was one of the construction of the Act, we must try to understand what it was meant to achieve, and in particular what the terms 'propir stankis' and 'loches' were meant to cover. This, in turn, involves looking at some wider aspects of the law relating to fish and other wild creatures.

The rump of the 1607 Act which remains in force today has been rechristened the 'Theft Act 1607' and now deals only with people who steal bees and fish. Originally it seems to have been called an 'Act Anent woddis parkis planting dowcattis et cetera'[8] and it covered a rather wide range of mischief, such as breaking down fences to pasture animals on the fenced land. In addition the Act confirmed previous legislation on similar topics. It has been observed that much of the legislation of the old Scots parliament was aimed at stamping out the destruction of game.[9] Doubtless the 1607 Act and its predecessors are to be seen in this context, but, even so, it is pertinent to ask why the measure was directed at fish in proper (*i.e.* private) stanks and lochs. In particular was there some legal difficulty relating to fish in such waters? In investigating this matter the term 'fish' will be used to refer to freshwater fish.

---

[8]A.P.S. III, 373, c. 6.

[9]J. Irvine Smith and I. Macdonald, 'Criminal Law', *Introduction to Scottish Legal History* (Stair Society Publications, Vol. 20, Edinburgh, 1958), pp. 286-287.

I. Occupatio

The starting-point of any inquiry is the basic rule of Scots law which classifies fish among creatures which are 'wild and free' and so 'in the property of none'.[10] This rule, like most of the Scots law on the topic, derives from Roman law.[11] Since fish in their natural free state are owned by nobody, it follows that they cannot be stolen.[12] On the contrary, a person who takes possession of such a wild creature becomes its owner by virtue of the doctrine which we call *occupatio*.[13] Of course, so long as a fish is owned in this way, it can be stolen like any other property. So if you take and eat a fish which is in my possession and ownership, you will unquestionably be guilty of theft at common law.[14]

Even though the theory behind the doctrine of *occupatio* is the same with wild creatures as with inanimate objects, none the less in practice it works rather differently.

In the first place, by definition inanimate objects cannot remove themselves from the possession of the person who has acquired them by *occupatio*. Wild animals and fish, by contrast, can and do escape from the possession of the person who acquired them. When that happens, they regain their natural state of freedom and are once more ownerless, *res nullius*. More precisely Stair says[15] that if wild

---

[10]Viscount Stair, *Institutions of the Law of Scotland* (2nd edn., Edinburgh, 1693) II.1.5.

[11]See for instance Justinian's *Institutes* 2.1.12-13, which derives from book 2 of the *res cottidianae* attributed to Gaius. See D.41.1.3 and 5, Gaius 2 *rerum cottidianarum* and Gaius' *Institutes* 2. 67.

[12]D. Hume, *Commentaries on the Law of Scotland respecting Crimes* (4th edn. by B. R. Bell, Edinburgh, 1844), i, 82.

[13]Stair, *Institutions* II.1.33. Roman jurists did not use the term in this connexion. See, for instance, D. Daube, *Roman Law Linguistic, Social, and Philosophical Aspects* (Edinburgh, 1969), p. 13. None-the-less there is a useful article on the topic under this term by M. Kaser in *Paulys Real-Encyclopädie der Classischen Altertumswissenschaft, Supplementband* 7 (Stuttgart, 1940), col. 682, especially at cols. 684 *et seq.*

[14]*Cf.* Hume, *Commentaries*, 1, 82.

[15]*Institutions* II.i.33.

creatures 'return to their ancient wildness', owners retain possession — and hence ownership — for as long as they pursue the creature, but once they give up, possession and ownership are lost. At that point, equally, the creatures cannot be the subject of theft.

In this connexion in Scots law a second peculiarity of wild creatures emerges. In *Valentine* v. *Kennedy*[16] Sheriff Younger argued *obiter* that if an owner in effect abandoned the possession of rainbow trout and someone else took them, 'the accused would still be liable to be convicted of theft as the trout having once been owned would not revert to being *res nullius* but would become the property of the Crown.'[17]

Doubtless any of Her Majesty's law officers would be pleased to think of the rivers and lochs of Scotland gradually filling with this new crop of royal fish, but in truth the sheriff's *obiter* remark is unsound. He is relying on the rule *quod nullius est fit domini regis,* "what belongs to no-one becomes the Crown's". This rule applies in Scots law when something which has been owned is "lost, forgotten or abandoned". [18] It certainly applies to animals which the law regards as tame, i.e. animals such as sheep or dogs. If, for instance, I abandon my dog, at common law he does not become a *res nullius* but like, say, an abandoned jewel, he becomes the property of the Crown.

This rule, however, has no application to freshwater fish and similar wild creatures.[19] None of the institutional writers applies it

---

[16]1985 S.C.C.R. 89.

[17]1985 S.C.C.R., at p. 91.

[18]G. J. Bell, *Principles of the Law of Scotland* (10th edn. by W. Guthrie, Edinburgh, 1899), para. 1291; *Lord Advocate* v. *University of Aberdeen* 1963 S.C. 533. The sheriff gives the doctrine a narrower scope than the *Aberdeen University* case vouches.

[19]Sheriff Younger (1985 S.C.C.R. 91) inclines to the correct view that a trout cannot be tamed. The classifications are fixed by law. So, for instance, Stair tells us that tame creatures 'are not comprehended' among free creatures: *Institutions* II.1.33.

to them and indeed Erskine says distinctly of wild creatures, including fish, that 'so soon as they get free from their confinement, he who shall have first laid hold of them, after the former proprietor has given over the pursuit, acquires their property.'[20] This reasoning presupposes that when the owner gives up the fish, they revert to being *res nullius*. The law takes that view because creatures of a species which it classifies as wild by nature are regarded as being in their ordinary state when they are wild. That ordinary state may be interrupted by the creature being taken into, and kept in, possession, but when the possession comes to an end the creature becomes once more 'wild and free'. It follows that, contrary to what Sheriff Younger says, if an owner were to abandon his rainbow trout by allowing them to escape, they would not become the property of the Crown. They would instead be ownerless. A person who took them would not be guilty of theft, but would become their new owner.

Since, then, fish are owned only so long as they are possessed, it is important to see in which circumstances a person may be said to possess a fish.

II. Possession of fish

Stair tells us that 'The creatures are understood to be free while they are not within the power of any; but fishes within ponds are proper, and fowls, though never so wild, while they are in custody.'[21] Stair's basic proposition seems to be that creatures lose their freedom when they are within someone's power, the examples of fish in ponds and fowls in custody being examples of that proposition being applied in practice. This corresponds broadly with what is said in the Roman texts which talk of creatures being possessed

---

[20]J. Erskine, *An Institute of the Law of Scotland* (8th edn. by J. B. Nicolson, Edinburgh, 1871) II.1.10, citing D.41.1.3.2, Gaius 2 *rerum cottidianarum*.
[21] *Institutions* II.1.33.

when they are in someone's *custodia*[22] — probably best translated in this context as 'control'.[23]

Stair says that fish in ponds are owned. The point is stated more precisely, if a trifle pedantically, in a manuscript version of the same passage which says that 'fishes within *proper* ponds are proper'.[24] In other words if you own a pond with fish in it, you own the fish because you possess them — they are within your power.

In the second edition of his *Institutions* Stair refers at the end of this paragraph to a number of Roman law texts, including D.41.2.3.14. This text comes from book 54 of Paul's edictal commentary where, for reasons which remain unclear, Paul inserted a major excursus on possession and *usucapio*.[25] The text, which was part of that excursus, records the views of the younger Nerva, a jurist who wrote in the first century A.D.[26] Just before this text the Digest bears to record Nerva's basic approach: we possess moveables as long as they are in our control (*custodia*). The Digest explains the idea of control: 'that is, as long as we can, if we wish, take natural possession of them'.[27] By 'natural possession' is meant physical possession and the passage is saying that we possess moveables if we could, if we wished, take physical possession of them.

Many modern scholars consider that this passage, and in particular the explanation referring to natural possession, have been altered

---

[22]See for instance Justinian's *Institutes* 2.1.12; D.41.2.3.13, Paul 54 *ad edictum.*

[23]So P. Birks, G. McLeod, *Justinian's Institutes* (London, 1987), p. 57.

[24]Adv. M.S. 25.1.10, National Library of Scotland. Emphasis added.

[25]See O. Lenel, *Das Edictum Perpetuum* (3rd edn., Leipzig, 1927), pp. 24 *et seq.*, and recently L. Winkel, '*Usucapio pro suo* and the Classification of the *causae usucapionis* by the Roman Jurists', *New Perspectives in the Roman Law of Property* (ed. P. Birks, Oxford, 1989), p. 215.

[26]W. Kunkel, *Herkunft und Soziale Stellung der Römischen Juristen* (2nd edn., Graz, Vienna, Cologne, 1967), p. 130.

[27]D.41.2.3.13, Paul 54 *ad edictum.*

to give the views of Justinian's sixth-century compilers rather than those of Nerva.[28] There is much to be said for that view on linguistic grounds and because, as we shall see, the reasoning in it does not seem to be applied in the text which follows and which particularly interests us. There is, however, no need to reach a final decision on that point.

At all events, having said that possession depends on control, and having given certain examples, in the passage cited by Stair the Digest continues:

> 'Likewise wild beasts which we shut up in pens (*vivaria*) and fish which we put in fish-ponds (*piscinae*) are possessed by us. But those fish which are in a stretch of standing water (*stagnum*), or wild animals which roam in woods with a boundary fence are not possessed by us since they have been left in their natural state of freedom: otherwise even if someone bought a wood, he would be considered to possess all the wild animals and that is wrong.'

Nerva's first examples are of animals shut up in pens (*vivaria*) and fish put into fishponds (*piscinae*). *Vivaria* are places constructed for keeping wild animals, usually for eating. *Piscinae* or artificial fishponds in particular were a common feature of grander Roman houses.[29] The examples are therefore far from academic. It is noteworthy that Nerva is contemplating animals which have been put into the pens and fish which have been put into the fishponds. Indeed since pens and fishponds are man-made, the creatures must have been put into them. Once in the pen or fishpond the creatures

---

[28]E. Levy, E. Rabel, *Index Interpolationum*, Vol. 3 (Weimar, 1935), col. 183.

[29]For *piscinae* and *vivaria* see for instance J.P.V.D. Balsdon, *Life and Leisure in Ancient Rome* (London, 1969), pp. 208 *et seq.* with references. D.41.2.3.14 was cited in *Copland* v. *Maxwell* (1868) 7 M. 142; (1871) 9 M. (H.L.) 1 and gave rise to discussion of what could be comprehended by the term *piscina*. See in particular the Lord Justice-Clerk (Patton) at 7 M. 148.

are under the control of the owner. Indeed the owner would pass the particular test of being someone who could at any moment take hold of an animal or net a fish.

Erskine seems to be following the approach in this text when he says that 'Deer inclosed in a park, fish in a pond, or birds in a volary, as they cannot be said to retain any longer their natural liberty, become the property of him who has brought them under his power; and consequently, whoever carries them off from the owner commits theft; 1474 c. 61'.[30] The reference to the statute seems *de trop* since common law theft would be committed by anyone taking the property of another. That was the view of Hume who argued that wild animals kept and confined in this way 'may certainly be stolen'.[31]

Nerva next proceeds to the more difficult case of fish which are in a *stagnum* or wild animals roaming in fenced woods. Even though '*stagnum*' in this passage has sometimes been translated as 'lake',[32] this is incorrect. A *stagnum* is an expanse of standing water, which may be a pool or a lagoon, and which can be natural or man-made.[33] As envisaged by Nerva the *stagnum* obviously differs from a fishpond. For one thing it is probably envisaged as being larger. Since the water cannot flow out, the fish in the water cannot leave the *stagnum*. Nerva therefore equates them to wild animals in a fenced forest. He holds that these fish are not possessed by the owner of the *stagnum* and the reason given is that they and the animals 'have been left in their natural state of liberty'.

---

[30] *Institute* II.1.10. See further F. von Savigny, *Das Recht des Besitzes* (7th edn. by A. F. Rudorff, Vienna 1865, reprinted, Darmstadt, 1967), pp. 342 *et seq.*

[31] Hume. *Commentaries*, i, 82.

[32] See for instance F. de Zulueta, *Digest 41, 1 & 2 with Translation and Commentary* (corrected reprint, Oxford, 1950), p. 90; J. A. C. Thomas in *The Digest of Justinian* (ed. A Watson, Philadelphia, 1985), Vol. 4.

[33] *Oxford Latin Dictionary* (Oxford, 1968), s.v. *stagnum* 1. Ulpian defines *lacus* and *stagnum* in D.43.14.1.3 and 4, Ulpian 68 *ad edictum*, where he is discussing the wording of a particular interdict. See O. Lenel, *Das Edictum Perpetuum*, p. 461, nn. 5 and 7.

It is noteworthy that the creatures in this second case are not said to have been put in the *stagnum* or forest. They would have been living there naturally, and the text suggests that nothing has been done to interfere with them, except that, in the case of the wild animals, the forest has been fenced. Within their somewhat restricted range both fish and animals 'have been left' (*relictae sint*) in their natural state of freedom. In this case, despite the limited area in which they can exercise this freedom, in Nerva's view the fish and animals are not under control and are not possessed.[34] Indeed there might well be little real control. An owner might have difficulty in finding, far less taking, a fish or animal in these circumstances. If, as Stair's citation suggests, this text were to be followed in Scots law, then fish in a *stagnum* and animals in a fenced forest would remain *res nullius* and could not be the subject of theft. Plainly at the very least the point must have been doubtful.

As Hume remarks,[35] we do not know what line the Scottish judges might have taken on fish 'in a stank or pond' because legislation, culminating in the 1607 Act, meant that the position in criminal law was regulated by statute.

In other countries lawyers had to deal with similar problems and it is clear that not all found Nerva's decision acceptable. For instance, in a work published in 1625, Grotius argued that there was only a difference of degree between the control over fish in a fishpond and fish in a *stagnum*. For this reason he approved the view — which he said was then dominant — that wild animals confined in private woods and fish confined in *stagna* are held to be possessed and owned.[36] One suspects that Nerva would have been alive to such an obvious argument and that Grotius, who ignores the

---

[34]Beseler would delete the *reductio ad absurdum* from the end of the text: G. von Beseler, 'Romanistische Studien' (1930) 10 *Tijdschrift voor Rechtsgeschiednis* 161, at p. 206. But Professor Daube has suggested that the *reductio* was a particularly popular argument at this period: *Roman Law*, 193.

[35]*Commentaries*, i. 82.

[36]H. Grotius, *de iure belli ac pacis* 2.8.2.

distinction between fish put into a fishpond and fish occurring naturally in a *stagnum*, has underestimated the subtlety of his reasoning. It is quite likely that some of Nerva's discussion has been omitted by Justinian's compilers. For present purposes it is sufficient to notice that there was uncertainty surrounding the legal position of such fish, and that the legislature seems to have stepped in to remove some of the practical difficulties caused by that uncertainty.

III. Stankis and loches

Having regard to this background, it is suggested that when the 1607 Act referred to 'stankis' it was referring to what the Roman texts refer to as *stagna*.[37] So 'stankis' would simply refer to areas of standing water.[38]

In *Pollok* v. *M'Cabe* on the other hand Lord Ardwall referred to Jamieson's Dictionary[39] which said that the word was 'used to denote a fishpond' and gave as an example the statute 1535, c. 13.[40] This refers to those who 'brekis dukatis cunyngares parkis stankis' and steal pyke and fish. On this basis Lord Ardwall concluded that in the 1607 Act 'propir stankis and loches' mean 'fish ponds belonging entirely to one proprietor and used for the purpose of keeping fish therein. . . . Of course this distinguishes fishes in proper stanks and lochs from fishes in rivers or large lochs. . . .'[41]

The reasoning is tortured to say the least. It involves saying that the term 'stankis' in the statute is limited to fishponds even though

---

[37]For the derivation see *The Oxford English Dictionary* (2nd edn., Oxford, 1989), Vol. 16, s.v. stank.

[38]*The Scottish National Dictionary*, Vol. 9 (Edinburgh, 1974), *s.v.* stank, gives as the primary definition 'A pond, pool, small semi-stagnant sheet of water, especially one that is overgrown and half solid with vegetation, a swampy place.' That dictionary covers the language from 1700.

[39]J. Jamieson, *An Etymological Dictionary of the Scottish Language*, Vol. 4 (Paisley, 1882), *s.v.* stank.

[40]A.P.S. II, 344, c. 11.

[41]6 Adam, at p. 143; 1910 S.C.(J.), at p. 26.

we can see that the ownership of fish in fishponds was not really doubtful. It would be strange to legislate for this case and not for the other more doubtful instances.

Lord Ardwall is also faced with difficulties over the absolutely ordinary word 'loches'. Having somehow also subsumed 'loches' under the category of fishponds, he then has to say that 'loches' are to be distinguished from 'large lochs'. Suffice it to say that the statute makes no such distinction.[42]

Finally, having settled on his narrow definition of a stank, Lord Ardwall is immediately forced to declare that the Lindean Reservoir should be regarded as a fishpond because Mr Scott Plummer stocked it with trout, and fish could not enter or leave it.[43] Lord Low takes his courage in both hands and says of the reservoir: 'in fact it is just a large fishpond. . . .'[44] This would, one imagines, have come as something of a surprise to the county council who thought that they had constructed a reservoir to supply water to local communities.[45]

When judges are obliged to strain common sense in this way there is usually something wrong with the basis of their argument. In this case the problem arises because of the narrow interpretation which they put on the word 'stankis'. It may well be, given the close connexion with dovecots, warrens and parks, that the 1535 statute cited by Jamieson's Dictionary was directed in particular at fishponds. None the less the basic meaning of the word 'stankis' is

---

[42]None the less the distinction duly turns up in a reference to 'small lochs' in G. W. S. Barry, 'Fisheries   Salmon and Freshwater Fisheries', *The Laws of Scotland, Stair Memorial Encyclopaedia*, Vol. 11 (Edinburgh, 1990), para. 47. One looks forward to seeing worked-out definitions of small lochs, lochs and large lochs.

[43]6 Adam, at p. 143; 1910 S.C.(J.), at p. 26.

[44]6 Adam, at p. 142; 1910 S.C.(J.), at p. 25.

[45]Loyally following *M'Cabe*, Sheriff Younger contemplated the situation where a reservoir would cease to be a stank if fish kept on escaping: *Valentine* v. *Kennedy* 1985 S.C.C.R. 89, at p. 90 and again at p. 91. Such unstable distinctions are hardly to be encouraged, especially in the criminal law.

simply a pond, pool or small sheet of semi-stagnant water. In the 1607 Act the repeated coupling of 'loches' and 'stankis' suggests that in this Act at least the wider meaning is intended. The statute can thus be satisfactorily construed as referring to ponds or pools which happen to contain fish. There is no need to describe them as fishponds.

Indeed if this wider meaning is adopted, the 1607 Act can be interpreted in a straightforward fashion. It makes it an offence to steal fish from any private ponds or standing water and from any private loch. It seems likely that the reservoir in *Pollok* v. *M'Cabe* would have been covered by one or other of those terms. It may well be that for the purposes of the statute at least there is no material distinction in principle between a stank and a loch and that a loch is really a larger version of a stank. If that is so, then the answer is perhaps that the Lindean Reservoir, which covers most of 33 acres,[46] should have been regarded as a 'loch' in terms of the 1607 Act.

IV. Ownership of fish in 'propir stankis and loches'

Finally, we may enter a word of caution about another remark of Lord Ardwall. He says that it is 'quite apparent' that the 1607 Act establishes and declares a right of property in bees and fishes in private stanks and lochs. The argument seems to be that because the Act makes it an offence to steal fish from such waters, the owners of such waters must have been made the owners of the fish.

The reasoning is not entirely persuasive. First, legislation can prevent the poaching of game on private land without making the landowner the owner of the game, and, as we saw above,[47] the legislation on fish was part of a larger tract of legislation which seems to have been more concerned with tackling abuses than with

---

[46]There is no finding-in-fact as to the size of the reservoir. The figure in the text is derived from a board at the former reservoir.

[47]Page 3.

establishing ownership. Secondly, the Act certainly does not in terms say anything about the ownership of the fish. Thirdly, if the Act really had the effect of vesting ownership of the fish in the owners of stanks and lochs, then Stair, for instance, when discussing the ownership of fish, should have mentioned the Act which would have made significant inroads into the area of application of the common law of *occupatio*. Yet he says nothing. Erskine indeed seems to proceed on exactly the reverse of Lord Ardwall's view: for him the Act 1474 c. 61 was applied to creatures precisely because they were owned.[48] Finally, if in fact the 1607 Act declared a right of property, then it would seem to follow that creatures falling within its terms could have been the object of common law theft. Yet the Act, which provides for a special minor penalty, is not interpreted as having such an effect. Indeed, if it had such an effect, for that reason alone, the procurator fiscal in *Pollok* should not have dropped the common law charge.

V. Conclusion

This article has been much concerned with rather ancient law, but the problems are as real today as in the seventeenth, or indeed the first, century. With the fall in value of the penalty under the Theft Act, there may yet be room for asking our judges to look more closely at the common law of theft in relation to fish. This would mean taking up the long-neglected discussion of the circumstances in which fish may be said to be in someone's control and hence possessed and owned. The concepts of possession and control are familiar from other areas of our law and the issues would not be entirely novel for their Lordships. One can only regret that Lord Emslie is not likely to join them in any such deliberations.[49]

---

[48] *Institute* II.1.10. Whether that view is correct is, of course, a different matter.

[49] The views in this article are expressed by me in my private capacity and are not to be taken as representing the opinion of Crown Counsel.

2

THE INTERACTION OF OBLIGATIONS AND CRIME

David M. Walker

The concepts of contract, delict and crime, and the bodies of principles and rules which cluster round each of them, are too frequently thought of as wholly distinct and mutually exclusive. But, in truth, there are considerable similarities and overlapping. The three bodies of rules are concerned, respectively, with duties to others, voluntarily assumed, to do or refrain from doing something, with duties to others, imposed by law, to refrain from causing them unjustifiable harm, and with duties to others, imposed by law, to refrain from unjustifiable or prohibited conduct, frequently harmful. Stated thus generally it is not very apparent that they are, or why they should be, distinct. In recent years these categories have increasingly been recognised as not being mutually exclusive. Some sets of facts fall clearly into one category or another but some may be treated in more than one way. Thus, it is now accepted that an individual's conduct may give rise to liability, alternatively or cumulatively, under two of these heads. Conduct may be both a breach of contract with A and a delict to him[1] and it may be practice rather than law which determines how the claim is formulated; or both a breach of contract with A and a delict against B;[2] or both a

---

[1] *E.g.* professional negligence by a solicitor: *Robertson* v. *Bannigan* 1965 S.C. 20, *per* Lord Wheatley at pp. 30-31; or injury to a passenger caused by a carrier of passengers.

[2] *E.g.* letting an insanitary dwelling to a tenant: *Cameron* v. *Young* 1908 S.C. (H.L.) 7; Occupier's Liability (Scotland) Act 1960, sec. 3.

breach of contract and a punishable crime, such as the sale of a vehicle which is unroadworthy, which is likely to be a breach of the Sale of Goods Act and is penalised by statute,[3] or both an actionable delict and a punishable crime. As early as 1845 a railway accident near Corstorphine gave rise to both an action for damages against the company[4] and a conviction of the persons involved for culpable homicide,[5] and today it is undeniable that such conduct as assaults and harm by driving a vehicle may give rise to both actions for delict and prosecutions.

An area which may be fruitful of problems of overlap is that of medical treatment. Medical treatment alleged to be unsatisfactory may be complained of as a breach of contract with the patient,[6] or a delict against him or her,[7] or may be a civil assault if done without reasonable explanation and real consent,[8] or might even be a criminal assault.[9] In fact, medical cases, while highly illustrative of the way in which particular conduct may be pleaded one way or another or in the alternative, are not very interesting on the point of differences in the concepts invoked and applied in judgment in cases on different grounds because medical negligence, etc. is not

---

[3]Road Traffic Act 1972, sec. 60(5), which expressly provided that this does not affect the validity of a contract. (See now sec. 75(7) of the Road Traffic Act 1988.)

[4]*Morton (Cooley's Factor)* v. *Edinburgh & Glasgow Ry.* (1845) 8D. 288.

[5]*H.M. Advocate* v. *Paton & McNab* (1845) 2 Broun 525. Interestingly enough Lord Justice-Clerk Hope's charge to the jury included a statement of the duty of care not unlike Lord Atkin's statement of the duty in civil law in *Donoghue* v. *Stevenson* 1932 S.C. (H.L.) 31, at p. 44.

[6]*E.g. Thake* v. *Maurice* [1984] 2 All E.R. 513, *per* Peter Pain J. at pp. 519-520; on appeal [1986] 1 All E.R. 497, *per* Kerr L.J. at pp. 500, 503 (point not reopened); *Clark* v. *Maclennan* [1983] 1 All E.R. 416 (negligent treatment).

[7]*E.g. Gold* v. *Haringey Health Authority* [1987] 2 All E.R. 888 (negligent misrepresentation).

[8]*E.g. Hills* v. *Potter* [1983] 3 All E.R. 716; *Freeman* v. *Home Office* [1984] 1 All E.R. 1036 (injection of drug).

[9]*Cf.* facts disclosed in *Lanford* v. *General Medical Council* [1989] 2 All E.R. 921 (doctor struck off register; he possibly could have been prosecuted).

different in principle from any other kind of professional negligence, or indeed any kind of physical damage by negligence; the concept is of failure to take the care which is reasonable in the circumstances. The application of the concept may be different because of the circumstances, but the concept itself is not different and does not have different meanings. It is, however, otherwise in the case of some concepts.

The salient difference is of course that those kinds of conduct which we deem contractual or delictual give rise to claims, usually for damages, enforceable by civil process, and those which we deem criminal give rise to prosecutions, enforceable by criminal process. The quantity of evidence and the standard of proof, moreover, differ.

It may, accordingly, be useful to explore some of these areas of overlap a little more fully, notably some points where either of the civil grounds of obligation overlaps with the criminal.

Consider first a general issue of responsibility, the responsibility of corporate bodies. It is abundantly clear that in contract a corporate body may, subject to the *ultra vires* rule, contract as an entity to the effect of binding itself and making its assets liable for bad performance or non-performance, and that, in delict, a corporate body may be made liable for its defaults as well as, vicariously, for the default of an employee acting in the course of his employment or of an agent acting within the sphere of his mandate. What is the situation in criminal law? The matter came up sharply in *Dean* v. *John Menzies (Holdings) Ltd.*[10] where a limited company was charged at common law with conducting itself in a shamelessly indecent manner by selling and having for sale a number of indecent and obscene magazines, likely to deprave or corrupt the morals of the lieges. The competency of the complaint was challenged and the High Court of Justiciary (Lords Stott and Maxwell,

---

[10] 1981 J.C. 23.

Lord Cameron dissenting) held that the complaint was incompetent as a body corporate was not capable of exhibiting the characteristics of shameless and indecent conduct. Lord Maxwell observed[11] that the crime involved, to an exceptional degree, a subjective judgment upon which reasonably held opinions could differ; a finding of guilt implied that the accused had used his judgment and discretion in an indecent and shameless fashion, and the crime involved knowledge of the contents of the particular magazines complained of. '[T]he company as a legal abstraction could not, as a matter of fact, have the knowledge, exercise the judgment and conduct itself in the manner alleged in the complaint.'[12] He declined to attribute to the company a fictional imputation of knowledge and reached the conclusion: 'I am not satisfied that the common law of Scotland recognises any clear single fiction which would, for purposes of criminal responsibility, in all matters attribute to a company the kind of human characteristics and conduct alleged in this complaint.'[13]

Lord Cameron, on the other hand, pointed out that a fictional body could exhibit an intention to act contrary to law, could form an intent and therefore incur criminal liability, at least in matters of statutory breach.[14] 'It has long been settled in our civil law that a company can be guilty of malice: malice implies a harmful intention deliberately directed against another person or persons. The parallel between malice and *mens rea* which is essential to criminal liability at common law appears to me close.'[15] Having referred to the criminal liability of a company upheld by the House of Lords in the English case of *Tesco Ltd.* v. *Nattrass*,[16] he continued:

---

[11] *Ibid.*, at p. 38.
[12] *Ibid.*, at p. 39.
[13] *Ibid.*, at p. 45.
[14] *Ibid.*, at pp. 25 and 28.
[15] *Ibid.*, at p. 29.
[16] [1972] A.C. 153.

'In both countries the rules and principles governing the civil liabilities of companies are the same; in both countries the rules and principles governing criminal liability in respect of statutory offences are the same and it is therefore not easy to see upon what principle of Scots criminal law a company created by statute should not be amenable to the common law in matters criminal . . . particularly as in both countries the capacity of a company to form an intent, to carry it into effect, to exercise a will and to make a conscious choice of courses of action or inaction is undoubted and is precisely the same.'[17] The test of criminality in that case was, he held, objective and not subjective; it was of the essence of the offence that the action was of an indecent character and directed to a person with certain intentions or knowledge of the consequences or likely consequences to that person or those persons, the intention or knowledge that it should corrupt or be calculated or liable to corrupt or deprave those towards whom the conduct is directed. To establish guilt it would have to be proved that the stocking of those magazines for sale was the result of a 'policy decision' to buy them in for retail sale in the knowledge of their contents.

Lord Cameron's view would have put the criminal liability of a corporation on the same basis as its civil liability; the majority view puts criminal liability, at least for alleged shameless and indecent conduct, on a different basis.

Another concept of wide application is causation, the term for the link between human conduct and consequence. Loss is recoverable for breach of contract only if caused by the breach; loss is recoverable for delict if the breach of duty caused the harm complained of; an accused can be held liable for criminal conduct if, in the case of a 'result-crime', his conduct actually caused the result. In every case the distinction is from the result being shown to have been brought about mainly by something else. It does not

---

[17] 1981 J.C., at p. 31.

appear that causation means anything different in the three classes of cases. Thus loss by late delivery of goods was held to have been mainly caused by the defenders' breach of contract in providing an unseaworthy ship;[18] a death was mainly caused by natural causes and not heavy exertion to avert the consequences of the defenders' employee's alleged negligence;[19] and, in a criminal context, a death was mainly caused by recklessly injecting a drug rather than by later switching off the victim's life-support machine.[20] In all cases the real cause was not the last-occurring event. In all three fields the court is conducting a practical enquiry with a view to determining responsibility and legal liability, and the main question is the fairly commonsense one: what predominantly brought about the situation alleged to be the loss or harm which grounds the action or prosecution?

Turning now to some more specific and particular issues, a point at which civil and criminal liability may overlap is conspiracy. So far as civil liability is concerned it is clear that there must be an agreement by two or more parties, it must be carried into effect to a greater or lesser degree, and some damage to the aggrieved party must have been produced thereby.[21] A mere agreement, even one to injure, if never acted upon and never leading to any result affecting the party complaining could not produce any damage and would not be actionable. So too even if the agreement were acted upon it would not be actionable if it failed to produce any damage.

In *Crofter Hand Woven Harris Tweed Co.* v. *Veitch*[22] the Lord Chancellor, Viscount Simon observed:[23] 'Conspiracy, when re-

---

[18] *A/B Karshamns Oljefabriker* v. *Monarch S.S. Co.* 1949 S.C. (H.L.) 1, at pp. 13 and 22.

[19] *Blaikie* v. *B.T.C.* 1961 S.C. 44, at p. 49.

[20] *Finlayson* v. *H.M. Advocate* 1979 J.C. 33.

[21] *Crofter Hand Woven Harris Tweed Co.* v. *Veitch* 1942 S.C. (H.L.) 1, *per* Viscount Simon L.C. at p. 5.

[22] 1942 S.C. (H.L.) 1.

[23] *Ibid.*, at p. 5.

garded as a crime, is the agreement of two or more persons to effect any unlawful purpose, whether as their ultimate aim,[24] or only as a means to it,[25] and the crime is complete if there is such agreement, even though nothing is done in pursuance of it . . . The crime consists in the agreement, though in most cases overt acts done in pursuance of the combination are available to prove the fact of agreement.' This formulation has been quoted in some recent Scottish cases.[26] The purpose must be unlawful.

After examining the tort (*sic*) of conspiracy the Lord Chancellor continued: 'The distinction between the essential conditions to be fulfilled by the crime and the tort respectively are conveniently set out by Lord Coleridge, C.J., in his judgment in *Mogul Steamship Co.* v. *McGregor, Gow & Co.*:[27] "In an indictment it suffices if the combination exists and is unlawful, because it is the combination itself which is mischievous, and which gives the public an interest to interfere by indictment. Nothing need be actually done in furtherance of it . . . It is otherwise in a civil action: it is the damage which results from the unlawful combination itself with which the civil action is concerned . . . If the combination is unlawful, then the parties to it commit a misdemeanour, and are offenders against the State; and if, as the result of such unlawful combination and misdemeanour, a private person receives a private injury, that gives such person a right of private action." . . . The appellants, therefore, in order to make out their case have to establish (a) agreement between the two respondents; (b) to effect an unlawful purpose; (c) resulting in damage to the appellants.'

---

[24] *E.g.* to blow up Kirk O'Field, Edinburgh, and thereby kill the Queen of Scots' husband.

[25] To kill the Queen's husband in order to enable one of the conspirators to marry her.

[26] *H.M. Advocate* v. *Wilson, Latta & Rooney* Glasgow High Court, Feb. 1968, *unreported* (see Gordon on *Criminal Law* (2nd edn.), p. 200); *H.M. Advocate* v. *Carberry & Others*, Glasgow High Court, Nov. 1974, *unreported* (see Gordon *op. cit.*, at p. 198).

[27] (1888) 21 Q.B.D. 544, at p. 549.

The difficulty, Lord Simon observed,[28] in the civil context was to determine what was meant by a combination to effect an 'unlawful purpose'. It need not be criminally unlawful. It would suffice if the predominant purpose was wilfully to damage the interests of the other rather than to advance the defenders' lawful interests in a matter where the defenders honestly believed that those interests would directly suffer if the action was not taken.

The cases have mostly related to rivalry in trade or attempts by trade unions to protect employment or maintain or secure conditions of employment, but the principle is not limited. If three academics work out a plan to damage the reputation of a fourth one by all writing unfavourable reviews of the fourth one's book, that would be actionable conspiracy if, in consequence, the fourth one fails to secure a better appointment. The necessary unlawful element in this case would be that the conspirators were not seeking to advance any interests of theirs, or in the expression of views which were not honestly held or could not be justified. (This would be extremely difficult to prove, given the considerable discrepancies which can, and do, exist between different academics' views of the merits of particular books.)

It is clear accordingly that 'conspiracy' means different things when considered as a basis for a civil claim and as the ground of a criminal charge.

Take next the concept of fraud. It has been recognised for a long time that if a person is induced to enter into a contract by what is deemed to be a fraudulent misrepresentation the contract is voidable at his instance and may indeed be totally void, if the misrepresentation has negated consent. A fraudulent misrepresentation is a materially inaccurate statement of fact communicated deliberately, in the knowledge of its material inaccuracy or at least with indifference to its accuracy or otherwise. Fraud is a state of mind involving knowledge of facts represented and their consistency or

---

[28] 1942 S.C. (H.L.), at p. 7.

otherwise with reality, and the intention with which they are communicated. It is clearly distinguishable from honest belief in their consistency with reality. In *Boyd & Forrest* v. *Glasgow & South Western Ry.*[29] it was affirmed that, for a representation inducing contract on the terms on which it did to be damned as fraudulent, it must have been made knowingly, or without belief in its truth, or recklessly, careless whether it be true or false. If made in the honest belief that it was true, it was not fraudulent, even if it were inaccurate. Material misrepresentation inducing contract, whatever the state of mind, justifies the court in reducing the contract, but only fraudulent[30] or negligent[31] misrepresentation justifies the court in awarding damages for the resultant loss.

But fraudulent misrepresentation by one to another is also an actionable delict.[32] 'Fraud gives remeid by reparation to all that are damnified thereby, against the actor of the fraud, either by annulling of the contract or other deeds elicited or induced by fraud, or by making up the damage sustained by the fraud, at the option of the injured.'[33] To induce a contract on unfavourable terms is only one of the ways in which the representee may be damnified.

Indeed, if the fraudulent misrepresentation induced a contract between the person defrauded and a third party, *not* the representor,[34] the contract is not voidable, at least on the ground of misrepresentation.[35] But damages can be claimed from the representor. The loss consists in being led to make a detrimental bargain with another.

---

[29]1912 S.C. (H.L.) 93.

[30]*Manners* v. *Whitehead* (1898) I.F. 171.

[31]Law Reform (Miscellaneous Provisions) (Scotland) Act 1985, sec. 10.

[32]*Tulloch* v. *Davidson* (1858) 20 D. 1045, at p. 1057; *Thin & Sinclair* v. *Arrol* (1896) 24 R. 198, *per* L. P. Robertson at p. 206.

[33]Stair I, 9, 4; *cf. Bryson & Co. Ltd.* v. *Bryson* 1916 1 SLT 361, *per* Lord Anderson at p. 364. See too Ersk. III, 1, 13.

[34]*E.g.* where A by fraudulent misrepresentation made to B induces him to contract with C who is innocent of the fraud.

[35]*Young* v. *Clydesdale Bank* (1889) 17 R. 231; *Thin & Sinclair, supra.*

Even where the contract is voidable the party defrauded may elect to claim damages without rescinding the contract.[36] So too, rescission of the contract is conditional on the possibility of making restitution *in integrum*; if the subject matter of contract has perished, *e.g.* an animal has died, restitution is impracticable. But the delictual remedy of damages may be pursued.

It does not appear that fraud or fraudulent misrepresentation is any different for these purposes. The avoiding of the contract is the contractual remedy and damages is the delictual one; in some cases both are appropriate. Fraud or dole is a machination or contrivance to deceive,[37] as by an inaccurate statement made in the knowledge of its falsity, or at least with indifference to its truth or falsity, with the intent actually to induce the conduct which in fact resulted, and with consequent detriment to the party affected by the fraud.

Indeed, in view of the overlap between contract and delict it would be strange and could give rise to difficulties if fraud meant something different in the contexts of contractual and delictual claims. The law should not emphasise differences between these grounds of obligations but rather promote uniformity. The remedies are different; reduction of the contract and damages respectively, but the facts which ground the different actions are the same.

There are some differences between fraud in contract and fraud in delict, notably in that if damages are claimed there must be specification of the person or persons who committed the fraud. Thus in the *Western Bank* v. *Addie*,[38] in which it was alleged that a purchase of shares had been induced by fraud and claims were made alternatively for reduction and for damages, in the claim for reduction of the contract it was relevant to sue the company, alleging misrepresentation by the directors, but if a claim had been

---

[36] *Smith* v. *Sim* 1954 S.C. 357.

[37] Ersk. III, 1, 16; Bell, *Prin.* s. 13; *Lees* v. *Tod* (1882) 9 R. 807, *per* L. P. Inglis at p. 853. *Cf. Brownlie* v. *Miller* (1878) 5 R. 1076, at p. 1091.

[38] (1865) 3 Macph. 899; (1867) 5 Macph. (H.L.) 80.

pressed for damages for fraud it would have had to be made against the directors personally, or also to have averred and proved vicarious liability of the company for fraud by its directors.[39] But these differences relate not to the concept of fraud, but to responsibility or liability for fraudulent communication.

But, the question arises: is fraud the same thing for contractual or delictual claims and for criminal purposes? For criminal purposes fraud is the bringing about of some definite practical result by means of false pretences,[40] though in some cases, notably the uttering of a forged document, the crime is constituted by the uttering even though no consequence follows. The requisites of simple fraud are a false pretence, and causation thereby of some practical consequence. The false pretence can be of many kinds including representing oneself to have certain attributes which one does not truly have *e.g.* to be a graduate, or to be able and willing to pay when one is not, or that some property has certain attributes which it does not truly have. The practical result is commonly the handing over of goods or money in reliance on the fraudulent representation or not getting goods of adequate value or value for money.

In *J. & P. Coats Ltd.* v. *Brown,*[41] the case which revived the long disused practice of a private party initiating a prosecution in the High Court of Justiciary by criminal letters without the concurrence of the Lord Advocate (which had earlier been refused) the basis for prosecution was falsehood, fraud and wilful imposition by having sold to the complainers coal under a specific description and supplied coal known not to be of that description, and certified it and invoiced it as such, and taken payment of the price as contracted for. There was no doubt that it was a relevant charge of

---

[39](1867) 5 Macph. (H.L.) 80, *per* L. C. Chelmsford at p. 85.
[40]Macdonald on *Criminal Law* (5th edn.) at p. 52, approved by Gordon *op. cit.*, at p. 588.
[41]1909 S.C. (J.) 29.

fraud. Was there any civil remedy? Could Coats have sued Brown for damages representing the difference in value between the coal as it had been represented to be and the coal as it actually was? There is a question whether, as the law was then understood, the complainers could have claimed damages without also rescinding the contract which, in turn, would have required that they returned the coal. But, as the law is now understood, could damages be claimed alone? It is thought that they could and, what is important for the present discussion, that what was relevantly charged criminally as fraud would also have been relevant to support a delictual claim for fraud. The defender had represented the coal to be A and had knowingly delivered and supplied coal of kind B, of lesser value.

Take another instance. In *Smith* v. *Sim*[42] Sim advertised for sale his hotel premises and the business carried on therein. His solicitors represented to Smith, an enquirer, that the turnover was £x p.a. Smith bought the premises and business and discovered that the turnover quoted was roughly double what it truly had been and that in consequence he had paid too much. He did not seek to rescind the contract but claimed damages for the excess payment; the claim was held competent as a delict. If he had reported the matter to the procurator-fiscal would these facts have founded a prosecution for fraud? It is thought that they would, and that Sim could have been charged with defrauding Smith of the excess price paid. The only difference would have been in the standard of proof, proof on balance of probabilities in the civil court, proof beyond reasonable doubt in the criminal court. The choice of proceedings adopted was dictated by the fact that the pursuer wanted damages, not to have the defender fined or imprisoned. If the defender had been impecunious, or the pursuer had felt *animus* against him, he might have elected to report him for prosecution as a swindler.

Take again the case of securing and retaining moveable property, which the former possessor did not intend to transfer. Is this a

---

[42] 1954 S.C. 357.

contract and breach thereof, or a delict, or a crime? The problems are well-illustrated by the very similar cases of *Morrisson*v. *Robertson*[43] and *McLeod*v. *Kerr*.[44] In *Morrisson*v. *Robertson* Morrisson took two cows to market. He was approached by one Telford, who falsely represented that he was young Wilson, son of one Wilson, a dairyman of Bonnyrigg, of good credit, with whom Morrison had previously had dealings, and that he had authority to buy two cows on behalf of his father. Morrisson handed over the cows to Telford, *alias* Wilson, on the usual credit. Telford quickly resold them to Robertson, who took them in good faith and for value. Morrisson then, having discovered what had happened, brought a civil claim against Robertson for recovery of the cows. He satisfied the court that he had been induced to contract with Telford by fraudulent misrepresentation inducing essential error in his mind as to the identity of the buyer and that in consequence the original sale was void. It followed that the subsale by Telford to Robertson was made by a putative seller (Telford) with no title to the cows and that it was void. Accordingly, Morrisson recovered his cows. Could Telford have been sued for the delict of fraud? Lord MacLaren observed: 'If there had been a contract of sale, then, although the pursuer might have had an action of damages against the person who obtained the goods by fraud, or might have had an action for reducing the sale, yet if in the meantime the property of the cows had passed by lawful subsale to a third person, then the right of the third person, the analogue of the defender in the present case, would be indefeasible.'[45] Could Telford have been sued for the delict of fraud? Clearly, yes. Could he have been successfully prosecuted for fraud? Yes, because he had deliberately misrepresented his identity and authority to buy and had thereby induced Morrisson to part with his

---

[43]1908 S.C. 332.
[44]1965 S.C. 235.
[45]1908 S.C. 332, at p. 336.

property. Could he have been successfully prosecuted for theft? No, because he obtained lawful possession of the cows with the consent of the true owner.

In *McLeod* v. *Kerr* Lord President Clyde pointed out that to constitute theft the fraudulent person would have had to take the goods without any intention on the owner's part to convey them and without his consent to the transfer.[46] He went to point out that Sir Thomas Smith had been incorrect[47] in suggesting that Telford was in the position of a thief, because Morrisson had voluntarily and intentionally delivered the cows to Telford, even though he was under a misapprehension when he did so as to who Telford was.

In *McLeod* v. *Kerr*, Kerr advertised his car for sale. One Galloway came to see it, gave his name as Craig, and having agreed to buy gave Kerr a cheque for the agreed price, signed 'L. Craig'. He then resold the car to Gibson, who took in good faith and for value, and from whom it was recovered by the police. The cheque was dishonoured. Galloway was prosecuted and convicted of fraud and theft of the car. This, it is thought, was correct as to fraud. What Galloway had done was deliberately to make a misrepresentation of his name and creditworthiness which induced Kerr to hand over his car in return for a worthless cheque.

On the civil issue of who was entitled to the car the court held that the first sale was not, as in *Morrisson* v. *Robertson*, a nullity, a void contract, vitiated by fraudulently induced error as to the identity of the purchaser, but a contract voidable at the instance of Kerr for Galloway's fraudulent misrepresentation of his name and consequent passing of a worthless cheque, but valid until set aside, and in the circumstances it had not been reduced or effectively challenged before Galloway had resold the car to Gibson. Conse-

---

[46]1965 S.C., at p. 255, citing Hume on *Crimes* (3rd edn.) i, 57; Alison, *Criminal Law*, i, 259.

[47] *Short Commentary on the Law of Scotland*, at p. 816.

quently, Galloway could pass, and did pass, good title to Gibson. The resale made the first sale unchallengeable.

Could Kerr have sued Galloway for damages for fraud? It is thought that he could, because he was induced to part with his car by false representations of intent and ability to pay. The practical answer is probably that Galloway was not worth suing.

In this case, moreover, the report discloses that Galloway had been charged with and convicted of fraud and theft. As to fraud, there is little doubt as to the justification for the conviction. But, as to theft there must be grave doubt, because Kerr had intended to transfer his car and did, in fact, voluntarily transfer it to Galloway, who he honestly regarded as purchasing the car. The facts, at least as they came out in the civil action, would appear to exclude guilt of theft.

In older Scots law such facts as arose in *Morrisson* or in *McLeod*, where a person finds that moveable property which he lawfully possessed, and frequently indeed owned, has come to be in the possession of another who may assert that he has justification for keeping the goods, would have been dealt with under the head of spuilzie. Spuilzie or spoliation was both a delict and a crime, and indeed it is hardly distinguishable from theft. Stair treated it under the general head of reparation and called it the taking away or inter-meddling with moveable goods without consent of the owner or order of law.[48] In the majority of cases goods spuilzied were really stolen. The obligation was to make restitution or to make reparation therefor. 'Thus things stolen or robbed, though they might be criminally pursued for as theft or robbery, yet they may be also civilly pursued for as spuilzie'. Spuilzie required a title of possession only, not necessarily property. 'Spuilzie *inurit labem realem* whereby the goods may be recovered from purchasers *bona fide*'. If, accordingly, *Morrisson* and *Macleod* had been argued on the basis of

---

[48]I, 9, 16.

spuilzie, ignoring the intermediate party, it seems that in each case the original owner would have recovered his property.[49] The property had come to be in the possession of a party who did not have the true owner's consent to possess or retain it; how he had come to possess it did not matter; he might have been, as he was in *Morrisson* and *Macleod*, an innocent party who had bought in good faith, or he might have been a thief or resetter. This suggests that it is a pity that this ancient ground of action and of prosecution has fallen into disuse and been forgotten. This is unjustified. It might still have utility, but a pleader who invoked spuilzie today might have a task to persuade the bench! It is likely to have utility particularly where the stages intermediate between the true owner's loss of possession and the goods turning up in the hands of the later possessor are uncertain. Suppose goods are lost, stolen or strayed, pass through various hands and turn up in an auction room, but are clearly identifiable. Is spuilzie not appropriate?

As the law developed the civil and criminal remedies in spuilzie separated and a person despoiled would bring a civil claim for restitution, or the procurator-fiscal would prosecute for theft. This obscures the essential identity of the wrong and crime and the similarity of the two claims.

Another point of contact is the area of industrial disputes, which is heavily influenced by statutory provisions. The Conspiracy and Protection of Property Act 1875, sec. 7, made it an offence to watch or beset the place where a person worked with a view to compelling him to abstain from doing anything. The Trade Union and Labour Relations Act 1974, sec. 13, made acts done in contemplation or furtherance of a trade dispute not actionable in tort on the ground only that they would interfere with performance of a contract. In *Galt* v. *Philp*[50] Philp and others were charged with watching and

---

[49]That is, the decision in *Macleod* would have been the other way.
[50]1983 J.C. 51.

besetting certain laboratories belonging to Fife Health Board with a view to compelling certain persons, employed by Fife Health Board, not to enter and do their work there. The question which arose was, there being in existence an industrial dispute and the exclusion being in furtherance thereof whether the 1974 Act provided a defence to the criminal charge. The High Court held without much difficulty that sec. 13 of the 1974 Act did not provide a defence to the criminal charge. Section 13 conferred on the doer of the wrongful act immunity from liability to damages or any other civil remedy in an action at the instance of a person who had suffered loss or damage in consequence of the act. It did not deal at all with immunity in any other type of action. It did not make the acts non-wrongful, but it gave protection to the persons responsible in civil claims only.

This would not be the only provision which operated as a total or partial defence in civil actions but not in criminal prosecutions. Contributory negligence was at common law a total defence, and is under statute a total or partial defence, to a claim of damages for negligent harm, but it never has been held that it has any application to criminal prosecutions.

Again there is the large area, discussed in many cases, where a statutory provision makes some act or omission criminal and the question has arisen whether harm resulting from the act or omission gives rise to a civil claim of damages on the ground of breach of statutory duty. It is in every case a question of the proper interpretation of the statutory provision in question[51] and various factors have been mentioned in different cases as persuasive one way or the other. But there is no simple rule applicable to all cases.

What determines in a particular case whether a person seeks to rescind a contract and/or claim damages, or claim damages for a

---

[51] *Cutler* v. *Wandsworth Stadium Ltd.* [1949] A.C. 398; *Pullar* v. *Window Clean Ltd.* 1956 S.C. 13; *Reid* v. *Westfield Paper Co.* 1957 S.C. 218; and see cases collected in *Solomons* v. *Gertzenstein* [1954] 2 Q.B. 243.

delict, or reports the matter to the procurator-fiscal for prosecution? It depends in the first place on what he wants, a remedy for himself, or the vindiction of right against the wrongdoing party. It may depend on whether the police are called or not; if they are the case is likely to have a criminal outcome. If many people have been prejudiced by the conduct prosecution may be simpler and more satisfactory.

What emerges then from this brief look at some of the points at which contract, delict and crime overlap? The first point is that the legal concept involved, such as conspiracy or fraud, may bear the same meaning in both the sets of principles involved, or it may bear quite materially different meanings in those sets of principles. It is dangerous to think of such concepts as having a single connotation, or to cite civil precedents in a criminal case or conversely. The second point is that a defence competent in one of these applications of a concept is not necessarily competent in another. Contributory negligence is a familiar defence in delict cases but not in contractual or criminal cases. The third point is that, obviously, the competency of particular kinds of evidence and the standard of proof differs as between civil remedies and criminal prosecutions. But, it is clear that in modern law it is wrong to think of contract, delict and crime as neatly separated from one another. That has never been, and certainly today is not, the case.

3

'AT THE MOUTH OF TWO WITNESSES': SOME COMMENTS ON CORROBORATION

Gerald H. Gordon

The requirement of corroboration is generally regarded by Scots lawyers as one of the most notable and precious features of Scots criminal law, and as something which they will defend religiously, perhaps because it is one of the last remaining links between Scots law and the Old Testament, or perhaps because it is a feature which Scots law shares with very few other legal systems, and which, in particular, it does not share with English law.[1] It is not the purpose of this paper to suggest that the requirement is anomalous, or old-fashioned, or in need of alteration or abolition. I merely want to explore some aspects of it, and perhaps to suggest that it is not quite so simple or straightforward as we sometimes think, or at least say when we pride ourselves on our superiority to the English.

The origins of the rule

The requirement of corroboration has its origins in Biblical and canon law,[2] and there are a number of Biblical formulations of it,

---

[1]It should be noted, however, that the Scottish Law Commission have begun to hint that they may yet consider sending it the way of corroboration in civil cases: see Report on the Evidence of Children etc., Scot. Law Com. No. 125, para. 3.3.: but I think that to do so will be much more difficult than it was to abolish corroboration in civil cases.

[2]See, *e.g.*, Bernard S. Jackson, *Essays in Jewish and Comparative Legal History* (Leiden, 1975), chaps. VI and VIII; 'Susanna and the History of Singular Witnesses', 1977 *Acta Juridica*, 37. Stair derives it from the Bible: see Stair, *Institutions*, IV, 43, 1. On the other hand Wigmore, in a paragraph headed

the most general being that in Deuteronomy, chapter 19, verse 15, which reads, in the King James version, as follows:

'One witness shall not rise up against a man for any iniquity, or for any sin, in any sin that he sinneth; at the mouth of two witnesses, or at the mouth of three witnesses, shall the matter be established.'

Its original rationale may have been that in a system where pursuer and defender both gave evidence, a decision could be come to only where the evidence of one of them was supported by that of another witness,[3] or it may have been that it was unsafe to rely on the evidence of one witness. Both reasons can be found in Philo Judaeus, writing in Alexandria in the first century, where he said:

'[Moses] added a splendid rule when he ordained a single person's testimony not to be admissible. First, because it is possible for a single person to see wrongly or hear wrongly or understand wrongly or be deceived. Secondly, because it is most unjust to make use of a single witness against more than one or even against one: . . . For why should one agree with the witness who details a case against somebody else rather than with the accused who speaks about himself? It is best, it would seem, to suspend judgment when neither side lacks or excels in anything.'[4]

These statements are not of merely academic interest, since one's view of the reason for the requirement of corroboration may determine one's view of what kind of evidence it desiderates: is it just a numerical rule requiring two witnesses (the 'two-witness rule'), or does it require that the corroborating evidence be such as

---

'History of Rules of Number', derives it from Roman law, *e.g.*, D xxii. 5.12, and from medieval notions of the oath as a formal act, necessarily efficacious, and quantitative in its nature: *Wigmore on Evidence in Trials at Common Law*, revd. Chadbourn, 1978, para. 2032.2

[3] *Cf.* Wigmore, *op. cit., loc. cit.*

[4] *Special laws*, 4.8.53, 54, quoted in David Daube, 'Witnesses in Bible and Talmud', Oxford Centre for Postgraduate Hebrew Studies, 1968, p. 5.

to provide some extra support for what would otherwise be the evidence of only one witness, who is, *ex hypothesi* (or, rather, *ex lege*), insufficiently reliable on his own[5] (which may be termed the 'unreliability principle')? Although Stair[6] and Burnett[7] are perhaps somewhat ambiguous, Hume comes out clearly in favour of the unreliability principle when he says

> 'No matter how trivial the offence, and how high soever the credit and character of the witness, still our law is averse to rely on his single word, in any inquiry which may affect the person, liberty, or fame of his neighbour; and rather than run the risk of such an error, a risk which does not hold when there is a concurrence of testimonies, it is willing that the guilty should escape.'[8]

Hume's statement shows clearly that what he was dealing with was an example of what is nowadays called 'rule-utilitarianism': we accept that sometimes a single witness can be reliable and that by refusing to believe him we may be doing injustice in the particular case; but we cannot always be sure about our judgments of reliability, and indeed we are so likely to be wrong, and the results of our error are likely to be so serious, that it is better to make it a rule that we shall never rely on only one witness, because, on the whole, that will lead to less injustice than will reliance on our ability to detect unreliability.[9]

---

[5] *Cf. McDonald* v. *Smith* (1978) S.C.C.R. Supp. 219, at p. 221.

[6] Who says that it follows from Deuteronomy, 'That one witness cannot make a sufficient probation, whatsoever be the quality or veracity of that witness; and yet the testimony of one witness may produce more faith in the judges than other two will do. This evinceth that every thing is not a sufficient proof that makes faith to the judge': Stair, *Institutions*, IV, 43, 2.

[7] Who says of the corroboration rule that it 'is founded both in reason and humanity. It is true, the denial of the party, and the presumption of innocence, is not equal to the assertion upon oath of a disinterested witness; yet it is such as to call for some additional circumstance to corroborate his testimony': Burnett, *Criminal Law*, p. 509.

[8] Hume on Crimes, ii, 383.

[9] For a discussion of rule-utilitarianism, see *e.g.* J. Rawls, 'Two Kinds of Rules' (1955) 64 Philosophical Rev. 3.

It might be thought that the 'quantitative' justification of corroboration, the bare two-witness rule, can now be forgotten, but the opposing ideas of corroboration as merely embodying a two-witness rule and as an expression of an unreliability principle still set up a tension in the modern law. When we require corroboration are we just saying that there must be two witnesses, that 'it will not do for the prosecutor to examine one witness and close his case';[10] or are we looking for evidence which will increase the strength of the evidence already led? There may, indeed, be yet another distinction. Even if we accept that corroboration is required because experience has shown that there is a real risk that an innocent person may be convicted unless the evidence against the accused is confirmed by other evidence,[11] what is the nature of the confirmation that is required? Is it evidence which 'confirms' or 'supports' or 'strengthens' other evidence,[12] or does it have to be in itself incriminating? Is it enough in the type of case where there is one direct or principal witness that the corroborating evidence be relevant and not inconsistent with the evidence of the first witness, or must it in itself be evidence pointing to guilt? These are questions which remain important in any discussion of the modern law on corroboration, as I hope to show.

The disadvantages of corroboration

Like any other example of rule-utilitarianism the requirement of corroboration has disadvantages. The primary disadvantage, of course, is the extent to which it allows the guilty to escape; a secondary one is that it puts an additional strain on scarce and expensive resources in that it lengthens trials, and requires police

---

[10]Alison's *Principles*, i, 89. Alison himself accepted the unreliability principle.

[11]*Cf. R.* v. *Kilbourne* [1973] A.C. 729, *per* L. Simon of Glasidale at p. 758 D-E.

[12]*Ibid.*, E-F.

forces to be large enough to send men out to hunt in pairs. Bentham, in his usual robust fashion, wanted to reject the rule because of the number of guilty people it allowed to escape. He referred to the security the rule offered against wrongful conviction, but said of that security that it was:

> 'Not so necessary as that you should pay so great a price for it as you do pay, and must pay, by the licence you thereby grant to commit the crime in the presence and with the aid of any *one*. . . . The innocent [*i.e.* the unjustly accused] who scarcely present themselves by so much as scores or dozens, engross the whole attention, and pass for the whole world. The innocent who ought to have presented themselves by millions [*i.e.* the victims of crimes unproved for lack of corroboration], are overlooked, and left out of the account.'[13]

The constraints imposed by a requirement of corroboration have been felt by all legal systems which have adopted it, and there are various ways of minimising them. One can decide that certain offences are so trivial that corroboration is wholly uneconomic on a cost-benefit basis, and abolish the requirement so far as they are concerned.[14] One can take the view that in some cases corroboration is so difficult to obtain, and the type of single witness likely to be called by the Crown so reliable, that the requirement can be dispensed with.[15] One can provide that some lesser form of conviction or penalty should follow in the case of a conviction obtained on uncorroborated evidence.[16] Conversely, one can decide that

---

[13] *Rationale of Judicial Evidence*, 9.6.1., quoted in Wigmore, *op. cit.,* para. 2033.
[14] See, *e.g.,* Road Traffic Offenders Act 1988, sec. 21.
[15] *Quaere* if this is why corroboration is not required in poaching offences, such as contraventions of the Poaching Prevention Act 1868.
[16] See Hume, ii, 383; *cf.* Maimonides, *Hilchoth Rotzeach,* 4.8. For the wider context of the latter passage see Daniel B. Sinclair, *Tradition and the Biological Revolution* (Edinburgh, 1989), chap. 2. Scots law does not now adopt this approach: an uncorroborated murder does not constitute culpable homicide, and the possible development of the not proven verdict into one available only where the jury are convinced of the accused's guilt but are prevented from convicting him because of the corroboration requirement did not happen.

only certain kinds of evidence are so suspect as to require corroboration, and limit the need for corroboration accordingly.[17]

The extent of the requirement of corroboration can also be limited by restricting it to the essential parts of the Crown case, as is done in Scotland, and/or by making it clear that it is not necessary that each fact relied on by the Crown be spoken to by two witnesses. As Alison puts it:

> 'Unquestionably the evidence of one witness will not in any case be sufficient. . . . But, on the other hand, the evidence of one witness, accompanied by a train of circumstances, each link of which is established by a single unexceptionable testimony, is unquestionably sufficient; nay, a chain of circumstantial evidence alone, proved in the same manner, of itself often amounts to the most conclusive legal proof.'[18]

Although Alison talks of a chain of circumstances, once the principle is accepted two circumstances, each spoken to by one, different witness, will be sufficient.[19]

More generally, one can adopt a flexible approach to just how much corroboration is necessary, varying the amount according to the circumstances of each case and the nature of the evidence to be corroborated. Such a flexible approach, of course, runs the risk of descending into arbitrariness or 'adhoccery', but it has the advantage that while the requirement can be relaxed in appropriate cases where the main evidence is strong, it remains available to be applied

---

[17]Scots law did not adopt this approach but English law did, in relation to the evidence of accomplices, evidence in sexual cases, and, until the coming into force of sec. 34 of the Criminal Justice Act 1988, in relation to the unsworn evidence of children: see Archbold's *Criminal Pleading, Evidence and Practice* (43rd edn.), chap. 16.

[18] Alison's *Principles*, p. 89. This approach is, of course, at the root of the *Moorov* doctrine: see Bernard S. Jackson, *op. cit.*, but a discussion of *Moorov* is outwith the scope of this paper.

[19]See *e.g. Neeson* v. *H.M. Advocate* 1984 S.C.C.R. 72.

in its full rigour in cases where that evidence appears to the court to be weak.

The corroboration requirement is also notable as being, apart from the hearsay rule, perhaps the last vestige of a system of evidence so riddled with distrust of juries that it excluded much evidence and many witnesses altogether on such grounds as consanguinity or interest. It is quite out of line with current ideas that all relevant evidence is competent, and that the jury can be trusted to determine its reliability. As Sheriff Wilkinson puts it, the requirement 'is at odds with the rejection of other safeguards formerly employed [against the fallibility of witnesses] and goes against the modern emphasis on the free assessment of evidence unencumbered by restrictive rules'.[20] It also sticks out like a sore thumb in a legal system which tends increasingly to leave even what were once thought of as questions of law to be determined by juries: the antithesis of rule-utilitarianism.[21]

The scope of the requirement

It is generally accepted that only the essential features of the Crown case need be spoken to by two witnesses. It is accepted that the identification of the accused as the offender must be corroborated,[22] and although there is some authority for saying that identification is the only matter which needs two witnesses,[23] it is generally accepted that all the essential features of the crime charged

---

[20]Wilkinson on *Evidence*, p. 204. We no longer even pay our last lingering lip-service to the rule that the evidence of *socii criminis* had to be treated *cum nota*, even though they could corroborate each other: *Docherty* v. *H.M. Advocate* 1987 S.C.C.R. 418.

[21]See, *e.g.*, *Low* v. *H.M. Advocate* 1987 S.C.C.R. 541.

[22]*Morton* v. *H.M. Advocate* 1938 J.C. 50.

[23]See *Gillespie* v. *Macmillan* 1957 J.C. 31, discussed *infra*.

have to be corroborated, *e.g.* that goods were stolen[24] or that, in the case where the crime charged can be committed only against persons of a certain age, the complainer was of that age.[25] Where the date of an offence is crucial it probably must be corroborated, but where it is immaterial it does not matter that the two eye-witnesses to the crime place it on different dates.[26] It is also a general rule that procedural requirements do not have to be corroborated, however essential they are,[27] but if an offence is so defined that it is committed only if it is discovered by certain procedures, then the fact that it was discovered by these procedures will have to be corroborated.[28]

It has also been long accepted that aggravations of a crime do not have to be corroborated. So if the charge is one of theft by housebreaking, the theft must be spoken to by corroborated evidence, but the housebreaking is sufficiently proved by one

---

[24]Where the stolen goods are recovered, their theft can be proved by the uncorroborated evidence of the complainer (or, presumably any one else who can speak to their loss). Strictly speaking, this rule should apply only where the circumstances in which the goods are recovered are themselves indicative of their being stolen, *e.g.*, that they were hidden or disguised, but in practice the rule may not always be subject to such a limitation. Where the goods are not recovered, their loss must be corroborated, and this means that there has to be corroboration both of their presence before the theft and of their absence thereafter: *McDonald* v. *Herron* 1966 S.L.T. 61; *Bennett* v. *H.M. Advocate* 1989 S.C.C.R. 608.

[25]*Lockwood* v. *Walker* (1910) 6 Adam 124.

[26]In *Morrison* v. *O'Brien* 1989 S.C.C.R. 689 the charge was of driving while disqualified on 23rd February 1988. One witness gave the date of the incident he witnessed as that in the complaint but the other gave it as a month later. It was held that as the accused was disqualified on both dates the sheriff was entitled to believe that both witnesses were talking about the same incident and to hold that they corroborated each other.

[27]*Farrell* v. *Concannon* 1957 J.C. 12.

[28]*MacLeod* v. *Nicol* 1970 J.C. 58; *cf. Carmichael* v. *Gillooly* 1982 S.C.C.R. 119 (Sh. Ct.). The fact that a circumstance is essential to *proving* the offence does not mean that it must be spoken to by two witnesses: *Gillespie* v. *Macmillan supra; cf.* W. A. Wilson, 'The Logic of Corroboration' (1960) 76 Sc.L. Rev. 101, 104.

40

witness.[29] But it is submitted that if the charge is one of housebreaking, or of opening lockfast places, with intent to steal, then both the breaking or forcing and the intent must be proved by corroborated evidence, since both are essential to there being any crime at all, although the intent can, of course, be inferred from circumstances.

Corroboration and contradiction

The most famous case in the history of corroboration is that of Susannah and the Elders, although its purpose was not to show the need for corroboration, which was well-established, but the importance of not allowing witnesses to hear each other's evidence.[30] Susannah, it will be remembered, was charged with adultery. The evidence against her consisted of statements from two eye witnesses who claimed to have seen her sinning under a tree in her garden. When they were separately cross-examined as to the kind of tree, they disagreed with each other, one describing it as one kind of tree and one as another. As a result, Susannah was triumphantly acquitted. Susannah's story shows what a godsend the two-witness rule is to a cross-examiner; it is only if there are two witnesses that their evidence can be probed for inconsistencies, which can then be prayed in aid as casting doubt on their evidence on the main point at issue. But if we transfer Susannah from Babylon to Bearsden (since she was a wealthy woman), pretend that adultery is still a crime in Scotland, and suppose that one of the witnesses placed the adultery under a fir tree and the other under an oak tree, but that she was nonetheless convicted, no one, I think, would give much

---

[29] *Richard Cameron* (1839) 2 Swin. 447, a case in which Lord Cockburn said, 'Indeed, there is no rule liable to so many exceptions and qualifications, as that whereby it is commonly said that two witnesses are requisite'; *Jas. Davidson* (1841) 2 Swin. 630.

[30] Another restrictive rule which has been discarded in Scotland: Criminal Procedure (Scotland) Act 1975, secs. 140, 343. For a discussion of the case of Susannah see Bernard S. Jackson's article 'Susannah and the Singular History of Singular Witnesses', *cit. supra*.

for her chances of a successful appeal. The question of what kinds of contradiction in the testimony of witnesses vitiated their evidence and what kinds did not, received a specific and formalised answer in Rabbinic law,[31] but modern legal systems are, of course, much more flexible, within, at any rate, fairly wide limits. Arguably, the effect of any discrepancies should be a jury question, but it seems that here, as in other types of case where corroboration is in issue, legal sufficiency is not clearly distinguishable from questions of weight and of the cogency of any inferences sought to be drawn from proved facts, and there comes, therefore, a stage at which an appeal court will say that the evidence is so weak that no reasonable jury could have regarded it as sufficient for conviction, and will quash the conviction, although they will probably justify their interference with the verdict in terms of legal insufficiency.[32]

One example of the way this works in practice in relation to discrepancies in evidence can be seen in the difference between *Reilly and Others* v. *H.M. Advocate*[33] and *Robertson* v. *H.M. Advocate*.[34] *Reilly* was a case in which three men accused of assaulting and robbing Mr and Mrs N were all positively identified by Mrs N, who said of one of them that he was masked and of another that he was unbearded, although by the time of the identification parade the latter man had grown a slight beard. The Crown sought to corroborate her identification of the masked man by a weak identification at the parade by Mr N and by the finding of a stocking mask in the accused's house. Unfortunately for the Crown, Mrs N said that the mask she saw was not of the stocking type but was one which left the features undistorted. In the case of the unbearded offender the Crown again relied on a weak identi-

---

[31] See Babylon Talmud, *Sanhedrin*, chap. 5.
[32] See further, *infra*.
[33] 1981 S.C.C.R. 201.
[34] 1990 S.C.C.R. 142.

fication by Mr N at the parade, but Mr N claimed that he picked out that accused at the parade as resembling one of the offenders because of his beard. The appeals against conviction were allowed, and the identification evidence was described by the court as lacking in the necessary 'character, quality and strength'. In later cases it became clear that the High Court regretted the use of these words, and were anxious to escape from any suggestion that they had substituted their own assessment of the reliability of evidence for that of the jury. It was accordingly explained in *Rubin* v. *H.M. Advocate*[35] that the reason the convictions had been quashed in *Reilly* was that the evidence relied on for corroboration was contradictory of the evidence it was supposed to corroborate.[36]

In *Robertson* the accused was identified by two witnesses, each of whom was positive in his identification, but who contradicted each other in the description of the offender's clothing to such an extent that, if both were right about the clothing they saw, they could not have seen the same person. The point was not crucial in that case since there was other evidence against the accused, and it was open to the jury to accept one of the identification witnesses and reject the other. But the Lord Justice-Clerk's opinion suggests that it would have been open to the jury to hold that while one or other or both of the witnesses were wrong about the clothing they were both correct in their identification, which was not based in either case on the clothing worn by the person seen by the witness.[37] If one is to look for a logical criterion, perhaps it is that if the discrepancy relates to the feature relied on by the witness for his identification,

---

[35] 1984 S.C.C.R. 96.

[36] See, *e.g.*, Lord Grieve at p. 110; *cf. Ralston* v. *H.M. Advocate* 1987 S.C.C.R. 467, 472.

[37] Oddly enough Professor Jackson, *op. cit.* p. 39, cites a Rabbinic dictum (Sanhedrin, 41a) that if in a murder charge one witness says that the killer used a sword and one that he used a dagger their evidence is inadmissible, but that if one says he wore black and another that he wore white their evidence is admissible; but contrast Maimonides, *Hilchoth Eduth*, 2.2.

it renders his evidence unacceptable as corroboration, but that if it relates to something on which he does not rely for identification then the effect of the discrepancy on the identification is a matter for the jury to determine.

Circumstantial and direct evidence

The requirement of corroboration can arise in a number of different situations. The classic case is where there are two eye-witnesses to some essential fact, and the question is whether or not they back each other up. Then there is the common case where there is one eye-witness, or at least one main witness, and corroboration is sought in some fact or circumstance spoken to by another witness. And then, of course, there is the case where the evidence is wholly circumstantial, and, provided there are two circumstances proved, albeit each by only one witness, the question is more properly one of weight and cogency of inference than one of legal sufficiency.

The distinction between direct and circumstantial evidence is not, however, all that sharp in practice, and indeed in the end of the day there may be no clear distinction between the two; it may just be that certain facts are so strongly indicative of guilt that they are sufficient on their own, provided they are spoken to by two witnesses, whereas other facts are not enough on their own, irrespective of however many witnesses speak to them, but require to be corroborated by other facts. Is evidence that the accused ran out of a house carrying a bloodstained knife direct or circumstantial evidence that he stabbed the man who was found immediately afterwards lying bleeding from a stab wound in the house?[38] In other words is it enough in such a case for the Crown to lead two witnesses who saw the man in order to identify him as the

---

[38]There is a further difficulty arising from the problem of describing a fact; is evidence that a man ran out of a house carrying a bloodstained knife evidence of one, two, or three facts?

perpetrator, or do they need evidence of some other circumstance as well? A fingerprint is only one source of evidence, but it can be sufficient in itself to prove guilt, however many witnesses may be needed to prove that the print belonged to the accused.[39] The finding of a print is equivalent to the sighting of its owner, and whether or not that is enough for conviction depends on the inferences which can be drawn from his presence where the print was found.[40]

In cases of the kind discussed, there is evidence, albeit of only one fact, from two witnesses, and the fact is in itself incriminating. Where the evidence is what is usually called circumstantial, no one piece of evidence need be in itself indicative of guilt. Corroboration is not really the issue in such cases, provided that more than two facts are spoken to, and that both are not spoken to by the same witness. Even if each piece of evidence is quite neutral in itself, but is nevertheless essential to proof of guilt, a conviction is justified if the two taken together support an inference of guilt. In the notorious case of *Gillespie* v. *Macmillan*[41] the accused was convicted of exceeding the speed limit over a measured distance. One police officer had been stationed at each end of the measured distance, and each of them gave evidence that as the accused's car passed him he pressed his stop-watch. Thereafter it was calculated on the basis of simple arithmetic that the speed over the distance had been excessive. *Gillespie* v. *Macmillan* is a full-bench case (convened to

---

[39] *Hamilton* v. *H.M. Advocate* 1934 J.C. 1; *Rolley* v. *H.M. Advocate* 1945 J.C. 155.

[40] A man can be convicted of murder on evidence that his bloodstained fingerprint was found in the same house as the body which must have been lying in fresh blood at the time the print was made: *Langan* v. *H.M. Advocate* 1989 S.C.C.R. 379. Similarly, a fingerprint spoken to by one witness may be sufficient to corroborate another single witness: *cf. McBeth* v. *H.M. Advocate* (1976) S.C.C.R. Supp. 123; conversely, the presence of a fingerprint on a cheque forged by the owner of the print not would evidence of uttering: be *Burke* v. *MacPhail* 1984 S.C.C.R. 388. See also *Welsh* v. *H.M. Advocate* 1992 S.C.C.R. 108:DVA profiling.

[41] 1957 J.C. 31.

reconsider *Scott* v. *Jameson*[42], in which the judges considered the authorities on corroboration. Lord Justice-General Clyde approved the statement in *Scott* v. *Jameson* by Lord Guthrie that:

> 'If, in order to establish a charge, evidence is only tendered regarding one fact, that fact must be proved by two witnesses. But, if several facts require to be proved and these form a consecutive chain, leading to one conclusion, then it may be that each of these facts will require to be proved by two witnesses.'

He also approved a statement by Lord McLaren in *Lees* v. *Macdonald*[43] to the effect that:

> 'All that the law demands is that there should be two witnesses to prove a case, and provided that is so, any fact in the case may be proved by the testimony of one credible witness.'

Lord Clyde also expressly disapproved a statement by Lord Cooper in *Bisset* v. *Anderson*[44] that:

> 'the evidence of a single witness, however credible, is insufficient at common law to establish the truth of any essential fact required for a criminal conviction,'

except in so far as it applied to the single issue of the identification of the accused. The most interesting *dicta* in *Gillespie* v. *Macmillan*, however, are those of Lord Justice-Clerk Thomson, who summed up the law on corroboration as follows:

> 'I do not think that the sufficiency of proof of a criminal charge can be any more precisely defined than by saying that there must be facts emanating from at least two separate and independent sources.'[45]

---

[42](1914) 7 Adam 529.
[43](1893) 3 White 468.
[44]1949 J.C. 106.
[45]1957 J.C., at p. 39.

The objections to *Gillespie* v. *Macmillan* are obvious — it was essential to the Crown case to establish both the time of entry to and the time of exit from the measured stretch of road, yet each was spoken to only by one witness.[46] Moreover, each constable's evidence was totally neutral, not to say meaningless, in itself, and went no way at all to confirming the truth of the other constable's evidence. One might say that *Gillespie* v. *Macmillan* abolished the need for corroboration in any real sense, that is to say as a requirement springing from the danger of relying on the evidence of a single witness. This result was recognised by the Lord Justice-Clerk in a characteristically pragmatic opinion, when he said:

> If law were an exact science or even a department of logic, there might be something to be said for this argument [that there was no independent check on the constables' evidence and that they did not support each other]. By relying on the disparate qualities of space and time the logician can prove that in a race the hare can never overtake the tortoise. But law is a practical affair and one has to approach its problems in a mundane common-sense way.... When one views that problem as a practical issue, the only risk is that the knob was not pressed at the precise moment; in other words, that the presser was unreliable for some reason or another. The safeguard against this risk is whether the tribunal believes the witness, and that is the safeguard which may operate whenever a link in the chain or a tile in the mosaic or a piece in the jigsaw is spoken to by one witness only. But this just shows that the appellant's argument depends on value rather than sufficiency.'[47]

That passage clearly rejects the unreliability principle, and leaves us with only a two-witness rule: if the car's entry to and exit from the measured distance had been observed from a vantage point by only one constable, there would have been insufficient evidence for

---

[46]See W. A. Wilson, *op. cit.*; and 'Corroboration of Evidence in Scottish Criminal Law', 1958 S.L.T. (News) 137.

[47]1957 J.C., at p. 40.

conviction, but as they were spoken to by different witnesses the two-witness rule was satisfied, and there was a legal sufficiency of evidence; the only remaining question was one of weight.

Although *Gillespie* v. *Macmillan* is a full bench decision, it has had little or no influence on later cases. This can hardly be because there was no real dispute as to the reliability of the evidence given in it, since it was decided on general principles.[48] It is authority that the law does not require the circumstances relied on for proof of guilt to be incriminating in themselves, or to be mutually support-ive in the sense that the evidence of each witness makes that of the other likely to be true. It also holds that the statement in *Morton* v. *H.M. Advocate*[49] that there must be evidence from at least two sources 'implicating' the accused with the commission of the crime is limited to the identification of the accused as the perpetrator. Be that as it may, later cases have not relied on *Gillespie* v. *Macmillan*, or even referred to it, and the idea that each source of evidence should somehow point to guilt has not been abandoned, even in cases which appear to contradict it. Lord Justice-Clerk Thomson himself, for all that he regarded corroboration as an out-dated requirement, referred to it in later cases as an 'independent check',[50] and spoke of the need for 'evidence from some other source which incriminates the accused', and of evidence which 'points to [the accused] as a participant'.[51]

---

[48]And compare the later history of *Sinclair* v. *Clark* 1962 J.C. 57, discussed *infra*, where the decision was more dependent on the facts of the particular case. For a similar development in an adjacent area of law, see the use made of *Miln* v. *cullen* 1967 J.C. 21 in the retreat from *Chalmers* v. *H.M. Advocate* 1954 J.C. 66. *Gillespie* v. *Macmillan* may have been regarded as special because it was a case of circumstantial evidence in which the inference to be drawn was not synthetic but analytic, which is a most unusual state of affairs.

[49]1938 J.C. 50, 55.

[50]*Sinclair* v. *Clark* 1962 J.C. 57, 62.

[51]*Connolly* v. *H.M. Advocate* 1958 S.L.T. 79, 80. One can see a certain inconsistency in judicial pronouncements on this matter. In *Miln* v. *Fitzgerald* (1978) S.C.C.R. Supp. 205, 207 the High Court said that where there was a clear

Confessions: simple confessions

One of the areas in which corroboration is most frequently in issue is that of confessions. Confessions for this purpose are divided into two classes — simple confessions and confessions disclosing 'special knowledge' of the circumstances of the offence.

It is undisputed that an accused cannot be convicted on the basis of a simple confession alone, however many times and to however many people he confesses. It is arguable that this rule does not arise necessarily from the requirement of corroboration, but is the result of a policy decision, a separate piece of rule-utilitarianism. The rule about confessions is sometimes spoken of as a corollary of the rule that guilt cannot be proved by evidence from one source only, in that however many times a man confesses, the source of all that evidence is still one and the same, the man himself.[52] That treats evidence of a confession as equivalent to direct evidence from the

---

admission from the accused that he was the driver of the car concerned in the offence, the question for the sheriff was whether there were any facts or circumstances which pointed 'unequivocally' to the truth of that statement, and in *McDonald* v. *Smith* (1978) S.C.C.R. Supp. 219, 221 the court said in a similar case that where the accused's admission was accepted as truthful, the issue was whether there were independent facts and circumstances pointing unequivocally to the truth of the admission, and also that very little was needed to corroborate it, and that the search was from some measure of independent support for an admission already accepted as credible and accurate.

[52]Evidence of distress is distinguished as having its source in the evidence of the observer of the distress and not in the complainer who displayed it. The fact that V told his story to W as well as to Y, or that the complainer gave an account of the offence to someone else soon after it had been committed, cannot corroborate his evidence of the incident, since he cannot corroborate himself, but evidence that he was in a distressed condition soon after the incident can corroborate his account of it. Evidence of distress is treated in the same way as evidence of physical injury. It is, of course, for the jury to say whether the distress was genuine or simulated, just as it is for them to determine the source of external injuries, but if they decide that it was genuine they can treat it as corroboration, and that not merely of lack of consent in rape, but of assault in a case of simple assault, and perhaps also of theft by housebreaking in appropriate cases: *Bennett* v. *H.M. Advocate* 1989 S.C.C.R. 608; *Stillie* v *H.M. Advocate,* 1990 S.C.C.R. 719; *Horner* v. *H.M. Advocate,* 1991 S.C.C.R. 248. For a discussion of the question, see *McLellan* v. *H.M. Advocate* 1992 S.C.C.R. 171.

accused himself, *i.e.* as evidence of the truth of its content,[53] but it is arguable that a confession is just a piece of circumstantial evidence, and that evidence from B and C that A said he killed V is not evidence from A that he killed V which requires to be corroborated from another source, but is evidence from B and C of a circumstance — a confession by A — from which guilt may be inferred. If that is correct, then, since that circumstance is spoken to by two witnesses, the two-witness rule will be satisfied, and all that will remain is the question of the cogency of the inference that may be drawn,[54] just as if B and C had given evidence that A's fingerprints were on the bloodstained knife. Equally the strength of the inference from confession to guilt would vary with the number of times the confession was made and the circumstances in which it was made: an inference from a series of confessions, spoken to by different people, whether or not each instance is spoken to by only one witness, will be stronger than one made from one confession, especially if some of the confessions are made to independent people or to friends of the accused, and not to police officers. In practice, however, the law does now treat a confession as equivalent to evidence given by the confessor.[54a] In any event the law, for whatever reason, requires corroboration of a simple confession, and that corroboration must come from a source other than the confessor; but it does not require all that much corroboration, declaring that where there is an 'unequivocal confession' very little else is required.[54b] The most recent cases do not appear to be concerned with the circumstances in which the confession is made, but only with its content, and the amount of corroboration required depends on the content of the confession, which indeed, as in the case of the special knowledge confession, may be such as

---

[53] *Cf. Morrison* v. *H.M. Advocate* 1990 J.C. 299; 1990 S.C.C.R. 235.

[54] Cf. Hume on *Crimes*, vol. ii, p. 325.

[54a] See note 53, *supra*.

[54b] But see now *Meredith* v. *Lees* Criminal Appeal Court, 18th March 1992; to be reported.

to require no real corroboration at all.[55] If the content is not clear
and unequivocal, if it is such that it might or might not be a
confession to the crime charged, it is treated as a circumstance like
any other, to be looked at along with other circumstances in
deciding the case.[56] But if it is clear and unequivocal, then all that
is needed is something to satisfy the rule that a confession in itself
is not enough.

The difficulty about this approach, when we come down to its
practical application, is that the main issue in many cases which
depend on confessions is not whether the contents of the confession
are such as to carry a convincing inference of guilt; it is whether the
accused made the confession, or whether, if he did make it, he made
it freely. The unreliability principle would lead us to require more
and not less corroboration than usual when the accused's case is that
the police forced the confession out of him, or are lying when they
say he made it. In order to satisfy that principle we would be looking
for independent evidence clearly linking the accused with the
crime, and the amount of evidence required to enable us to make
a cogent inference of guilt should depend not so much on the
content of the confession as on the extent to which the circumstances of its alleged making are doubtful. In that context there is
all the difference in the world between a driver who goes into a
police station to report an accident involving the car he was driving,
as happened in *Sinclair* v. *Clark*,[57] and a seventeen year old boy of
low intelligence who confesses to a murder at two o'clock in the
morning after having been in police custody for twelve hours
without any sleep, as happened in *Hartley* v. *H.M. Advocate*.[58] Yet
these two situations were equiparated in *Hartley* where, although
Lord Grieve said that there must be evidence other than the

---

[55] See *infra*.
[56] *Greenshields* v. *H.M. Advocate* 1989 S.C.C.R. 637.
[57] 1962 J.C. 57.
[58] 1979 S.L.T. 26

confession pointing to the accused as the murderer, all the judges said that very little corroboration was required, and Lord Dunpark went so far as to stress that the court was looking only for extrinsic evidence consistent with the confession.[59]

One can but marvel, with respect, at the mental agility displayed by the 'quantum leap' from *Sinclair* to *Hartley*, especially as the degree of corroboration required was said in *Sinclair* to be related to the circumstances of the making of the confession. What Lord Justice-Clerk Thomson said there was:

> 'There is a rule in our law — a somewhat archaic rule — the merit of which in modern conditions is not always obvious, at all events where the admission is made in circumstances beyond suspicion, that short of a solemn plea of guilt, an admission of guilt by an accused is not conclusive against him, unless it is corroborated by something beyond the actual admission. One reason for this rule is to ensure that there is nothing phoney or quixotic about the confession. What is required by way of independent evidence in order to elide such a risk must depend on the facts of the case, and, in particular, the nature and character of the confession and the circumstances in which it is made.'[60]

Out of this dictum there has developed what sounds more like a catch-phrase than a rule of law[60a]: a confession needs very little in the way of corroboration. Generations of advocates-depute have by now happily and successfully stood up in the appeal court and said, 'All that is required for conviction is a confession and very little else, and that is what we have here'. The attitude of the court towards the corroboration of confessions in recent times is perhaps comparable to their attitude to the related question of the admissibility of confessions made by suspects to police officers. As I have said, the decision not to convict on the basis of confessions alone may be, in

---

[59]See 1979 S.L.T. at pp. 31 and 33.

[60]1962 J.C., at p. 62.

[60a]It has now been said not to be a rule of law: *Meredith* v. *Lees* Criminal Appeal Court, 18th March 1992; to be reported.

the end of the day, a policy decision that certain inferences will not be regarded as sufficiently cogent to satisfy the standard of proof beyond reasonable doubt. But this, like the corroboration requirement itself, creates difficulties in convicting the clearly guilty, and the extent to which the law will limit the corroboration needed may itself be a function of the same kind of considerations as govern the extent to which it will enforce exclusionary rules relating to the admissibility of confessions at all — and both questions arose sharply in *Hartley*. Perhaps in this context I may be allowed to quote what I said in another *Festschrift*:[61]

> 'It is easy to tolerate a few criminals and a few unjust acquittals (or any other group or practice to which one feels a degree of antagonism) in the name of freedom and fair play; it is different when the criminals are many and look like getting the upper hand. There is, too, when punishments are less severe, and especially now that capital punishment has gone, less need to weight the law of evidence in the accused's favour. It is, it may be said, all very well being fair to the criminals, but their victims, present and potential, are entitled to a little fairness too.'

The approach of the court to the confession in *Hartley* raises another interesting point, particularly as it is typical of the approach of the court to all questions of corroboration where what is in issue is whether there is enough other evidence to corroborate the one source of evidence which points clearly to guilt, such as a confession. The admissibility of the confession in *Hartley* was challenged on the ground that it had been unfairly obtained. The court dealt with that point first, and then, having held that the jury were entitled to accept that it was fairly obtained, dealt with corroboration on the basis that the confession was as reliable as that in *Sinclair* v. *Clark*. The court, that is to say, assumed that the jury had first

----

[61]'The Admissibility of Answers to Police Questioning in Scotland', in *Reshaping the Criminal Law*, ed. Glazebrook (London, 1978) 317, at p. 318.

looked at the confession in isolation and been satisfied of its reliability, and had then looked for corroboration. In that case, of course, any corroboration required would have been minimal, since it would have been required only to satisfy the rule that a confession has to be corroborated, reliability being no longer in issue.[62] But that is not how corroboration works, at least in the context of the unreliability principle. If corroboration is required in that context because it is held to be unacceptably dangerous to rely on a confession alone, one has to allow for the situation in which the jury are initially unsure of the reliability of the confession, and become satisfied of it only because it is sufficiently corroborated. A jury may hover between believing the police and believing the accused in relation to whether, or how, or why the confession was made, and eventually decide to convict because there is other evidence of guilt. The amount of corroboration required in such a case may well be greater than that required in one where, as in *Sinclair* v. *Clark* and many of the other road traffic cases, the accused does not deny making the confession and the trial is really about whether his lawyer is clever enough to persuade the court that there is insufficient evidence of his client's manifest guilt.[63] Similar considerations apply to that other suspect source of evidence — eye-witness identification — whose history is not unlike that of confessions.[64]

This particular aspect of the law of corroboration does not seem to have engaged the Scottish courts. It has, however, been discussed in some House of Lords and Privy Council cases, which were concerned with whether a jury had to accept the main witness as reliable before they could look for corroboration. The cases culmi-

---

[62] *Cf. McDonald* v. *Smith* (1978) S.C.C.R. Supp. 219, 221: 'The search is for some measure of independent support for an admission which is ex hypothesi of the argument one which has already been accepted as credible and accurate.'

[63] See *e.g. McDonald* v. *Smith, supra; Lockhart* v. *Crockatt* 1986 S.C.C.R. 685.

[64] *Infra.*

nated in *Attorney-General of Hong Kong* v. *Wong*,[65] where Lord Bridge of Harwich said:

> 'Evidence which a witness first gives and then admits to have been false is no longer his sworn testimony and, if a criminal prosecution depends on it, the judge should direct an acquittal. But, apart from such extremes, any tribunal of fact confronted with a conflict of testimony must evaluate the credibility of evidence in deciding whether the party who bears the burden of proof has discharged it. It is a commonplace of judicial experience that a witness who makes a poor impression in the witness box may be found at the end of the day, when his evidence is considered in the light of all the other evidence bearing upon the issue, to have been both truthful and accurate. Conversely, the evidence of a witness who at first seemed impressive and reliable may at the end of the day have to be rejected. Such experience suggests that it is dangerous to assess the credibility of the evidence given by any witness in isolation from other evidence in the case which is capable of throwing light on its reliability; it would, to their Lordships' minds, be surprising if the law requiring juries to be warned of the danger of convicting on the uncorroborated evidence of a witness in one of the suspect categories should have developed to the point where, in some cases, the jury must be directed to make such an assessment of credibility in isolation.

The concluding sentence in the passage which their Lordships have cited from the speech of Lord Hailsham of St Marylebone L.C. in *Reg.* v. *Kilbourne* [1973] A.C. 729, 746, seems to point directly against the suggested two stage process. The passage as a whole, their Lordships think, is primarily emphasising what is plainly correct, viz. that the evidence of a suspect witness, even though it receives some independent support in a form capable of providing corroboration, cannot found a conviction unless itself accepted as true.

More difficulty arises from the passage cited from the speech of Lord Morris of Borth-y-Gest in *Reg.* v. *Hester* [1973] A.C. 296, 315, particularly the last sentence. It is possible to read the sentence as supporting the proposition that corroborative evidence cannot 'give validity or credence to evidence which is . . . suspect'. If this was

---

[65] [1987] A.C. 501.

indeed a proposition which Lord Morris of Borth-y-Gest intended to enunciate, it is one from which their Lordships feel constrained respectfully to dissent. It is precisely because the evidence of a witness in one of the categories which their Lordships for convenience have called 'suspect witness' may be of questionable reliability for a variety of reasons, familiar to generations of judges but not immediately apparent to jurors, that juries must be warned of the danger of convicting on that evidence if not corroborated; in short because it is suspect evidence. The corroborative evidence will not, of course, necessarily authenticate the evidence of the suspect witness. But it may at least allay some of the suspicion. In other words it may assist in establishing the reliability of the suspect evidence.

Their Lordships attach particular significance to the words of Lord Reid in *Reg.* v. *Kilbourne* [1973] A.C. 729, 750: "There is nothing technical in the idea of corroboration. When in the ordinary affairs of life one is doubtful whether or not to believe a particular statement one naturally looks to see whether it fits in with other statements or circumstances relating to the particular matter; the better it fits in, the more one is inclined to believe it. The doubted statement is corroborated to a greater or lesser extent by the other statements or circumstances with which it fits in".'[66]

Confessions: special knowledge

There is, however, one kind of confession which is sufficient in itself for conviction, provided at least that there is other evidence that the crime was committed by someone, and that is the so-called 'special knowledge' confession, sometimes, and not entirely inaccurately, called a 'self-corroborating' confession. It can best be described by quoting the *locus classicus* on the subject in Alison's *Practice*.[67]

---

[66]At pp. 510D-511E. It may be of interest to note that the most recent case on corroboration (which dealt with a *Moorov* – type situation) was one in which the majority of their Lordships consisted of former High Court judges, including Lord Emslie, and in which the leading speech was given by Lord Mackay of Clashfern, L.C., with whom the other members of the Appeals Committee concurred: *D.P.P.* v *P.* [1991] 2 A. C. 447.

[67]At pp. 580-581.

'Thus, if a person is apprehended on a charge of theft, and he tells the officer who seized him, that if he will go to such a place, and look under such a bush, he will find the stolen goods; or he is charged with murder or assault, and he says that he threw the bloody weapon into such a pool, in such a river, and it is there searched for and found; without doubt, these are such strong confirmations of the truth of the confession, as renders it of itself sufficient, if the *corpus* is established *aliunde*, to convict the prisoner.'

What is important about this kind of confession is not that it is a confession, but that it reveals that the accused knew various things about the crime. The law says that where the accused knew certain details of the crime it is permissible to infer that he committed the offence, if that is the only reasonable explanation of how he came by the knowledge in question. That knowledge is a single circumstance, and the evidence led from other witnesses that the accused's knowledge was correct, that what he described was indeed the fact, does not corroborate his possession of the knowledge, it merely enables us to describe what he said as constituting knowledge. It certainly gives us no help at all in determining the source of that knowledge, yet the identity of that source is the vital element in the Crown case, since if the accused knew of the facts disclosed in his statement because, *e.g.* the police told him about them, his knowledge is worthless as a circumstance indicating guilt, and his statement will be at most no more than a simple confession. What matters in a special knowledge confession is not that the accused confessed to the crime, but that he knew certain things about it. The knowledge need not even be displayed in a confession; it can be displayed in an exculpatory statement and still be sufficient to allow of an inference of guilt. If the accused says he was innocent of the crime, but gives an account of it which discloses special knowledge, which he says he obtained from X, and if it can be shown that his knowledge could not have come from X, the fact that he had that knowledge may suffice to convict him.[68]

---

[68] *Cf. Moran* v. *H.M. Advocate* 1990 S.C.C.R. 40.

Because everything depends on the only reasonable explanation of the accused's knowledge being his involvement in the crime, one might have expected the inference of guilt to be allowable only where there was evidence that the facts disclosed by the accused were not known to the police. That was the situation described by Alison, and it was the situation in the leading modern case on the subject, *Manuel* v. *H.M. Advocate*,[69] where the accused revealed the burial place of one of his victims to the police. To restrict the cases in which it is competent to convict on the basis of a special knowledge confession alone to cases of this kind would, of course, be a policy decision, depending on the view that it would be too dangerous to allow a jury to decide that the police were telling the truth when they gave evidence that although the matters spoken to by the accused were already known to them, they did not pass that information on to him.[70] It was, I believe, fairly generally thought at one time that special knowledge confessions could be relied on as sufficient proof only in cases where the information disclosed in them was unknown to the police, but if that ever was the law it ceased to be so in 1982 when it was settled that it was not necessarily fatal to the application of the rule about special knowledge confessions that the facts concerned were known to persons other than the accused. The question is not whether anyone else knew, but whether the accused had any reason to know unless he was guilty. There are no legal limitations on the circumstances in which an inference of guilt can be drawn from such confessions, and it is for the jury in each case to determine whether the only reasonable explanation of the accused's knowledge is that he was guilty.[71] All

---

[69] 1958 J.C. 41.

[70] One might have expected special knowledge confessions to be insufficient for conviction where the knowledge displayed was of facts which were public knowledge, or in cases where the accused included incorrect 'facts' in his statement as well as correct ones, but neither of these restrictions applies: see *Wilson* v. *H.M. Advocate* 1987 S.C.C.R. 217; *Gilmour* v. *H.M. Advocate* 1982 S.C.C.R. 590.

[71] See *McAvoy* v. *H.M. Advocate* 1982 S.C.C.R. 263; *Wilson* v. *McCaughey* 1982 S.C.C.R. 398.

that is left of what used to be a proud boast that Scots law was superior to English law because no-one could be convicted in Scotland on the basis of his confession alone, is that no-one can be so convicted unless his confession includes some details about the crime which are sufficient to persuade the jury that the only reason he was able to mention them is that he is guilty. As a protection against possible police abuses that is, of course, quite worthless.[72]

To turn to less polemical matters, it should be noted that although one thinks of special knowledge confessions as containing details of the crime, that is not necessary, at least in principle. If a man comes into the police station and simply says that he has just murdered his wife, but gives no details at all, and if up to that time no-one had any idea that his wife was anything but alive and well, that is a special knowledge confession. The fact, if it be one, that this confession is unlikely to be treated as a special knowledge confession is due to the influence of the classic examples of such confessions, which do contain details, and perhaps also to a lingering feeling of unease about this type of evidence, which leads us to look for a little more than a bare statement of guilt.

---

[72]A recent case, does, however, suggest that the High Court may be prepared to take a stricter view, at least in summary cases. In *Woodland* v. *Hamilton* 1990 S.C.C.R. 166 the charge was one of theft, and the special knowledge displayed was that the stolen goods had been in the possession of a named person, in whose possession they were indeed proved to have been. But the accused's statement was made a year after the theft and shortly after he had been speaking to a co-accused (who was acquitted). The appeal court applied the proposition that the Crown had to show that the only reasonable explanation for the accused's knowledge was guilt, and held that in the circumstances the sheriff was not entitled to hold that the Crown had done this and quashed the conviction. The case may be special in that evidence was led of an actual opportunity which the appellant had to obtain innocently the knowledge relied on by the Crown, but it does raise questions as to how far there is a duty on the Crown to exclude such opportunities, and what duty there is on an accused to introduce into evidence facts indicating the existence of an innocent opportunity to acquire the relevant knowledge. See also *Robertson* v. *H.M. Advocate* 1990 S.C.C.R. 142.

Since the only source of evidence against the accused in this kind of case is his own knowledge, it is necessary to lead two witnesses to speak to the making of the confession, just as it needs two witnesses to speak to the finding of fingerprints. It is not so clear that two witnesses are required to speak to the fact of the commission of the crime itself, at least where the special knowledge is accompanied by an admission of guilt. Alison speaks of proving the crime '*aliundè*', but does not elaborate the point. If the accused says he committed the crime, and goes on to display special knowledge, it is not clear why that statement, which includes a statement that the crime was committed, should require to be corroborated by two witnesses to the commission of the crime. Even if A's extrajudicial confession that he committed the crime is not direct evidence of the commission of the crime,[73] it is a circumstance from which the commission of the crime can be inferred, just as it is a circumstance from which it can be inferred that it was committed by him. There is indeed some ground for supposing that the crime does not need to be spoken to by two witnesses, so that if A says he broke into a particular house and there stole certain articles, that is enough to corroborate the evidence of one witness that the house was broken into and the articles taken.[74] On the other hand, it can be argued that as the correctness of the accused's knowledge is essential to the Crown case it should (*pace, Gillespie* v. *Macmillan*[75]) be proved by two witnesses.

Identification

The position with regard to identification is remarkably similar to that with regard to confessions. The result is that the requirements of corroboration are at their weakest when what is to be corrobo-

---

[73]See *supra*.

[74]See *Smith*v. *H.M. Advocate*(1978) S.C.C.R. Supp. 203, although the matter is not made explicit; in *Sinclair*v. *Tudhope* 1987 S.C.C.R. 690 there was no other evidence of the commission of the crime at all.

[75]1957 J.C. 31.

rated is evidence of a kind regarded by most people as highly suspect. In relation to identification evidence, as in the case of confessions, a dictum in a minor road traffic case where the main evidence was clearly reliable has been extended to cover quite different situations and evidence which is far from so clearly reliable. The identification of a driver by his workmate who was a passenger in the vehicle clearly requires only formal corroboration,[76] but it is in a different world from an identification by a stranger who caught only a fleeting glimpse of the culprit.[77] Yet the same rule, that where there is one positive identification very little corroboration is required, is applied in both cases. And it is applied on the same view of how the jury approached the evidence as is taken in confession cases.[78] The appeal court, that is to say, assume that the jury accepted the identification as reliable and then looked for corroboration, rather than asking whether any particular identification was so weak as to be unlikely to have been accepted without corroboration, and then asking if there was any evidence from which sufficiently strong corroboration could be obtained. The cases talk of positive identifications, by analogy perhaps with unequivocal confessions, but a positive identification is just one that the witness was positive about, not one which was obviously reliable, like the identification of one friend by another. That is to say, the positive nature of an identification is a function of the obstinacy or self-assurance of the witness, rather than of his reliability or the circumstances in which the identification was made. It is true, of course, that juries are warned of the dangers inherent in identification evidence,[78a] but they are free to accept such evidence, and once they have accepted a positive identification

---

[76] *MacNeill* v. *Wilson* 1981 S.C.C.R. 80.

[77] *Cf. Ralston* v. *H.M. Advocate* 1987 S.C.C.R. 467.

[78] *Supra.*

[78a] On the degree of warning necessary, see *McAvoy* v *H.M. Advocate,* 1991 S.C.C.R. 123; contrast the English requirements, as applied in *Reid (Junior)* v. *The Queen* [1990] 1 A.C. 363, and the authorities referred to therein.

of the accused, all that remains for them to do is to find the necessary minimal corroboration required by the two witness-rule.[79]

Sufficiency and weight

It is sometimes said that sufficiency is a question of law while weight is one of fact, so that if a conviction is obtained on insufficient evidence the appeal court will quash it, whereas matters of weight are jury questions with which the appeal court will not interfere. That, however, is not strictly accurate, although it must be said that the term 'sufficiency' is somewhat vague. In relation to corroboration, the matter is further complicated by the consideration that what is sufficient corroboration depends on whether we are thinking of the two-witness rule or of the principle of unreliability. Within the confines of the two-witness rule sufficiency is a matter of arithmetic, but once reliability is brought into the equation it is impossible to disentangle sufficiency from weight.

It is clear that if the two-witness rule is breached the conviction will be quashed.[80] It is equally clear that the appeal court will not interfere with the jury's assessment of the credibility and reliability of the witnesses.[81] The evidence offered as corroboration must also be relevant, but that relevance is sometimes tested in the context of an exercise of checking the evidence of the main witness,[82] and at other times is related to the requirements of the law. An interesting example of the latter situation can be seen in *Quinn* v. *H.M. Advocate*.[83] In that case the complainer gave evidence that the appellant was a participant in a rape which took place in his house. The Crown sought corroboration in evidence of the appellant's

---

[79]Indeed a witness who says he is 80 per cent sure of his identification can be corroborated by another witness who is 75 per cent sure: *Nolan* v. *McLeod* 1987 S.C.C.R. 558.

[80]*Morton* v. *H.M. Advocate* 1938 J.C. 50.

[81]*Rubin* v. *H.M. Advocate* 1984 S.C.C.R. 96.

[82]See, *e.g., Hartley* v. *H.M. Advocate* 1979 S.L.T. 26.

[83]1990 S.C.C.R. 254.

presence on the scene, his involvement in an indecent assault on the complainer in the same place a few hours earlier, and his denial to the police that any one had been in his house at the relevant time. Each of these matters was rejected by the appeal court, since mere presence is not enough for art and part guilt, involvement in an earlier offence is irrelevant to proof of involvement in a later one,[84] and there is no such thing as corroboration by false denial. *Quinn* does not go so far as to say that corroboration must take the form of evidence in itself incriminating, but it goes some way towards doing so.

One interesting example of an appeal court considering the weight of evidence can be seen in *Bennett* v. *H.M. Advocate.*[85] In that case three men were charged with assaulting and robbing a taxi-driver in the course of a journey in his taxi: although they put him out of the taxi and drove off in it, they were not charged with robbery of the taxi. The element of robbery was held to be uncorroborated, so that what was left was an assault on the driver in which one of the men pointed a knife at him. The complainer identified all three men, L, B, and C. There was no problem regarding L. In the case of B there was evidence from another witness that one of the men who got into the taxi was wearing a bonnet, and evidence from other witnesses that B was seen near where the taxi was abandoned, walking towards his home in the company of two unidentified men, and wearing a bonnet. In the case of C there was evidence from another witness that he had got into the taxi at the beginning of its journey, along with the two other accused and a girl, but no evidence of his whereabouts thereafter. The appeal court held that in the case of B it 'was very much a jury question as to whether the facts and circumstances' were sufficient to corroborate the complainer, and refused his

---

[84] *Cf. Carrick* v. *H.M. Advocate* 1990 S.C.C.R. 286.
[85] 1989 S.C.C.R. 608.

appeal. In the case of C, however, it was held that, as there was no evidence to corroborate the complainer's statement that he was still in the taxi at the time of the assault, there was insufficient corroboration, and his conviction was quashed. One would, with respect, have thought that the 'very little' needed to corroborate a positive identification was provided by the witness who spoke to C's being in the taxi at the beginning of the journey,[86] there being no evidence to suggest that he left it in mid-stream, so to speak, but one would have been wrong. If the decision was unexpectedly favourable to C, it might be argued that it was by the same token unexpectedly unfavourable to B. There were three men and a girl in the taxi along with the complainer. There was some corroboration that the complainer had been the victim of a knife attack which the court held to be sufficient, but there was no corroboration of his account that all three male passengers were party to the assault, or as to which man did what; and in that situation it is arguable that the involvement of none of the accused in the attack was corroborated, even if there was corroborated evidence that two of them were in the taxi at the relevant time.[87] What we appear to be left with is that the appeal court thought that the corroboration of the identification of B was sufficiently strong, whereas that of the identification of C was not.

Conclusion

It is difficult to summarise the law relating to corroboration. Perhaps all that can be said is that, apart from special cases such as the proof of loss in theft, the only firm rule is that there must be two

---

[86] *Cf.* Alison's statements that the evidence in robbery usually consists of that of complainer 'coupled with that of persons who saw [the accused] near the scene of violence, or in company with the principal witness shortly before the robbery,' and that 'the direct evidence of the person robbed, coupled with very slender adminicles' is usually enough for a conviction of stouthrief: *Principles*, pp. 242, 249.

[87] *Cf. Quinn* v. *H.M. Advocate* 1990 S.C.C.R. 254.

witnesses to prove guilt. Beyond that, and within the limits of relevance, it is all a matter of circumstances. As Burnett put it:[88]

'What those circumstances are which ought to confirm and render complete the *semiplena probatio* of *one* witness, it is impossible to determine by any rule, as the result depends upon the nature and quality of each circumstance, and their joint effect when combined; and also on the view taken of them by those who are to judge of the case. . . .

. . . what modification of circumstances ought to mark the line between that *legal certainty*, which in such cases ought to warrant a finding of guilt, and that *suspicion* merely, which is no ground to warrant a *conviction*, it is impossible to ascertain. They must lie in the breasts and in the consciences of those who are to judge of them; and are in their nature so various and complicated, as to be beyond the reach of precise legal rules.'

---

[88]Burnett's *Criminal Law*, pp. 519, 523.

4

HEARSAY: A SCOTTISH PERSPECTIVE

A. B. Wilkinson

Origins

In the *Berkeley Peerage* case Lord Mansfield said:

'In Scotland and in most continental countries, the judges determine about the facts in dispute as well as on the law; and they think
that there is no danger in their listening to evidence of hearsay
because when they come to consider of their judgment on the merits
of the case they can trust themselves to disregard entirely the hearsay
evidence, or give it any little weight which it seems to deserve. But
in England, where the jury are the sole judges of the facts, hearsay
evidence is properly excluded because no man can tell what effect it
might have upon their minds.'[1]

Yet the Scottish lineage of the rule against hearsay is ancient.
Stair put it simply: 'testimonies *ex auditu* prove not', and Balfour,
Hume and Burnett were to the same effect.[2] Nor, if there had been
no rule against hearsay, would the absence of jury trial have been an
adequate explanation. Lord Mansfield spoke before jury trial was
introduced, or re-introduced, to Scottish civil practice[3] but the
criminal jury was already long-established and had similar historical roots to its English counterpart. Lord Mansfield's views are,

---

[1](1811) 4 Camp. 401, at p. 414.
[2]Stair, IV, xliii, 15; Balfour, *Practicks*, 381; Hume on *Crimes* (3rd edn.), ii, 406;
Burnett, *Criminal Law*, 600.
[3]Jury Trials (Scotland) Act 1815.

however, of interest for two reasons. First, he may from experience of Scottish appeals in the House of Lords have acquired some impression of how, at least in civil cases, hearsay evidence was handled by Scottish courts. Lord Devlin has said that the law of evidence as expounded on the basis of the authorities bears the same relation to the law of evidence as practised in the courts as the King's English bears to pidgin English.[4] Lord Mansfield is, perhaps, an eloquent if unwitting witness to that dichotomy. Closing or reducing the gap between law and practice may be a legitimate object of reform. Secondly, however mistaken Lord Mansfield's comparative researches may have been[5] — and the continental sources give little more support to his thesis than do the Scottish — he is of interest as an early exponent of the view that the rationale for the rule against hearsay is to be found in the jury. That view was taken up by Thayer and controversy has since flourished on whether it is to the jury or to adversary procedure that the common law legal world should look for the origins of the rule.[6]

The controversy on origins, if pursued on traditional lines, is largely sterile. The material from early sources, such as the explanation of the exclusion of evidence on the ground that the author of the statement had not been on oath or was not available for cross-examination, is now usually thought to support the adversary, rather than the jury, theory, but none of the material is unequivocal. The exigencies both of jury trial and of adversary procedure have doubtless influenced later developments but, at least so far as Scotland is concerned, it is difficult to accept that either was a formative source. Until 1686 civil procedure was essentially in-

---

[4]Cross, *Some Proposals for Reform of the Law of Evidence* (1961) 24 M.L.R. 31, at p. 65.

[5]See: Hammelmanm, *Hearsay Evidence, A Comparison* (1951) 67 L.Q.R. 67.

[6]Thayer, *Preliminary Treatise on Evidence at the Common Law*; Morgan, *Law of Evidence: Some Proposals for its Reform* (Yale, 1927) and also *Introduction to the American Law Institute's Model Code of Evidence.*

quisitorial and it retained something of that character until the reforms at the beginning of the nineteenth century. Yet the rule against hearsay is at least as old as the early seventeenth century. On the other hand, as juries were unknown to post-mediaeval civil procedure until 1815, distrust of, or lack of confidence in, the jury is unlikely to have played a determinant part. The search for origins can be pursued more profitably elsewhere. The dominant historical influence here, as in much of both the substantive and adjective law, seems to have been civilian. Indeed, nowhere is civilian (or canonist) influence stronger than in pre-nineteenth century adjective law, as can be seen from the forms of procedure and proof. There are traces of a rule against hearsay in the Novels and the Digest.[7] Conservative and liberal interpretations may be found in the later civilian tradition. In eighteenth century German law *testimonium de auditu* was regarded as worthless and so, with an exception for questions of blood relationship in matrimonial disputes, the *testis de auditu* was excluded.[8] Pothier too considered that hearsay testimony could not make proof,[9] and pre-Napoleonic French law admitted hearsay only in exceptional circumstances. Voet, on the other hand, was more liberal. He discusses hearsay only in connection with public rumour and broadcast reports. These, he says, are not properly evidence but 'only provide a kind of token by which in criminal matters the judge may direct his further tracking down of the truth.' They may also strengthen other evidence. But 'for the rest rumour is as much a grasper at what is made up and is evil as it is a messenger of the truth.' His conclusion, while acknowledging that the commentators he cites would narrow the discretion of the judge in various ways, is that 'the extent of belief to be given to rumour must be left to the discretion of a cautious judge.'[10] Scots law, it seems

---

[7]Nov. 90, 2; D.22, 3, 28; *cf.* C.4, 21, 13.

[8]Hammelmanm, p. 69.

[9] *Traite des Obligations* No. 786.

[10] *Commentary on the Pardects,* XXII, 3, 4 (Gane's transl., vol. 3, p. 727).

clear, inclined to the conservative side of the civilian debate, although a place was found for proof by reputation in questions of marriage and legitimacy and other cases in which reliance could be put on public report so as to yield at least *prima facie* proof.[11]

If one looks for the rationale on which civilian ideas were assimilated and applied it is to be found, quite simply, in an ancient distrust of oral testimony. That distrust is typical of Roman law and found its way into the civilian tradition.[12] It has also influenced the historical course of English law.[13] It was a marked feature of Scots law as reflected in the numerous categories of witnesses who were for long excluded from giving evidence.[14] Some of these excluded categories may in part be explained by a reluctance to burden men's consciences with a conflict between their own interests, or the interests of those to whom they were bound by familial or other allegiance, and the duty of speaking the truth under oath, but the main reason was that oral testimony was thought so unreliable that any feature which might heighten the risk of falsehood or error led to the witness's exclusion. 'Yet great caution,' says Stair, 'hath been always adhibited in admitting of witnesses; because many are apt to mistake, through inadvertency or precipitancy, and through the secret insinuation of favour or hatred, which even the witnesses themselves do not perceive.'[15] The same distrust of oral testimony, if in a more acceptable form, may be seen in the requirement of corroboration and in the rules that writing is necessary for the constitution of certain obligations and that the writ or oath of the party having the interest to deny the obligation is necessary for the proof of others. In the latter connection Erskine's comment is of

---

[11] Stair, III, iii, 42 and IV, xlv, 4.

[12] Morrison, *Some Features of the Roman and the English law of Evidence* (1959) 33 Tulane L.R. 577, 585; Voet, XXII, 5 (Gane's transl. vol. 3, pp. 760 *et seq.*).

[13] Cross on *Evidence* (7th edn.) pp. 201-206.

[14] Stair, IV, xliii; Erskine, *Institute* IV, ii, 22-25; Hume, ii, 339.

[15] Stair, IV, xliii.

interest that, when the art of writing was rare, proof by witnesses was admitted in almost every case, but 'after writing became a more general accomplishment, the lubricity and uncertain faith of testimonies made it necessary to bring the doctrine of parole evidence within narrower limits.'[16] Our ancestors were very conscious of the fallibility of testimony and until the nineteenth century was well advanced there was little of the modern confidence, perhaps now waning, in the ability of the trier of fact, whether judge or jury, to separate the true from the false. At the beginning of the modern development More commented:

> 'According to the old notions entertained in Scotland, all persons were incompetent as witnesses whose testimony was supposed to be liable to any bias, or to whose evidence full and implicit credit might not be given. Every person admitted as a witness was not only presumed to tell the truth, and the whole truth, but the capacity of every witness for accuracy of observation, and distinctness of recollection, seemed to be placed on the same footing, so that no room was left for the exercise of that discrimination, perhaps the most essential, as it is undoubtedly the most difficult, duty of those who are called upon to judge of evidence, which consists in giving to the testimony even of the most upright witnesses, only that degree of weight to which their opportunities and accuracy of observation entitle it. But when, instead of exercising this discrimination, every person admitted as a witness was held to stand upon the same level, and the evidence of each was received with the same attention, and held to be entitled to the same weight, it is obvious that much precaution was necessary as to the persons who should be allowed to give evidence.'[17]

Reluctance to admit oral evidence went then hand-in-hand with reluctance to evaluate it once admitted. More stood at the dawn of the modern era and although he saw some of the hazards he did not shrink from the challenge. His confidence in the trier of fact was well-nigh complete. Grotesque though some of the results were, the

---

[16] Erskine, IV, ii, 19.
[17] More's *Notes on Stair*, cccix, note on IV, xliii.

distrust of oral testimony was not, however, in itself irrational. Witnesses lie. Memory fails. Sentiments of loyalty or compassion, hatred or repulsion, cloud the mind. Threats or inducements, sometimes subtle, sometimes almost unconscious, play a part. Reflection on what was perceived leads imperceptibly to reconstruction. To close the door on all that, or most of it, by shutting out all but the stoutest testimony was intelligible policy. However much we may reject it, or believe we have progressed beyond it, we cannot deny its claim to reason. For long, thinking of that kind underlay attitudes to evidence. It is as old as Justinian or older. A climate of opinion which severely restricted the scope of direct oral testimony and erected elaborate safeguards around it would also, of necessity, be impatient of the reception of indirect testimony dependent on the narrative of others. The authority of the civil law and native caution combined in support. It is there, rather than in the specialities of jury trial or adversary procedure that the *fons et origo* of the rule against hearsay lie.

The question may be asked why, if the rule had its origins in a distrust of oral testimony, it continued to flourish when that distrust had declined. Here, no doubt, the exigencies of adversary procedure, and perhaps also of the jury, played a part. The new confidence in the capacity of the trier of fact to evaluate oral testimony, went hand-in-hand with, was largely based on, confidence in cross-examination as the key to truth. The new era was the era of the great advocates. They were great pleaders and also great cross-examiners. Evidence which was not susceptible to the test of cross-examination remained suspect.

Definition and scope

Until very recently Scots law has lacked an authoritative statement of what is meant by hearsay. Walkers defined hearsay, very simply, as 'evidence of what another person has said'.[18] That is etymologically

---

[18]Walker and Walker, *Law of Evidence in Scotland,* para. 370.

exact but requires a division of hearsay into primary and secondary hearsay only the latter of which is properly hearsay for the purpose of evidentiary rules. Dickson's definition may be better: 'Hearsay evidence is testimony delivered by one who depones, not from his personal knowledge of a fact, but from his recollection of what another told him regarding it.'[19] Neither definition, however, directs attention to the assertion of the truth of the matter stated as the critical feature in the exclusion of hearsay evidence. What was said in the Irish case of *Cullen* v. *Clarke*[20] underlies all the Scottish decisions as well.

> 'There is no general rule of evidence that a witness may not testify as to the words spoken by a person who is not produced as a witness. There is a general rule, subject to many exceptions, that evidence of the speaking of such words is inadmissible to prove the truth of the facts they assert.'

The lack of an authoritative Scottish formulation has been supplied by *Morrison* v. *H.M. Advocate*[21] in which the court adopted as representing the law of Scotland a definition derived from Cross:[22] 'An assertion other than one made by a person while giving oral evidence is inadmissible as evidence of any fact asserted.' Objection to hearsay lies in its assertive character. Utterances which are non-assertive or which have a relevance independent of what they assert are not struck at and a reported assertion is objectionable irrespective of the means by which the assertion was made or reported. The commonplace use of documentary records, especially hospital records, even in criminal trials sometimes seems to overlook that assertions in documents (or in electronic recordings or computer-

---

[19]Dickson, *Law of Evidence in Scotland* (1st edn.), p. 56, para. 83; (3rd edn.), p. 185, para. 244.

[20][1963] I.R. 368, *per* Kingsmill Moore J.

[21]1990 J.C. 299, *per* Lord Justice-Clerk Ross at p. 312.

[22]Cross, *Evidence* (6th edn.) p. 38, now (7th edn.), p. 42. The adoption of this definition with the addition of a reference to opinion had been advocated by the present writer (Wilkinson, *The Scottish Law of Evidence* p. 34).

ised information) are no less objectionable than assertions in reported speech. Moreover, although expert opinion will often and necessarily be based on accumulated knowledge derived from the experience of others[23] an assertion of the opinion of someone other than the witness bearing specifically on the particular facts in the case is as objectionable as is an assertion of fact. Nor is evidence taken out of the category of hearsay by the fact that the original communication was not in words. Intentionally assertive or negatory conduct (*e.g.* where something is indicated or denied by gesture) may be the subject of hearsay no less than the written or spoken word. The rule against hearsay is concerned to exclude evidence of extrajudicial assertive or negatory statements and their equivalent in conduct when tendered in proof of the matter asserted or disproof of the matter denied.

The abolition by the Civil Evidence (Scotland) Act 1988[24] of the rule against hearsay in civil cases makes any detailed analysis of the exceptions formerly applicable to such cases of little interest except, perhaps, for the purpose of weighing evidence or of determining whether the admission in evidence of a written statement is subject to the procedural rules governing written hearsay. They are, however, included in the following list for the sake of completeness. A good deal of confusion seems to exist about the extent of the

---

[23]See: *Wilson* v. *H.M. Advocate* 1988 S.C.C.R. 384 where, in the course of W's trial for being concerned in the supply of cannabis resin in the form of cannabis oil, evidence was adduced from drug squad officers and forensic scientists as to the common method of importing cannabis resin in this form. That evidence had been timeously objected to on the ground that, as it was derived from information conveyed at seminars and from discussion with customs officers, it constituted hearsay evidence. The appeal court, however, refused the appeal against conviction, the Lord Justice-General (Lord Emslie), holding that the evidence given by the drug squad officers and the forensic scientists 'could be described as simply disclosure of the received wisdom of persons concerned in drug enforcement, wisdom which they were bound to have picked up in various ways in order that they might perform their duties'. (1988 S.C.C.R. at p. 385).

[24]Sec. 2.

exceptions whether civil or criminal. It has been said that 'apart from the statutory exceptions relating to documentary hearsay the only recognised exceptions to the rule that hearsay is inadmissible as evidence of the facts alleged in the statement occur when the maker of the statement is dead or permanently insane, and at least in a civil case, a prisoner of war.'[25] That view is, it is submitted, untenable. The following additional common law exceptions applicable, unless otherwise noted, to both criminal and civil cases, may be listed:

(1) *Res gestae* statements.[26]

(2) Statements regarding the physical or mental condition of the maker in the sense of sensations experienced or the content of the mind.[27] This exception is affirmed by Dickson[28] but lacks judicial authority except in the case of statements indicative of a particular disposition towards a party[29] and *Hall* v. *Otto*[30] affords some, if slender, authority against admitting statements indicative of physical pain. But the admission of statements of this kind accords, it is thought, with Scottish practice and is well-recognised in England.[31] It can be justified on the ground that, in the absence at least of inference from conduct or of evident reactions as of pain, pleasure, sorrow or anger, what someone says about his thoughts, sensations or emotions is the only evidence that can be obtained. The statement if it is to be admissible must refer to the maker's

---

[25]Scottish Law Commission, Memo. 46 — *Law of Evidence* (1980) p. 136, para. T.04. It is clear from later passages that the Scottish Law Commission is aware of other exceptions but their list is incomplete. Cf. Walker and Walker para. 371.

[26] *O'Hara* v. *Central S.M.T.* 1941 S.C. 363; Hume, ii, 406; Dickson (3rd edn.), p. 189, para. 254.

[27]Dickson (3rd edn.), p. 186, para. 249 *et seq;* Cross on *Evidence* (7th edn.), pp. 674-676.

[28]At p. 186.

[29]*King* v. *King* (1841) 4 D. 124; *Rose* v. *Junor* (1846) 9 D. 12.

[30](1818) 1 Msc. 144.

[31]Cross on *Evidence* (7th edn.), pp. 674-676.

contemporary state. There is here an analogy with the admission of *res gestae* statements.

(3) Statements against interest made by a party to a civil action or by an accused person.[32]

(4) Statements made by an accused person prior to his trial which are capable of being both incriminatory and exculpatory and which are led in evidence by the Crown or by the defence without objection from the Crown. Statements which are purely exculpatory are inadmissible as evidence of the facts asserted, although they may be admissible for other purposes, but the whole of a mixed statement is admissible as evidence of the facts it contains. This view of the law, formulated in *Morrison* v. *H.M. Advocate,*[33] is criticised later in this article.[34]

(5) Statements made in the presence of a party to a civil action or of an accused person in circumstances in which a reply or other reaction was to be expected.[35]

(6) Statements forming part of or relating to a tradition concerning family pedigree, right of way, or other ancient right[36] (applicable only to civil cases and now therefore superseded by the Civil Evidence (Scotland) Act 1988).

(7) Evidence of reputation in questions of marriage and legitimacy[37] (applicable only to civil cases and now therefore superseded by the Civil Evidence (Scotland) Act 1988).

(8) Statements forming part of records kept under statutory or

---

[32]Walker and Walker, ch. IV, pp. 27 *et seq*, and authorities cited therein.

[33]1990 J.C. 299.

[34]See discussion *infra*. pp. 86 to 90.

[35]*Dowling* v. *Henderson & Son* (1890) 17 R. 921; Walker and Walker, pp. 32, 33, para. 34.

[36]*Alexander* v. *Officers of State* (1868) 6 M. 54; *Macpherson* v. *Reid's Trs.* (1877) 4 R. (H.L.) 87; Stair, IV, xlii, 16; Erskine IV, ii, 7.

[37]Clive, *Law of Husband and Wife in Scotland* (2nd edn.), p. 487, *De Thoren* v. *Wall* (1876) 3 R. (H.L.) 28; *Jones* v. *McLennan* 1971 S.L.T. 162.

other public authority for the purpose of recording the facts to which the statements relates.[38]

(9) Statements admitted on grounds of fairness in view of the admission of evidence of other statements. The sole authority for this exception is *O'Hara* v. *Central S.M.T.*[39] in which it was held that as a result of the admission of a *res gestae* statement fairness required the admission of a subsequent statement. What constitutes fairness for this purpose, and what its limits are, await elaboration. Although fairness is nowhere else treated as a general ground of admissibility, considerations of fairness underly other specific exceptions.

(10) Statements identifying accused persons made shortly after the crime by a witness who at the trial fails to identify the accused.[40]

(11) Entries in business books regularly kept and tendered as evidence, for the party by or on whose behalf they were kept, of matters of account properly within their purview[41] (applicable only to civil cases and now therefore superseded by the Civil Evidence (Scotland) Act 1988).

(12) Evidence of facts falling within the received wisdom of the specialism of a witness testifying from special knowledge. An exception along these lines is required by *Wilson* v. *H.M. Advocate*[42] in which it was held that officers of the police drugs squad and forensic scientists might give evidence of methods of secretion commonly used in the illegal importation of a controlled drug,

---

[38]Dickson (3rd edn.), chs. V-IX; Walker and Walker, ch. XVIII. The subject is attended with some technicality and falls outwith the scope of this essay but the law may be broadly stated in the terms which have been indicated.

[39]1941 S.C. 363, *per* Lord Fleming at p. 386 and Lord Carmont at p. 394.

[40]*Muldoon* v. *Herron* 1970 J.C. 30. This is the leading case but there is earlier authority: trial of *Thomas Wright*, Feb. 22, 1836, briefly reported in Bell's *Notes on Hume*, p. 288.

[41]Erskine, IV.ii.4; *Wood* v. *Kello* (1672) M. 12728; *Ivory & Co.* v. *Gourlay* (1816) 4 Dow 467; *British Linen Co.* v. *Thomson* (1853) 15 D. 314; Walker and Walker pp. 241, 242, para. 228.

[42]1988 S.C.C.R. 384.

cannabis, although that evidence was not based on their own experience but on information derived from seminars and discussions with officers of the Customs and Excise service. A similar exception is required to accommodate opinion evidence by experts, who must often have to rely, at least in part, on the general state of knowledge within their field as well as on their own experience. The source of that knowledge is, inevitably, assertions of fact made by others.

The admissibility of statements in most of the above categories is well-settled and it is clear that they constitute exceptions to the rule against hearsay. In the cases, however, of *res gestae* statements[42a] and of statements identifying accused persons, the view has been expressed that statements in these categories do not constitute hearsay and so are not exceptions to the rule. So far as *res gestae* statements are concerned this view may in part be based on the vivid, but perhaps unguarded, description of such statements as a species of real evidence.[43]

The compelling reasoning of *Ratten* v. *R.*[44] now puts beyond doubt that *res gestae* statements are admitted as an exception to the rule against hearsay but the matter had, in any event, always been clear in principle. Statements admissible as original evidence, *i.e.* independently of the truth or falsity of any fact they assert, will often be part of the *res gestae* but their admissibility is not determined by that fact. They are admissible, provided they are relevant, whenever and in whatever circumstances they are uttered.[45] There

---

[42a] Walker and Walker, *The Law of Evidence in Scotland* paras. 371, 375 and 377. *Res gestae* statements are discussed by Walker and Walker as instances of primary hearsay which, on their terminology, is not hearsay at all in the sense at present under consideration.

[43] *O'Hara* v. *Central S.M.T.* 1941 S.C. 363, *per* Lord Moncrieff at p. 390; *Teper* v. *R.* [1952] A.C. 480, *per* Lord Normand at p. 487.

[44] [1972] A.C. 378. Cf. *Morrison* v. *H.M. Advocate supra* at p. 312.

[45] Dickson (3rd edn.), p. 186, paras. 247, 248.

is no need for a category of *res gestae* statements to cover their admissibility. The point is driven home by the fact that in many of the cases in which statements have been admitted as part of the *res gestae* they have been admitted as evidence of the fact asserted and if regarded independently of their truth or falsity would have been of little or no relevance.[46]

In *Muldoon* v. *Herron*[47] an attempt was made to treat the act of identification of an accused person on an occasion prior to his trial as an event or occurrence distinct from any question of its accuracy and so not susceptible to the rule against hearsay. It is, however, difficult to escape the conclusion that, despite its high authority, that reasoning is mistaken. An identification is an assertion that a person seen on one occasion, usually the occasion on which the identification is made, is the same as a person seen on another occasion, usually the commission of the crime or some event closely connected with it, and its assertive character is not diminished by the fact, if it be such, that the identification is made by gesture rather than by words. It is adduced as evidence of the fact asserted and in that situation the question of whether the assertion was made cannot be divorced from a consideration of its accuracy. To say that evidence of a prior identification is primary and direct evidence of 'who is in fact identified'[48] is to beg the question. A witness's evidence of what was said in his hearing is always primary and direct evidence that the statement he heard was made but, in order to determine whether or not it is hearsay, one has to go on to ask for what purpose the evidence is to be used. Evidence of who was in fact identified is irrelevant, where identification is in issue, unless used

---

[46] *E.g.*, *The Schwalbe* (1861) Lush. 239. The distinction between the use of a statement as original evidence and its use as a *res gestae* statement is brought out in *Ratten* v. *R.*, *supra*, n. 44.

[47] 1970 J.C. 30, *per* Lord Justice-Clerk Grant at p. 36 and *per* Lord Walker at p. 43; *cf. Maxwell* v. *H.M. Advocate* 1991 S.L.T. 63, at p. 64

[48] 1970 J.C., at p.36.

to prove the truth of the assertion, implicit or explicit, in the identification. To admit evidence of prior identification is, therefore, to admit evidence of statements or the equivalent of statements as an exception to the rule against hearsay.

To the above list of exceptions, must, of course, be added the 'recognised' exceptions for statements made by a person who is deceased, permanently insane or a prisoner-of-war at the time of trial or proof, although only the first of these can be said to be undoubtedly recognised,[49] and also the various statutory exceptions. The most important of the latter, and the only instance of general application, is the exception created by the Criminal Evidence Act 1965.[50] Specialised exceptions exist, however under a number of statues of which the Merchant Shipping Acts 1894 to 1988[51] the Army Act 1955[52] and the Education (Scotland) Act 1980[53] are notable examples.

Statements bearing on credibility

The rule against hearsay applies to the extrajudicial statement of a witness adduced in court, no less than of a person who is not called to give testimony, if the statement is tendered in proof of the fact asserted. It does not, however, strike at extrajudicial statements of a witness tendered solely for the purpose of supporting or destroying his credibility. Such statements require separate consideration. The general rule, clear in principle however imperfectly understood and indifferently applied in practice, is that while a witness may be cross-examined on a wide range of matters bearing on his credibility, evidence cannot be adduced, otherwise than by way of such cross-

---

[49]See: Wilkinson, *Scottish Law of Evidence*, pp. 49-50; *H.M. Advocate* v. *Monson* (1893) 21 R. (J.) 5; Dickson, paras. 266-273; *Ranking of Cleland's Creditors* (1708) M. 12634.

[50]Sec. 1.

[51]1894 Act, secs. 691, 695(1);

[52]Sec. 198.

[53]Sec. 86.

examination, if it would not constitute competent and relevant evidence for any purpose other than its bearing on the credibility of the witness. On that principle, a witness might be cross-examined on his prior inconsistent statements but otherwise his prior statements, whether consistent or inconsistent with his evidence, could not be admitted to proof. As long ago as 1852, however, statute provided that a witness's prior statements inconsistent with his evidence might be proved, provided a foundation for doing so has been laid in cross-examination, and it seems that our law has come to accept that prior consistent statements might also be admitted.[54] In *Barr* v. *Barr*[55] Lord President Normand said: 'Evidence that A made a statement to C may be useful as showing that A's evidence *in causa* was true evidence, and may be useful to set up his credibility' and in *Gibson* v. *National Cash Register Co.*[56] a letter and telegram sent by a witness were held to have been properly admitted for the purpose of supporting his credibility. The admissibility of evidence of such prior statements by a witness was also affirmed in the Outer House case of *Burns* v. *Colin McAndrew & Partners Ltd.*[57] In England, apart from the specialities introduced by the Civil Evidence Act 1968, and also in some jurisdictions influenced by English common law, it is a prerequisite for the admission of a previous consistent statement that the witness should have been challenged in cross-examination with fabrication of his evidence; and it is not sufficient that it has been suggested merely that his evidence is untruthful or inconsistent.[58] But of the

---

[54] Evidence (Scotland) Act 1852, sec. 3, now, so far as criminal proceedings are concerned, repealed by the Criminal Procedure (Scotland) Act 1975, Sched. 10, Pt. I, and substantially re-enacted in secs. 147 and 349.

[55] 1939 S.C. 696, at p. 699.

[56] 1925 S.C. 500.

[57] 1963 S.L.T. (Notes) 71.

[58] *R.* v. *Coll* (1899) 25 L.R. Ir. 522, *per* Holmes J. at p. 541; *Fox* v. *General Medical Council* [1960] 3 All E.R. 225; *Flanagan* v. *Fahy* [1918] 1 I.R. 361; *R.* v. *Roberts* [1942] 1 All E.R. 187, *per* Humphries J. at p. 191; *R.* v. *Oyesiku* (1971) 56 Cr. App. R. 240; *R.* v. *Benjamin* (1913) 8 Cr. Appl. R. 146; *Nominal Defendant* v. *Clements* (1961) 104 C.L.R. 476, *per* Dixon C.J. at p. 479; but *cf. Ahmed* v. *Brumfitt* (1967) 112 Sol. Jo. 32.

Scottish authorities only *Burns* v. *Colin McAndrew & Partners* mentioned that qualification. For civil cases the law is now contained in the Civil Evidence (Scotland) Act 1988 which provides that a statement made, otherwise than in the course of the proof, by a person who at the proof is examined as to the statement shall be admissible as evidence in so far as it tends to reflect favourably or unfavourably on that person's credibility.[59] There is no requirement that the witness should have been challenged with fabrication. A doubt, however, remains about the state of the criminal law. Are prior consistent statements by witnesses generally admissible in criminal trials? The question is touched on in *Morrison* v. *H.M. Advocate*,[60] but all the other authorities, as already noted, are civil. Before 1988, however, the general pattern was that evidentiary rules applied, with some special exceptions, to civil and criminal cases alike. If such statements are admissible in criminal trials, is it a condition of admissibility that the witness should have been challenged with fabricating his evidence? *Morrison,* in contrast with the civil precedents, suggests an affirmative answer. And what relationship does any rule admitting a witness's prior statement bear to the rule admitting *de recenti* statements? In *Morton* v. *H.M. Advocate*[61] it was said that in cases of assault and sexual offences against women and children, evidence of the victim's *de recenti* statement was admissible for the purpose only of supporting the victim's credibility. But the question of support for the victim's credibility can arise only if the victim is a witness. Is a rule about *de recenti* statements required if a witness's prior consistent statements are in any event admissible? Or, are victims excluded from any general rule about witnesses' prior statements? Or does a *de recenti* statement differ from other prior statements in being admissible although there has been no challenge of fabrication? And is the

---

[59]Sec. 3.
[60]1990 J.C. 299, at p. 313.
[61]1938 J.C. 50, *per* Lord Justice-Clerk Aitchison at p. 53.

admissibility of *de recenti* statements restricted, as *Morton* v. *H.M. Advocate* seems to suggest, to cases of assault and sexual offences against women and children? The expression is certainly used, perhaps loosely, in other contexts.[61a] These questions may often be circumvented by a certain latitude of practice but they await authoritative answers. A narrower rule than that now laid down for civil cases may be appropriate to the more stringent requirements of a criminal trial. The primary need is for clarification.

Self-serving statements by parties

The extrajudicial statements of parties if against their interest constitute, as already noticed, an exception to the rule against hearsay. If favourable to a party's interest they are, when tendered in proof of a fact asserted, obnoxious to the rule. When a party testifies as a witness, use may be made for credibility purposes of his prior consistent or inconsistent statements on the principles already discussed. Some special problems concerning the self-serving statements of accused persons arise, however, from *H.M. Advocate* v. *Forrest*,[62] *H.M. Advocate* v. *Pye*,[63] *Brown* v. *H.M. Advocate*[64] and *Morrison* v. *H.M. Advocate*[65] and from the views of Hume, Alison and Macdonald canvassed in these cases. These problems, even if rather peripheral to the main concerns of criminal evidence in a modern setting, have been the subject of extensive recent judicial consideration and may merit correspondingly extensive examination. The law up to and including *Brown* is considered before turning to the effect on it of *Morrison*. *Forrest* may be taken as the starting point.

In *Forrest* the accused, who was charged with culpable homicide arising out of the discharge of a firearm, had made a *res gestae*

[61a] e.g. *Morrison infra* at p. 312.
[62] (1837) 1 Swin. 404.
[63] (1838) 2 Swin. 187.
[64] 1964 J.C. 10.
[65] 1990 J.C. 299.

statement that the firearm had been discharged accidentally by a blow from the deceased, and he had later emitted a judicial declaration to similar effect. Evidence was admitted of a statement made by the accused on the night of the incident, but not part of the *res gestae*, which again told the same story. The evidence was admitted as showing the consistency of his account. In *Pye*, where the accused, who was charged with the theft of bank notes, had made a statement to her mother shortly after the event which consisted with her later judicial declaration, that she had found the notes. The ground of admission seems to have been the same as in *Forrest.* Both cases belong to the era before 1898 when the accused could not give evidence and it was the common practice, if the accused had emitted a declaration, for the Crown to read it to the jury if to do so served the interests of the prosecution or if the accused so requested. A means was thus afforded by which the accused's version of events could be put before the jury and so in some degree compensate for his inability to give evidence in the ordinary way. Yet in the view of the older authorities as represented by Alison, the declaration was not evidence of the facts asserted in it if these favoured the accused, although, of course, if it amounted to a statement against interest, it might constitute evidence against him.[66] But, it might be 'a material circumstance in his favour'.

The distinction between the use of a declaration as a circumstance favourable to the accused, which was allowed, and the use of a favourable declaration as evidence of its contents, which was excluded, is elusive. Alison says: 'Though a prisoner is no more entitled to refer to a declaration as evidence of the truth of what it contains, than the prosecutor is to found on the libel for the same purpose, yet he is fully entitled to found upon the declaration as a material circumstance in his favour, if it contains a full, fair, and candid statement, such as bears probability on its face, and if it is

---

[66] Alison, ii, 555.
[67] *Ibid.*

confirmed by what the witnesses, either on one side or the other, prove at the trial.[67] To that, it may be objected that, if it is a circumstance in the accused's favour, it must in some sense be evidence. If it is evidence, it must either be evidence of the facts asserted, which Alison denies, or evidence bearing on the credibility of other testimony, which Alison does not affirm. Alison says rather that it is the other testimony which may make the accused's declaration worthy of credit. On that view it is difficult to avoid the conclusion that, despite the authorities to the contrary, the declaration when supported by other evidence becomes evidence of the facts it asserts; that is, evidence in the accused's favour in the full sense. The problem cannot be circumvented by saying that the only purpose for which the accused can rely on the declaration is as evidence showing merely that a statement in those terms was in fact made.[68] The making of a statement in such terms is of no significance or relevance unless the contents of the statement can be used as evidence at least for the purpose of supporting the credibility of testimony, if not as positive evidence *in causa*. It is, however, profitless to pursue this analysis further. The kind of distinction Alison seeks to make is of little value in a question with a party who bears no *onus*. Once it is allowed that the matter may competently be admitted to the knowledge of the jury and that the jury may attach weight to it, it is obvious that, however one classifies its evidentiary status, it may serve the only interest which the accused has to pursue; that is, to cast doubt on the Crown's case. The point which seems to emerge, put in broad practical terms, is that a declaration on its own is of no avail to the accused (although it is not clear that even then the jury should, or can, be directed to disregard it) but that if consistent with evidence adduced it may form part of a pattern to which weight may be attached. *Forrest* and *Pye* are authority for admitting statements of the accused consistent

---

[68] *Brown* v. *H.M. Advocate* 1964 J.C. 10 *per* Lord Justice-Clerk Grant at p. 13.

with and preceding his declaration in order to reinforce that pattern and *Brown* is authority for treating the accused's reply when cautioned and charged as analogous to his declaration. Alison's ambiguities and uncertainties, however, remain.

Unfortunately, the opinions in *Brown* do not recognise the analytical weakness of Alison's treatment and so do nothing to resolve the resultant problems. They also lay what seems an unwarranted stress on the fact that the accused's statement was led in evidence by the Crown.[69] When cautioned and charged with causing death by dangerous driving, contrary to section 1 of the Road Traffic Act 1960, the accused had made a reply which tended to exculpate him and evidence of that statement was led by the Crown. A parallel was pointed with the declaration which could be read only at the instance of the Crown. That was the common law and, although it was usual to read the declaration if the accused asked for it, he had no right to insist on that being done. The Criminal Procedure (Scotland) Act 1887 provided, however, that the declaration of the accused should 'be received in evidence without being sworn to by the witnesses, either for the prosecution or for the defence'.[70] The concern was with the proof, rather than with the use, of declarations but it is difficult to read the statute in any sense other than contemplating, if not directing, that the declaration might be put in evidence by, and used as evidence for, either the prosecution or the defence. In any event, the analogy between declaration and reply to caution and charge is not complete. The latter does not enjoy the special status of the former within the judicial process. It is but an item in the ordinary course of evidence and if in principle a reply favouring the accused is competent evidence, as *Brown* acknowledges, it is anomalous to

---

[69] 1964 J.C., *per* Lord Justice-Clerk Grant at p. 14 and *per* Lord Strachan at p. 18.

[70] Sec. 69. Similar provisions are now contained in the Criminal Procedure (Scotland) Act 1975, secs. 151 (1) and 352.

deny the right of leading such evidence to the defence. *Forrest* and *Pye* vouch that a statement made by the accused, and consistent with his subsequent declaration, may be led in evidence by the defence and it is difficult to see why the same rule should not apply to a reply to caution and charge which will necessarily precede any declaration, if emitted, and, more importantly in modern practice, will precede judicial examination.

Perhaps inconsistently with the stress laid on the fact that the evidence there in issue was elicited by the Crown, there are *dicta* in *Brown* which would seem to support the admission of any statement, however self-serving, made by the accused at any time, however late, after the commission of the crime. In particular, a passage from Alison that 'the principle of law and the rule of common sense is, that every deed done, and every word spoken by the prisoner subsequent to the date of the crime charged against him, is the fit subject for the consideration of the jury, and that if duly proved, it must enter into the composition of their verdict'[71] is cited with approval. That passage is used in *Brown* to justify the admission of statements favourable to the accused. It is, however, reasonably clear that Alison, although ambiguous, is to be understood in context as referring to the use of deeds and words as evidence against the accused. In any other sense the passage is inconsistent with Hume, also cited with approval in *Brown*: 'There are obvious reasons why a pannel's *denial of* his guilt, or his statements, *in conversation afterwards*, of his defences against the charge, or his narrative of the way in which the thing happened, cannot be admitted as evidence on his behalf.'[72] The general admission of exculpatory extrajudicial statements made by the accused even if subsequent to his judicial examination or declaration would go beyond what the authorities before *Brown* vouched and is not necessary for the decision in that case.

---

[71] Alison, *ibid.*
[72] Hume, ii, 401.

In *Morrison* v. *H.M. Advocate* the court was concerned with the admissibility of a mixed statement, capable, it was said, of being both incriminatory and exulpatory. Perhaps more accurately, a mixed statement is a statement capable of being either incriminatory or exculpatory, exculpatory if it is accepted as a whole but incriminatory if part of the statement necessary to its exculpatory character is rejected. The statement at issue in *Morrison,* which was a case of rape, had been made by the accused to the police and was to the effect that he had had intercourse with the alleged victim but with her consent. The Court was, however, concerned to lay down principles of general application to mixed statements as they defined them and that definition is apt to cover statements with a range of inculpatory and, possibly disconnected and contradictory, exculpatory elements. *Brown* too can be regarded as a case of a mixed statement but no stress had been laid on that and no distinction drawn between the admissibility of such a statement in its exculpatory aspect and of a purely exculpatory statement. For *Morrison* that distinction was critical and the decision turned on the specialities of mixed statements. But the opinion of the court, although in passages not strictly necessary for the decision, also sets down principles for the admission of purely exculpatory statements. Some *dicta* suggest that the only purpose for which such statements can be used is to show the consistency of the accused's story if he gives evidence and his evidence is challenged as a late invention. That accords, as has been seen, with what may be the general rule where a witness's testimony is challenged and it is submitted that it would have been best to have left the matter there. But it seems that is not all. 'A prior statement of an accused which is not to any extent incriminatory is admissible for the limited purpose of proving that the statement was made, and of the attitude or reaction of the accused at the time when it was made which is part of the general picture which the jury have to consider, but it is not evidence of the facts contained in the statement.'[73] But if an exculpa-

---

[73] *Morrison* v. *H.M. Advocate* 1990 J.C. 299, *per* Lord Justice-Clerk Ross at p. 313.

tory statement is not evidence of the facts contained in it, what part
does proof of its having been made, and of the accused's attitude
and reaction at the time (other than guilty reactions), have to play
in the general picture which the jury have to consider? The answer
given in *Morrison* is that it is evidence (a) admissible at the instance
of the accused where he gives evidence and is charged with
fabrication, and (b) on which the accused may rely, if evidence of
the statement is led by the Crown, for the purpose of showing the
consistency of his line of defence even if he does not give evidence.
That, of course, accords with *Forrest, Pye* and *Brown* and, although
the reasoning of *Brown* in so far as based on Alison is rejected and
the difficulty is recognised of distinguishing between a statement of
an accused person as evidence of the truth of its contents and as 'a
material circumstance in his favour', the decision in *Brown* is
approved and some of its ambiguities remai.n. And in *Morrison* as
in *Brown*, although the purposes for which a prior exculpatory
statement is admissible are limited, it seems that it is admissible
irrespective of the time at which it was made.

It was held in *Morrison* that mixed statements led by or with the
acquiescence of the Crown were, in contrast with purely exculpatory statements, admissible as evidence of the facts asserted whether
these were incriminatory or exculpatory. The jury was to be
directed to 'consider the whole statement, both the incriminating
parts and the exculpating parts, and determine whether the whole
or any part of the statement is accepted by them as truth'.[74] That
goes beyond what was decided in *Owens* v. *H.M. Advocate*,[75] that
an admission must be taken with its qualifications, that the Crown
cannot take advantage of the admission without displacing the
explanation or at all events presenting to the jury a not less strong
case that shows that the explanation is false.[76] It is, of course, true

[74] *Ibid.*
[75] 1946 J.C. 119.
[76] 1946 J.C., at p. 124.

as is said in *Morrison* that it is unfair to admit the admission without also admitting the explanation. *Owens* allowed for that; *Hendry* v. *H.M. Advocate*[77] which was overruled in *Morrison* had appeared to overlook it. Where *Morrison* goes beyond *Owens* is in the use which is allowed of the explanation. According to *Owens* its only use was to qualify the admission; if the explanation was not displaced, the admission could not be used as a confession of guilt. But according to *Morrison* the jury is to determine 'whether the whole or any part of the statement is accepted by them as truth'. It is therefore open to the jury to attach positive value to the exculpatory part of the statement. There was no warrant for that in *Owens*. What *Owens* required was that, where an extrajudicial statement by the accused contained an admission accompanied by a qualification, no weight should be given to the admission unless the other evidence in the case justified the rejection of the qualification. The merits of the statement itself, whether incriminatory or exculpatory, did not enter into that process. Only if on a consideration of the other evidence, the qualification was rejected, did the incriminatory part, the admission, become evidence. If the qualification was not rejected, no part of the statement became evidence. At no stage did the exculpatory part itself, the qualification, become evidence of its contents whether as evidence *in causa* or as evidence to be weighed on the question of receiving the admission as evidence. According to *Morrison*, however, it seems that the jury may treat the exculpatory part as evidence of the truth of its contents for the purpose both of weighing it against the other evidence to decide whether or not the statements' true character is an admission and, if it is not, of receiving it as evidence *in causa* in the accused's favour. That, although an innovation, may not be of major importance where the exculpatory part is a true qualification of the admission, but *Morrison* appears to warrant similar treatment of all exculpatory parts of a mixed statement however remote the exculpatory feature

---

[77] 1985 J.C. 105.

may be in its bearing on the admission. It is difficult to see either the fairness or logic of that. Fairness does not require that an accused person should be able to make positive use of an explanation for which there is no evidence and which he has not chosen to support by his own testimony and it is illogical that he should be unable to rely on a purely exculpatory statement but able to rely on a mixed statement which has taken on a purely exculpatory character.

In civil litigation self-serving statements by parties will now be admissible as hearsay under the Civil Evidence (Scotland) Act 1988 although the value to be attached to them where the party does not give evidence must generally be slight. The authority for the admission of such statements at common law was slender and *obiter*.[78]

In criminal cases *Morrison* has left the law in a state of some complexity and ambiguity when simplification and clarity could have been achieved. Most of the difficulties are traceable to the problems of an earlier age. The pre-1898 law has cast a long shadow. In modern conditions it is difficult to justify the admission of self-serving statements by accused persons unless, where the accused testifies as a witness, on the principles applicable to witnesses already discussed or unless one of the exceptions to the rule against hearsay, other than the exception now introduced for mixed statements, applies. So far as mixed statements are concerned, it is respectfully submitted that *Morrison* would have reached a more satisfactory conclusion if it had restored the law to where it stood under *Owens*.

---

[78] *Apthorpe* v. *Edinburgh Street Tramways* (1882) 10 R. 344, *per* Lord President Inglis at p. 351. The statement in issue was excluded as opinion and was, in any event, adverse to the interests of the party on whose behalf it was uttered.

Conclusion

A possible solution for all problems of hearsay is abolition of the rule. That is the solution in civil causes adopted by the Civil Evidence (Scotland) Act 1988. On the resultant freeing of proof from the restraints, sometimes artificial, to which it was previously subject, testimony can follow a more natural course, documents whose contents have not been agreed or proved but whose reliability there is no real reason to doubt, can be accepted and a new facility is given for the admission of valuable evidence which would formerly have been excluded. Perhaps, the most noticeable example of that facility is the admission in proceedings concerning compulsory measures of care, of the extrajudicial statements of children who have been victims of abuse. But there are disadvantages. There is no principle on which unreliable evidence can be excluded. As a result the proof may be burdened and prolonged by evidence of little value, evidence whose reliability cannot be adequately tested may be admitted and judgment may proceed on apparently impressive evidence which is in fact highly suspect. It may be answered that these dangers will be controlled by the court but some may not be apparent to the court and others beyond its control. The dangers are enhanced by the admission of hearsay of whatever degree and by the possibility of judgments based on remote hearsay which, where appeal lies only on questions of law, will not be subject to review. Not surprisingly, Parliament shows little sign of embarking on a similar course for the admission of hearsay in criminal cases.

It is sometimes said that if one is thinking of reforming the law the first thing to do is to study the existing law thoroughly and, if one does that, it will often be found that the law does not need to be reformed at all. The author does not wholly subscribe to the latter part of that view but it may have some relevance to a consideration of reform of the rule against hearsay.

A leading handicap of much discussion of the rule against hearsay in Scotland is the failure to recognise adequately the scope of the rule.[79] Because it is inadequately understood, it is often represented as being either more restrictive or more technical than it is. The purpose of the preceding discussion has been to remedy these defects and to identify the main features of the present law. It has comprehended, in addition to the rule against hearsay proper, a consideration of statements bearing on credibility and self-serving statements of parties which are often conflated with hearsay and are integral to any satisfactory treatment of it. What then is the result?

Some anomalies, particularly in relation to self-serving statements by accused persons, have been noticed and remedies suggested. So far, however, as the rule against hearsay proper is concerned, it is submitted that the overall picture is of a generally rational and coherent code. A policy directed to the exclusion of unreliable and the admission of the most reliable available evidence, although now abandoned for civil cases, underlies both the rule and its exceptions. Most of the latter can be justified on one or other of the twin principles postulated by Wigmore, the necessity principle and the principle of circumstantial probability of trustworthiness.[80] By the necessity principle Wigmore meant, to paraphrase him, that the admission of evidence was justified on the ground of necessity when it came from a source which would otherwise be lost or when it was such that we could not expect to get other evidence of the same value from the same or other sources. By circumstantial probability of trustworthiness he meant that the evidence was of a kind to which such a degree of probability of accuracy and trustworthiness attached as to make the reported statement an adequate substitute for evidence tested by cross-examination in the conventional manner. These principles Wigmore applied not to the admission of particular items of evidence but to the explanation

---

[79] *E.g.*, by the Scottish law Commission in Memo No. 46 — *Law of Evidence* (1980).

[80] Wigmore, *Evidence in Trials at Common Law*, Bk. I, p. 204, paras. 1421, 1422.

of the various exceptions to the exclusion of hearsay. The admission of the statements of deceased persons constitutes a strong example of the application of the first principle, the *res gestae* exception of the second. Some of the Scottish exceptions represent the application of these principles in a form which has been diluted or lost in the Anglo-American legal world. Wigmore comments: 'There was a time, in the early 1800s, when it came near to being settled that a general exception should exist for all statements of deceased persons who had competent knowledge and no apparent interest to deceive; but this tendency was of short-lived duration and was decisively negatived. Nevertheless, such an exception, uniting as it does the essential requirements of an exception to the Hearsay rule, commends itself as a just addition to the present sharply defined exceptions, and represents undoubtedly the enlightened policy of the future.'[81] The law of Scotland is in this respect close to what Wigmore regarded as the *optimum*. The Scottish exception, now obsolete, for the regularly kept business books of a party was known to English law until 1609 when it was abolished by statute.[82] It was also known to the Civil law.[83] English and American jurisdictions until recently made good the loss of this exception in piecemeal fashion.[84] The Scottish position represented an older and, because more integral, arguably a better solution.

Necessity and circumstantial probability of trustworthiness, with their echoes of the best evidence rule, represent, it is submitted, along with the concern for fairness embodied in *O'Hara* v. *Central S.M.T.* and *Morrison* v. *H.M. Advocate,* important keys to both the understanding and the reform of the rule against hearsay. The necessity principle, it is true, may require to be applied with caution. Evidence may be too untrustworthy to merit admission

---

[81] Bk. I, p. 435, para. 1576.
[82] Wigmore, *op. cit.*, Bk. I, p. 347, para. 1518.
[83] Voet, *op. cit.*, XXII, 4.12 (Gane's transl. vol. 3, pp. 751, 752).
[84] Wigmore, *op. cit.*, Bk. I, p. 351, para. 1519.

even if no other evidence of the same value can be obtained. Necessity and trustworthiness interact and justice to one must at times be at some expense to the other. The main criticism of the rule against hearsay in criminal cases is that although based on these principles it does not carry the search for reliability of testimony within the constrictions of availability and fairness far enough. In particular it does not do full justice to the perception that not only may hearsay sometimes be the best available evidence but it may be better evidence than other evidence which is available, *i.e.* the hearsay report may be superior in its evidentiary value to the testimony of the witness. *Muldoon* v. *Herron*[85] illustrates the point well and contains the hidden logic of reform. As already indicated it is difficult to accept that case in so far as it treats the evidence of identification as other than hearsay evidence. Regarded as constituting an exception to the rule against hearsay, the decision has, however, a cogent rationale. An identification made by a witness shortly after the event may be much better evidence than identification, or failure to identify, much later in court. The passage of time not only increases the risk of intimidation — a factor recognised in *Muldoon* — but also of faulty recollection. It is on that basis, of the intrinsic value of the evidence, that the decision can be justified. Once, however, that is accepted as the true *ratio*, it is difficult to restrict its application to questions of identification alone. A strict separation of identification evidence from evidence of the commission of the crime is, in any event, problematic. Often evidence of identification and of the commission of the crime will be necessarily and inextricably combined. Evidence that it was the accused who struck the blow is also evidence that a blow was struck. If, at an identification parade, a witness has identified the accused as the man who struck the blow, a jury can scarcely be invited to exclude that from their consideration in a question of whether the

---

[85] 1970 J.C. 30.

blow was struck but to accept it as evidence of identification. From the standpoint of accuracy of recollection, what a witness says soon after the event, whether about identification or about any other pertinent matter, is likely to be more reliable evidence than the witness's testimony on these matters in court. It is less likely to be affected by tutoring, intimidation or other external influences, or by unconscious reconstruction, and the opportunity for deliberate distortion or concoction is somewhat reduced. The development of the law requires a wider application of the insights which *Muldoon* v. *Herron*, properly understood, represents.

The principles which have been indicated are, it is submitted, the appropriate guides both for such judicial assessment and control of hearsay as the Civil Evidence (Scotland) Act 1988 permits and for development of the rule against hearsay in criminal cases. Their application would give effect to the practical dynamics of the present law freed from the constraints imposed by the defective perception of principle and by artificial distinctions. The result would at the same time, be more scientific than the abandonment of any legal barrier to hearsay or the entrusting of its control to judicial discretion. Our law lacks a science of proof. That is a task, perhaps, for the future. In the meantime, it is well to make such beginnings as we can. The admission or exclusion of evidence according to categories which can be perceived as based on principles of necessity or trustworthiness is a first step in that direction. At the same time a contribution is made, by simplification, to closing the gap between precept and practice and the best perceptions of a continuous tradition founded on a concern for the reliability of testimony are respected.[86]

---

[86]This is a substantially amended text of an article shewn in its original form under the title of 'The Rule Against Hearsay in Scotland' at 1982 J.R. 213. Grateful acknowledgment is made to the publishersm Messrs W. Green & Son Ltd, Edinburgh, for permission to base the present essay on that article.

5

JURISDICTION AND CRIMINAL LAW IN SCOTLAND AND ENGLAND

P. W. Ferguson

Introduction

Jurisdictional questions do not often arise in the criminal courts in Scotland. This, it could be unconvincingly argued, is because jurisdiction is held generally to be territorially limited.[1] The *locus classicus* on this issue is to be found in Macdonald:

'Every person who commits a crime in Scotland against the law of Scotland is amenable to the jurisdiction of the High Court of Justiciary because the proper *forum* in criminal matters is the *forum delicti*.'[2]

However, since there has been some consideration given to the question of the ambit of criminal law in England[3] and the question

---

[1]See Renton and Brown, *Criminal Procedure* (5th edn.), para. 1-07; Gordon *Criminal Law of Scotland* (2nd edn.), p. 93. That is supposed to be the general rule but there are exceptions, the most notable being that any British subject who commits murder or culpable homicide (as Scots law defines these crimes) in a country outside the United Kingdom may be proceeded against, indicted, tried and punished for the crime in Scotland: Criminal Procedure (Scotland) Act 1975, sec. 6(1) and (3). Any offence punishable on indictment which is committed in a foreign country by a British subject while employed in the service of the Crown is likewise justiciable in Scotland: sec. 6 (2) and (3).

[2]*Crimes* (5th edn.), p. 190.

[3]See Law Com., *The Territorial and Extraterritorial Extent of the Criminal Law*, (No. 91) (1970); Hirst, 'Territorial Principles and the Law Commission' [1979] Crim. L.R. 355.

of jurisdiction has been raised in a number of cases including the House of Lords' decision in *R.* v. *Berry*[4] and the Court of Appeal's opinion in *Attorney-General's Reference (No. 1 of 1982)*,[5] it is perhaps timely to compare the English approach with the Scots approach as represented by the decisions of the High Court of Justiciary in *Laird* v. *H.M. Advocate*[6] which is itself not free from difficulty and *Clements* v. *H.M. Advocate*.[6a] But before a comparison is attempted, it is proposed to consider precisely what part of the law is the cause of the difficulty.

Result-crimes and conduct—crimes

Problems of jurisdiction do not arise in cases of crimes which are wholly occasioned in Scotland. The difficulty exists in cases where only part of the crime is committed within the jurisdiction of the Scottish courts. The basic distinction which was introduced by Sheriff G. H. Gordon in the first edition of his *Criminal Law of Scotland*,[7] to provide for the crimes which occur partly in one country and partly in another and those which occur only in one country, is founded on the somewhat unphilosophical view that some crimes require a consequence whereas others do not. The latter category are consequently termed 'conduct-crimes' and the former class are known as 'result-crimes'. Sheriff Gordon explains: 'the *actus reus*, the situation forbidden by law, is separable in time and/or place from the criminal conduct creating it.'[8]

In the case of the so-called conduct-crimes, the court which has jurisdiction is the court of the jurisdiction where the conduct

---

[4][1984] 3 W.L.R. 1274.

[5][1983] 1 Q.B. 751. See also *R.* v. *Beck (Brian)* [1985] 1 W.L.R. 22 and *R.* v. *Tomsett* [1985] Crim. L.R. 369.

[6]1985 S.L.T. 298. See commentary at 1984 S.C.C.R. pp. 474-476.

[6a] 1991 S.L.T. 388.

[7](1st edn.), p. 61. Professor Glanville Williams erroneously ascribes this classification to Professor J. C. Smith: *Textbook of Criminal Law* (2nd edn.), p. 78.

[8]Gordon, *Criminal Law of Scotland* (2nd edn.), p. 63.

occurs. However, to take the classic example, if A, standing in Scotland, shoots at and kills B who is standing in England, is A amenable to the jurisdiction of the Scottish courts? If one follows the principle of territoriality, as there is no crime in Scotland until B is killed, thus A cannot be tried by the Scottish courts. There are, however, several difficulties with this two-fold classification, notwithstanding the fact that the terminology of result- and conduct-crimes has been judicially (albeit half-heartedly) adopted.[9]

First, the distinction infers that result-crimes do not require conduct on the part of the accused. As Lord Diplock said in *R. v. Treacy*:[10] 'this nomenclature, though convenient in drawing attention to the distinction, tends to blur the fact that the conduct of the accused is an essential ingredient of a "result-crime" as it is for a "conduct-crime".'[11]

Secondly, the terminology also suggests that conduct-crimes do not have consequences. The crime of uttering, for example, is a conduct-crime, but it cannot be argued that there is not also a consequence of the conduct, namely the making public of the document which is forged. Thus it is that there is a difficulty which Professor Ganville Williams has illustrated.[12] In the case of murder, the crime is either a result-crime or a conduct-crime; the question is dependent on linguistics for its answer. Is murder the act of killing, in which case it is a conduct-crime, or is it the act of causing death and thus a result-crime? This difficulty has been especially marked in academic circles by the controversy over the offence of abduction contained in sec. 20 of the Sexual Offences Act 1956

---

[9]See *R. v. Treacy* [1971] A.C. 537, *per* Lord Diplock at p. 560; *R. v. Markus* [1975] 2 W.L.R. 708, *per* Viscount Dilhorne at p. 713 and Lord Diplock at p. 716; *R. v. Miller* [1983] 2 W.L.R. 539, *per* Lord Diplock at p. 542; *R. v. Berry* [1984] 3 W.L.R. 1274, per Lord Roskill at p. 1279; and *Clements* v. *H.M. Advocate* 1991 S.L.T. 388, *per* Lord Coulsfield at p. 397.

[10][1971] A.C. 537.

[11] *Ibid.*, at p. 560.

[12] *Textbook of Criminal Law* (2nd edn.), p. 78.

which constitutes it an offence for a person acting without lawful authority or excuse to remove an unmarried girl under the age of 16 from the possession of her parent or guardian against her will. Professor Williams maintains that such an offence is a conduct-crime,[13] while Professors Smith and Hogan[14] insist with some considerable justification that the removal of the girl is the result of the accused's act of taking which is only part of the prohibited *actus reus*.

Thirdly, the differentiation endorses the view that an offence is either one type or the other whereas in truth there are crimes such as shameless indecency which cannot be categorised at all. For example, in the well-known case of *Watt* v. *Annan*,[15] was the showing of the pornographic film a conduct-crime or did the showing have to have a result? In *McLaughlan* v. *Boyd*,[16] on the other hand, there was quite clearly a result-crime.

Fourthly, doubt must also exist with regard to criminal attempts. Is attempted murder, for example, a conduct-crime? If it is not, is the result the negative one of failure to commit murder? Omissions which the law punishes are also an area of uncertainty. If a father kills his child by a failure in duty towards the child, is this homicide a result-crime or a conduct-crime? It is rather odd to describe inactivity as conduct; but equally, it is odd to talk in terms of results where there is no conduct to give rise to a result.

While the distinction between conduct- and result-crimes is thus imprecise, it is however nonetheless of practical assistance in resolving questions of jurisdiction. Most, though not all, crimes can be categorised as either a conduct- or a result-crime. The question is therefore whether Scots law follows the principle of territoriality

---

[13]See 'The Problem of Reckless Attempts' [1983] Crim. L.R. 365 at p. 368.

[14]*Criminal Law* (6th edn.), p. 39. See also Buxton, 'Circumstances, Consequences and Attempted Rape' [1984] Crim. L.R. 25 at p. 29.

[15]1978 S.L.T. 198.

[16]1934 J.C. 19.

and grants jurisdiction to its criminal courts only in respect of result-crimes which have their proscribed results in Scotland. In order to effect a comparison between Scots law and English law, it is necessary to consider English law and this shall be done first. As shall be seen, the theory underlying the two jurisdictions' approaches is considerably different.

Jurisdiction in English law

The general principle in English law is that the English courts have jurisdiction only in offences committed within the territory of England and Wales.[17] The English courts have in general adhered to this territorial limitation although on occasion, while the principle has been readily asserted, the judicial decision has failed to comply with it.

In the leading modern authority of *R. v. Treacy*,[18] which concerned a charge of demanding money with menaces contrary to sec. 21 of the Theft Act 1968, the appellant wrote and posted a letter in England to his victim in West Germany where the victim received the letter. At his trial, the appellant objected that the court had no jurisdiction as the offence was committed in West Germany where the letter was received. The Court of Appeal dismissed the appeal;[19] and on appeal to the House of Lords it was decided by a majority of three-two that the appeal should be dismissed. Two of the Law Lords in the majority[20] held that the offence had been committed by the appellant when he wrote and posted the letter in England. Both Lord Reid and Lord Morris of Borth-y-Gest dissented on the ground that no demand could properly be said to have been made in England as receipt of the letter was required for a

---

[17]See Williams, *Textbook of Criminal Law* (2nd edn.), pp. 164-165 and 'Venue and Ambit of Criminal Law' (1965) 81 L.Q.R. 518.

[18][1971] A.C. 537.

[19]*Ibid.*, at pp. 541-545.

[20]Lord Hodson (at p. 557), with whom Lord Guest (at p. 558) concurred.

demand to be made; and consequently the demand could only be said to have been made in West Germany. The implicit view of two of the Law Lords in the majority[20] was, however, that if the demand was made in West Germany, then the courts could not have jurisdiction.

Lord Diplock was the only dissentient voice in the majority in regard to the governing principle. In his view the role of the courts is to ensure that the domestic law is interpreted in accordance with the rules of international comity which, Lord Diplock held, requires only that when both an accused's conduct and its harmful consequences occur outwith England, the English courts' jurisdiction is ousted. 'But I see no reason in comity,' Lord Diplock said, 'for requiring any wider limitation than that upon the exercise by Parliament of its legislative power in the field of criminal law'.[21]

It is here submitted that Lord Diplock erred in arrogating to the English courts the jurisdiction to try a crime which only originated in England but had its result in another country; and furthermore, that the majority of the House of Lords erred in interpreting the at least arguably ambiguous phrase 'makes any unwarranted demand' against the interests of the appellant. A demand is *prima facie* only made when the person of whom it is intended to make the demand, learns of it. It is of course true that Parliament could, if it so chose, apply its laws to acts done outwith the jurisdiction. However, as Lord Reid observed: 'the presumption is well known to draftsmen, and where there is an intention to make an English Act or part of such an Act apply to acts done outside England that intention is and must be made clear in the Act'.[22] Consequently, the only proper remedy in *Treacy* was legislation.

---

[21] [1971] A.C. 537, at p. 561.
[22] *Ibid.*, at p. 551. See also Lord Morris of Borth-y-Gest at p. 552.

The territorial principle has also been applied in the unique crime of conspiracy. In *Board of Trade* v. *Owen*,[23] the respondents were convicted on an indictment which libelled a conspiracy in London to defraud a West German export control department by inducing the department to issue licences to export certain metals from West Germany by fraudulently misrepresenting that the metal was destined for Ireland although in truth it was for export to countries behind the Iron Curtain. Lord Tucker, who delivered the judgment of the House of Lords, said:

> 'a conspiracy to commit a crime abroad is not indictable in this country unless the contemplated crime is one for which an indictment would lie here . . . and . . . it necessarily follows that [the conspiracy charge] . . . is not triable in this country, since the unlawful means and the ultimate object were both outside the jurisdiction.'[24]

Lord Tucker was not, it may be added, impressed by the argument based on the comity of nations in the field of criminal law, as such interests would, in his opinion, be best served by treaties of extradition.

This territorial approach is moreover not contradicted by the subsequent decision of the House of Lords in 1972 in *R.* v. *Doot*[25] in which the respondents, a group of American citizens, had agreed abroad to import cannabis into the United States of America *via* England. The respondents were charged with conspiracy to import dangerous drugs and were convicted. The Court of Appeal,[26]

---

[23][1957] A.C. 602. See also *R.* v. *Governor of Brixton Prison, ex.p. Rush* [1969] 1 W.L.R. 165 and *R.* v. *Tomsett* [1985] Crim. L.R. 369. What the House of Lords held as regards jurisdiction in cases of conspiracy is now codified in section 1 (4) of the Criminal Law Act 1977: see Smith & Hogan, *Criminal Law* (6th edn.), pp. 268-269.

[24][1957] A.C. 602, at p. 634.

[25][1973] A.C. 807.

[26][1972] 3 W.L.R. 33.

however, quashed the respondents' conviction on the ground that, as the crime of conspiracy is complete on the reaching of *consensus in idem* among the conspirators, no criminal act was committed in England. The House of Lords, however, unanimously upheld the convictions on the basis that a conspiracy, while it is complete for the purposes of prosecution at the stage of agreement, is also a *crimen continuum* and so if anything is done in furtherance of the plan within England, the courts have jurisdiction. In *Doot*, therefore, the House of Lords did observe Lord Halsbury L.C.'s maxim[27] that: 'All crime is local.' Lord Salmon best expressed the principle so far as conspiracy is concerned:

> 'It was unusual until recently to have any direct evidence of conspiracy. Conspiracy was usually proved by what are called overt acts, being acts from which an antecedent conspiracy is to be inferred. Where and when the conspiracy occurs is often unknown and seldom relevant.'[28]

By seeking to justify the view that the punishment of conspiracies is possible where there have been overt acts done in furtherance of the conspiracy, the House of Lords demonstrated that it did not intend to create an exception to the rule that criminal jurisdiction is territorially limited.

In *Attorney-General's Reference (No. 1 of 1982)*,[29] the principle of territoriality was again emphasised in regard to conspiracy. In that case, the Court of Appeal held that a conspiracy to defraud companies by 'passing-off' whisky as the produce of other companies was not indictable in England and so the English courts had no jurisdiction (on the authority of *Board of Trade* v. *Owen*) even though there would be an incidental consequence of economic

---

[27] *Macleod* v. *Attorney-General for New South Wales* [1891] A.C. 455, at p. 458.
[28] [1973] A.C. 807, at p. 833.
[29] [1983] 1 Q.B. 751.

harm to companies and persons in England. In the course of holding that Lord Tucker's *obiter dictum* in *Board of Trade* v. *Owen* to the effect that a conspiracy wholly executed abroad could perhaps be indictable if it caused a 'public mischief' in England[30] was unacceptable, Lord Lane C.J. remarked tellingly: 'If it is necessary to enlarge the present jurisdiction, which we think it is not, then that is a matter for Parliament.'[31]

Thus it is clear that the English courts conceive of the criminal jurisdiction as being limited to result-crimes which have their results in England. There is, however, one area of difficulty. In the interpretation of penal statutes, while issues of jurisdiction should be present to the minds of the judiciary, there is a marked tendency on the part of the courts not to regard the jurisdictional issue as anything more than an exercise in statutory interpretation. Even in *Treacy,* both Lord Hodson and Lord Guest believed that the question could be answered by construing the statutory provision, although clearly that was not all that was required. In the construction of statutory offences, the courts sometimes, almost unwittingly, trespass on jurisdictional issues which are occasionally consequently answered improperly. *R.* v. *Markus,*[32] *R.* v. *El-Hakkaoui*[33] and *R.* v. *Berry*[34] are illustrations of this difficulty.

In *Markus,* the appellant was indicted for *inter alia* conniving at a corporation inducing the investment of money by false representations as to the genuineness of a management company, contrary to sec. 13(1)(*b*) of the Prevention of Fraud (Investments) Act 1958 as amended. The appellant had been a director of the management company which was formed and registered in London. Prospective

---

[30][1957] A.C. 602, at p. 634.
[31][1983] 1 Q.B. 751, at pp. 758-759.
[32][1975] 2 W.L.R. 708.
[33][1975] 1 W.L.R. 396, applying *R.* v. *Hornett,* Court of Appeal (Criminal Division), July 21, 1974 (*unreported*).
[34][1984] 3 W.L.R. 1274.

investors living in West Germany were visited by salesmen from the company. These salesmen induced the would-be investors to apply for shares, which share applications were brought back to London by the salesmen to be processed there. It was held by a majority of four-one that the offence was committed when the forms were processed in London. Viscount Dilhorne dissented on the basis that the offence, being one of inducing persons to take part in arrangements, was completed on the persons in West Germany forwarding their application forms; nothing was done thereafter in London.

Clearly, the majority gave an extended meaning to sec. 13(1)(*b*). The House of Lords chose to understand the offence as a continuing one and not, as it was no doubt conceived by the draftsmen, as a complete offence on the person being induced to do something. At the very least, as there could be said to have been a genuine doubt as to the meaning of the offence, the section should have been read in favour of the appellant. Furthermore, Lord Diplock was wrong when he said: 'To answer this question in the instant case does not . . . call for any wide-roving inquiry into the territorial ambit of English criminal law.'[35] Obviously, jurisdiction was a relevant consideration.

A difficulty in interpretation has particularly arisen in respect of offences in which the accused must do a prohibited act with a specified intention which extends beyond the mere prohibited act. In sec. 16 of the Firearms Act 1968, for example, the accused must possess a firearm with intent to endanger life or cause serious injury to property. In *El-Hakkaoui*, the appellant maintained that while his possession of the firearm was in England, his intention at that time was to use the weapon to endanger life in France. The Court of Appeal in dismissing the appeal held that a present intention to

---

[35][1975] 2 W.L.R. 708, at p. 716. Lord Kilbrandon and Lord Salmon concurred in Lord Diplock's speech.

use the weapon to endanger life was all that was necessary and that it was irrelevant where the intention was to be carried out or indeed whether or not the intention was ever given effect to by the appellant. This being the Court of Appeal's view, it is odd therefore that Browne L.J. indicated that the court in *El-Hakkaoui* considered the dissenters' views in *Treacy* as correct and Lord Diplock's as wrong. However, Browne L.J. also said: 'What Lord Reid and Lord Morris of Borth-y-Gest are saying is that where the acts constituting the crime are done entirely outside England they will not be punishable in England, either at common law or under statute, in the absence of express provision.'[36] This is manifestly erroneous: what Lord Reid and Lord Morris insisted was that the result should occur in England for the English courts to have jurisdiction.

However, the decision in *El-Hakkaoui* even contradicts Browne L.J.'s understanding of the dissent in *Treacy*, for there is no express provision in the Act of 1968 which allowed the courts to try cases in which the offence which the Act aims at preventing is intended to be committed abroad. It should therefore be a good defence to the charge that the firearm is intended for use abroad; and the jury ought to be the judge of this defence. In *El-Hakkaoui* the court was concerned with the possibility of facile defences being advanced and believed by juries. The solution is not however for the judiciary to extend the scope of the statutory offence, but for Parliament to make express provision either for the application of the statute to intentions to commit crime abroad or the exclusion of the availability of such a defence under the Act. But it would be most improbable that juries would accept such a facile defence.

The same problem arose in *Berry*,[37] where the House of Lords held that the offence of making explosive substances in circum-

---

[36][1975] 1 W.L.R. 396, at p. 401.

[37][1984] 3 W.L.R. 1274. See Cooper 'Explosives for Use Abroad', (1985) 49 J.C.L. 137 and commentary at [1985] Crim. L.R. 102.

stances which give rise to a reasonable suspicion that they are not being made for a lawful object, contrary to sec. 4 of the Explosive Substances Act 1883, was justiciable in England even though the object for which the substances were being made was to be executed in France. Where the substances were to be used was held to be irrelevant. Lord Roskill, in delivering the opinion of the House of Lords, said that the question was not one of jurisdiction but one of determining the true construction of the section.[38]

Once again, this view of the judicial function in *Berry* is inaccurate, as the decision entitles juries to convict people who fail to prove on a balance of probabilities that their object was not unlawful under foreign law. It is to be wondered whether such a requirement can be imposed on accused persons without the jurisdiction of the courts being called into question. The jurisdiction of the English courts, after all, does not include the interpretation and administration of French criminal law.

It would appear therefore that English law wishes to be taken as holding to the territorial limitation, but in practice exercises itself so as to give a strained and unrealistic meaning to words in statutory offences in order to hold that acts have occurred within jurisdiction. Such judicial acrobatics do, however, demonstrate that the English view is that jurisdiction is territorially limited unless statute provides to the contrary. The problem in this respect is that the English courts have, however, tended to accept that statutes import an extra-territorial jurisdiction without expressly so providing.

That having been said, the very recent decision of the Privy Council in an appeal from the Court of Appeal of Hong Kong requires brief notice. In *Liangsiriprasert* v. *Government of the United States of America*[39] an American undercover drug enforcement

---

[38] [1984] 3 W.L.R., at p. 1278.
[39] [1990] 3 W.L.R. 606.

agent had arranged with the appellant, a Thai national, to supply him with heroin for importation into the United States of America. The appellant was arrested in Hong Kong where he and another person had gone to collect payment. The United States government sought extradition of the appellant who was charged with trafficking in a dangerous drug and also committing acts preparatory to trafficking contrary to the Dangerous Drugs Ordinance 1988. The board held that as the appellant's activities in relation to both offences took place in Thailand they could not constitute a breach of the Ordinance which properly construed, had no extra-territorial effect. Lord Griffith explained the board's approach thus:

> 'When approaching the construction of a statute, particularly a criminal statute, there is a strong presumption that it is not intended to have extra-territorial effect and clear and specific words are required to show the contrary: see *Air-India* v. *Wiggins* [1980] 1 W.L.R. 815 and *Holmes* v. *Bangaladesh Biman Corp.* [1989] A.C. 1112. This presumption arises from the assumption that the legislature does not intend to intrude upon the affairs of other countries which should be left to order affairs within their own boundaries by their own laws.'[40]

It is, however, of importance to note that in a review of the relevant English and Commonwealth authorities including, *inter alia, Board of Trade* v. *Owen* and *Doot*, the Board quoted with evident approval La Forest, J.'s statement in *Libman* v. *The Queen*,[41] to the effect that the English courts have decidedly begun to move away from technical formulations to an application of English criminal law where a substantial measure of the activities constituting a crime take place in England.

Lord Griffith continued by stating:

---

[40] *Ibid.*, at pp. 621-622.
[41] (1985) 21 C.C.C. (3d) 206, at p. 221.

'Unfortunately in this century crime has ceased to be largely local in origin and effect. Crime is now established on an international scale and the common law must face this new reality. Their Lordships can find nothing in precedent, comity or good sense that should inhibit the common law from regarding as justiciable in England inchoate crimes committed abroad which are intended to result in the commission of criminal offences in England.'[42]

The technical limitation of the English criminal law is thus being replaced by a less strict restriction. In due course it can but be wondered whether the territorial restriction will not cease to be in any sense meaningful.

Scots law and the 'main act' theory

Lord Wilberforce observed in *Doot*: 'the starting point of legal discussion in this case, is the proposition that all crime is territorial. In following this principle derived from the *Digest* and modernised by Huber, common law jurisdictions have been consistent — more so, I believe, than systems of the civil law'.[43] As far as the mixed legal system of Scotland is concerned, this view is undoubtedly correct. The principle which governs Scots law is not, as it might at first appear, represented by the quotation from Macdonald at the start of this essay. The ruling principle, also supplied by Macdonald, is: 'It is not essential . . . that the whole of the acts constituting the crime should have been done in Scotland. If the main act is committed in Scotland . . . there is jurisdiction.'[44]

---

[42] [1990] 3 W.L.R. 606, at p. 620.

[43] [1973] A.C. 807, at p. 817.

[44] *Crimes* (5th edn.), p. 191. See also Renton and Brown, *Criminal Procedure* (5th .edn.), para. 1-70; *Encyclopaedia of the Laws of Scotland*, vol. v *sub. nom.* 'Crime', p. 222. The only authority given in the *Encyclopaedia* is Macdonald. See also *Stair Memorial Encyclopaedia of Laws of Scotland*, vol. vi, *sub. nom.* 'Courts and Competency,' para. 867 which oddly omits reference to *Laird* v. *H.M. Advocate* 1985 S.L.T. 298.

This view of jurisdiction (the 'main act' theory) has been applied by the High Court of Justiciary in *Laird* v. *H.M. Advocate*.[45] It has, however, to be said that until *Laird*, there was no real authority for this theory except one earlier case, *H.M. Advocate* v. *Semple*, [46] which is principally an authority for the proposition that it is not a crime to attempt to abort a woman who is not pregnant and it is thus only indirectly an apparent authority for Macdonald's main act theory.

In *Laird*, the appellants were indicted for a complex fraud which, though conceived in Scotland, was performed partly in Scotland and partly in England. It was libelled that in pursuance of the fraudulent scheme, the appellants pretended to certain representatives of the defrauded company, uttered as genuine certificates relating to steel and delivered to the defrauded company a quantity of substandard steel. All the utterings took place in England, the pretence was made in Glasgow or, as the indictment narrated 'elsewhere in Great Britain'; the steel was delivered in Scotland. Thus, if the territorial principle were to have been applied, the Scottish courts would not have had jurisdiction because the fraud was worked upon the defrauded company in England; such a view would be consistent with the view that fraud is a result-crime in that it is established by proof *inter alia* of a practical result whereby the 'dupe' is induced to do what he would not otherwise have done.[47]

However, applying (it would appear) the main act theory, the High Court unanimously held that the Scottish courts had jurisdiction. Lord Justice-Clerk Wheatley, with whom Lord Robertson and Lord Dunpark concurred, said in explanation:

'[W]here a crime is of such a nature that it has to originate with the forming of a fraudulent plan, and that thereafter various steps have

---

[45] 1985 S.L.T. 298.
[46] 1937 J.C. 41. *Semple* is the only relevant authority cited by Macdonald for his main act theory: see Gordon, *Criminal Law of Scotland* (2nd edn.), pp. 97-99.
[47] *Adcock* v. *Archibald* 1925 J.C. 58.

to be taken to bring that fraudulent plan to fruition, if some of these subsequent steps take place in one jurisdiction and some in another, then if the totality of the events in one country play *a material part in the operation and fulfilment of the fraudulent scheme as a whole* there should be jurisdiction in that country.'[48]

Lord Dunpark's reasoning was however somewhat different.

'When a fraudulent scheme is formulated in Scotland by two men . . . and the initial step of offering to sell goods . . . is made from Scotland . . . [t]he fact that some of the further acts take place in England, including the exchange of the goods for the purchase price, cannot, in my opinion, deprive the High Court of Justiciary of jurisdiction.'[49]

Lord Dunpark would therefore appear to be arguing that the Crown need only establish that the initiatory step in a result-crime has occurred in Scotland for the Scottish courts to have jurisdiction. But this is inconsistent with Lord Justice-Clerk Wheatley's view with which Lord Dunpark expressly concurred.

There are other difficulties with the opinions in *Laird.* First, when it is said that the totality of events plays a material part, is it therefore impossible for the main act theory to allow more than one law district to have jurisdiction? This would not appear to be the case, for the Lord Justice-Clerk remarked that in the two cases of *H.M. Advocate* v. *Allan*[50] and *H.M. Advocate* v. *Bradbury*[51] the judges were inclined to hold that the courts in England and Scotland could have jurisdiction in cases where frauds were practised upon people in Scotland by persons in England;[52] and as the

---

[48]1985 S.L.T. 298, at p. 300 (emphasis added).

[49]*Ibid.,* at p. 301.

[50](1872) 2 Coup. 402.

[51](1872) 2 Coup. 311.

[52]See Lord Ardmillan at p. 407 and Lord Justice-Clerk Moncrieff at p. 408 in *Allan*; and Lord Neaves (with whom the Lord Justice-Clerk concurred) at p. 318 in *Bradbury*.

court of six judges in *H.M. Advocate* v. *Witherington*[53] approves the decisions in both *Allan* and *Bradbury*, the Lord Justice-Clerk considered that the approval in *Witherington* could be deemed to cover the passages in the earlier cases relating to dual jurisdiction because the judges in *Witherington* had not seen fit to exclude this point from their approval. Such an exercise in deeming is, however, wholly novel and a breach of the accepted canons of *stare decisis* since the issue of duality of jurisdictions did not enter into the *ratio* of *Witherington*, or for that matter, *Laird*. Secondly, this decision misapplies the main act theory in that the facts of *Laird* did not merit the view that the main acts were committed in Scotland. The only important act in Scotland indeed was the formation of the scheme. But this factor cannot be equiparated with the facts of *Allan*, *Bradbury* or *Witherington*. In all three cases, the most important element in the frauds was the uttering of false documents upon their receipt by the people who were defrauded by being induced in Scotland to send money onwards to the accused in England. (Scotland was also the place of the result-crime of fraud in each case.) In *Laird* it was the forged certificate as to the standard of the steel that in truth induced the company to pay the money to the appellants' and that inducing occurred in England.

Thirdly, because their Lordships in *Laird* chose to speak in terms of frauds and not more generally in respect of any result-crimes, it may be possible to restrict the application of the main act theory (especially as it is extended in *Laird*) to crimes of fraud. However, this expectation will probably prove unrealistic. What is much more probable is that the High Court shall not apply principle (just as it did in *Laird* by going beyond what the main act theory permits) but hold that each case falls to be determined on its own facts; and thus the case law shall be ignored. An example of this rejection of precedent — as has been shown already, it occurs in England as well

---

[53](1881) 4 Coup. 475, at p. 491.

— is to be found in the 1983 decision in *Smith* v. *Inglis*[54] where the High Court decided that when a company, which has its registered office in Dundee, fails to deliver documents required by the Companies Act 1976 to be delivered to the Registrar of Companies in Edinburgh, the offence is committed in Edinburgh on the basis that 'the omission which constitutes the offence is failure to deliver the documents to the Registrar of Companies whose office is in Edinburgh'.[55] The High Court decided that it was not necessary to analyse the general law on jurisdiction as had been canvassed by Sheriff C. G. B. Nicholson (as he then was) in his earlier decision in *P.F. (Edinburgh)* v. *Jamieson* which the sheriff appended to the stated case in *Smith* in explanation of his decision, 'since the short answer here,' said the High Court, 'is to be found in the wording of section 1(7) itself'[55] of the Companies Act 1976. Thus the rule in *Lipsey* v. *Mackintosh*,[56] which provides that if a criminal act is done through the medium of the post, it is committed at both ends of the transmission, the postal service being the accused's innocent agent, was not expressly applied in order to render the failure liable to prosecution in both Edinburgh and Dundee — the conclusion which would have been appropriate as the rule in *Lipsey* is nothing other than a particular application of the main act theory in that it treats an act done between two jurisdictions as of equal significance in either jurisdiction.

Fourthly, there is the question whether or not Lord Dunpark intended to require that the main act should be a *sine qua non* of the crime in order for it to found jurisdiction when he said: 'it is obvious that this fraudulent scheme was formulated in Scotland and that it could not have succeeded *without* some of the acts which subsequently took place in Scotland.'[57] This would seem a reasonable test

---

[54] 1983 S.L.T. 160. *cf. H.M. Advocate v. Mentiplay,* 1938 J.C. 117
[55] 1983 S.L.T., at p.161
[56] 1913 2 S.L.T. 77. *cf. Wm. Jeffrey* (1842) 1 Broun 337
[57] 1985 S.L.T. 298, at p. 302 (emphasis added).

since it would appear that it is applied as the test in order to determine whether or not the Crown should be permitted to lead evidence of a crime committed exclusively abroad when that crime has been libelled in the indictment as 'an integral part of the crime which is libelled as having taken place in Scotland:' *Dumoulin* v. *H.M. Advocate.*[58]

However that may be, the decision in *Laird* applies a variant of the main act theory and the Lord Justice-Clerk's opinion, being supported by Lord Robertson without further comment, must be taken as the *ratio decidendi.* The proposition that the Scottish courts have jurisdiction in crimes on a territorial basis and thus only in respect of result-crimes which have their result in Scotland is therefore set at naught. Yet the main act theory is without authority in Scots law.[59]

Witherington was in truth a fraud which had its result in Scotland and on that basis the Scottish courts had jurisdiction. Lord Justice-General Inglis in a well-known passage indicated that the basis of the decision in *Witherington* was the distinction between conduct- and result-crimes:

> 'In all the examples which I have adduced the commencement of the criminal action is in one country and the completion of it in another. But in most of these cases the perpetrator's success in his criminal object is necessary to complete the crime. In the case of the poisoners there would have been no murder if the victim had not swallowed the poison . . .'[60]

Thus *Laird* was decided *per incuriam*, as *Witherington* did not support the main act principle of jurisdiction; the only support is

---

[58] 1974 S.L.T. (Notes) 42, at p. 43. See also *H.M. Advocate v. Joseph,* 1929 J.C. 55.

[59] *Cf.* Hume, *Commentaries,* ii, 54. Alison, *Criminal Law,* ii, 74-75.

[60] (1881) 4 Coup. 475, at p. 491.

to be found in *H.M. Advocate* v. *Semple.*[61]

In *Semple*, an indictment was held to be relevant when it libelled an attempt at abortion but did not specify where the abortion was to take place. However, because *Semple* rejected the need for specification of the place of the proposed abortion, it lends support to the idea that Scottish courts can claim jurisdiction when the main act takes place in Scotland, because in *Semple* the main act of supplying abortifacients took place in Scotland. However, if it be accepted that in Scots law no attempt at crime can be criminal unless the completed crime can be prosecuted in Scotland, then *Semple* was wrongly decided and thus does not support Macdonald's proposition concerning the main act. Moreover, it is difficult to see how *Semple* can be said to be correctly decided as the propriety of *Semple* would entail in the case of conspiracy, for example, that a conspiracy which is complete at the moment of agreement,[62] to commit a crime in France would be indictable in Scotland. While the Scottish courts can have every reason to claim jurisdiction over conspiracies to commit crimes in Scotland even when the conspiracy is formed outwith Scotland, the converse is not true. Indeed, until recently only Lord Diplock[63] has ever advocated such a course.

---

[61]The decision in *J. W. Nicol* (1834) Bell's Notes 149 to the effect that theft in England may be prosecuted in Scotland can be ignored as it concerns a *crimen continuum* and the main act theory is concerned with crimes which have a conclusion in one country but also have elements committed in other countries. In any case, secs. 7 and 292 of the Criminal Procedure (Scotland) Act 1975 make statutory provision for *Nicol.* See Hume, *Commentaries*, ii, 54-55 and Alison, *op. cit.*, ii, 78-79.

[62]See *Maxwell* v. *H.M. Advocate* 1980 J.C. 40; *Crofter Hand Woven Tweed Company Limited* v. *Veitch* 1942 S.C. (H.L.) 1, *per* Lord Viscount Simon L.C. at p. 5; Macdonald, *Crimes* (5th edn.), pp. 185 *et seq.*

[63]See [1971] A.C. 537, at p. 561.

Statutory offences

Since this article was published in its original form in 1987 the High Court has been required to consider a difficult jurisdictional question arising out of contraventions of the Misuse of Drugs Act 1971. In *Clements* v. *H.M. Advocate*[64] the appellants were charged with being concerned in the supply of cannabis resin contrary to sec. 4 (3) (*b*) of the Misuse of Drugs Act 1971. The indictment libelled the *loci* as being at various addresses in Essex, Kent and London, on a train travelling between London and Edinburgh and at various addresses in Edinburgh. The only evidence against the appellants (so far as was relevant for the purpose of their appeals) was their actings in London whereby they collected a holdall containing seven kilogrammes of cannabis resin and gave it to a co-accused who had travelled down by train to London and thereafter promptly returned to Edinburgh by train. Before the High Court it was contended under references to the judgment of Lord Griffith in *Liangsiriprasert*[65] that there was a strong presumption that a criminal statute was not intended to have extra-territorial effect, and that there was nothing in the 1971 Act to overcome that presumption. Accordingly it was submitted that the High Court did not have jurisdiction to try the appellants. This argument was rejected. Lord Justice-General Hope dismissed as irrelevant the presumption referred to by Lord Griffith in *Liangsiriprasert*, and explained:

'I do not think that we are concerned here at all with the extra-territorial effect, if any, of the Misuse of Drugs Act 1971. All the activities in this case took place in the United Kingdom, within the jurisdiction of the United Kingdom Parliament. The problem in this case is one as to territorial limitation as between the different jurisdictions within the United Kingdom. This depends on constitutional practice, not on international comity. . . . But for the purposes of the present case it is, I think, sufficient to look only to

---

[64] 1991 S.L.T. 388. See Sheriff Gordon's Commentary at 1991 S.C.C.R. 280-281.
[65] [1990] 3 W.L.R. 606, at pp. 621-622.

the situation within the United Kingdom and to ask why the courts of one part of it should be denied jurisdiction if the activities of persons elsewhere in the United Kingdom are seen to have their harmful *effects* in that part.'[66]

Thus the High Court in *Clements* construed sec. 4(3)(*b*) of the 1971 Act. There need be no supply unlike the offence in sec. 4(1)(*b*) of the 1971 Act and accordingly, Lord Justice-General Hope said, 'it seems to follow that each person who participates in the chain of distribution commits a self-subsisting statutory offence.'[67] Both of the appellants were involved in a 'single enterprise', namely obtaining the drug from source and transmitting it to the point of supply. Lords Wylie and Coulsfield in separate opinions agreed with Lord Justice-General Hope's conclusions.

The decision in *Clements* is interesting. First, it asserts that the appeals were not concerned with the extra-territorial effect of the 1971 Act. However, it is here submitted that there is no distinction to be drawn between a cross-border issue arising between Scotland and England and the same issue arising between Scotland and Germany. Certainly, such an approach was not mentioned by the court in *Laird* where the actings were both in England and Scotland. As Professor Williams said, for the purpose of the criminal law, Scotland is treated as a foreign country.[68] England is therefore a foreign country. Secondly, it is of no consequence, it is here submitted, that the particular offence was enacted in a United Kingdom statute. Nor is it relevant that all of the criminal conduct occurred within the jurisdiction of the United Kingdom Parliament. The appeal was concerned with the jurisdiction of the High Court of Justiciary to try crime; not the jurisdiction of Parliament

---

[66] 1991 S.L.T. at p. 393 (emphasis added).

[67] 1991 S.L.T. at p. 392; and see *Kerr* v. *H.M. Advocate* 1986 S.C.C.R. 81, *per* Lord Hunter at p. 87.

[68] *Textbook of Criminal Law* (2nd edn.), p. 165. See also Sheriff Gordon's view at 1991 S.C.C.R. 280 (para. 1).

to make criminal law. For both these reasons, accordingly, the presumption noted by Lord Griffith should arguably have applied in *Clements*. Had the presumption applied, the court would have been obliged thereafter to consider whether a conduct-crime executed in England by the appellants was intended by Parliament to be justiciable in Scotland. This question could only be answered by applying the main act theory which according to *Laird* is the test to be applied. Lord Coulsfield undoubtedly recognised this fact when he referred to the proposition by Macdonald that there might be jurisdiction in Scotland if an act done outside Scotland had a practical effect in Scotland[69] since that proposition was advanced by Macdonald in the context of the main act theory. Lord Coulsfield could see nothing in principle or authority to prevent the application of the rule stated by Macdonald.

On the main act theory, the question would have been what was or were the main act or acts of the offence under sec. 4 (3) (*b*) of the 1971 Act? Lord Justice-General Hope concluded that the determinative factor for jurisdiction was the place where the drugs were to be supplied.[69a] The underlying mischief at which sec. 4 of the 1971 Act stuck was the supply of, or offer to supply, a controlled drug to another. Thus, to regard the place of the mischief as the place where jurisdiction could be established against all persons involved in the offence was consistent with the idea that the courts of the place where the harmful acts occur may exercise jurisdiction even over those whose acts elsewhere have these consequences (although this did not confer exclusive jurisdiction on the courts of that particular place). While this reasoning has, as Lord Justice–General Hope noted, the advantage of serving the interests of justice by allowing the prosecution together of all participants in the chain of supply, it also, however, may sit uneasily with the main act theory since it may infer that in all result–crimes the harmful effect is always the main

---

[69] *Crimes* (5th edn.), p. 191.
[69a] 1991 S.L.T. at p. 394.

act. However, as has been observed already, the distinction between result–crimes and conduct–crimes is sometimes difficult to apply. Thus, it is surely arguable that the offence under sec. 4 (3) (b) is a conduct–crime giving jurisdiction to the English Courts. On the other hand, applying the main act theory and selecting the point of supply as the main act (in preference to any other possibility), jurisdiction falls to the Scottish Courts. It was in the circumstances a difficult question for the High Court to resolve in *Clements* and it may therefore be that an underlying policy of the 1971 Act was instrumental in the eventual answer given by the High Court.

Conclusion

It has been submitted that at common law the jurisdiction of both the English and Scottish courts should be limited to offences committed inside the geographical boundaries of the respective kingdoms. Thus only result-crimes which have their harmful consequences in Scotland should be indictable in Scotland. This would be in accordance with the view expressed at one point by Macdonald (and concurred in by both Hume[70] and Alison[71]): 'There may even be jurisdiction if an act done out of Scotland take practical effect in Scotland.'[72] However, Macdonald also gave expression to the principle that if the main act in an offence occurs in Scotland, the Scottish courts will have jurisdiction. This was not the view adopted by the courts in the older cases of *Allan, Bradbury* and *Witherington*, but is apparently the view now favoured by the High Court. The Scots law position as represented by *Laird* is therefore obviously at odds with English law as represented by the principles expressed in *Board of Trade* v. *Owen* and advocated by

---

[70]Hume, *Commentaries*, ii, 54.

[71]Alison, *Criminal Law*, ii, 74-75.

[72]*Crimes* (5th edn.), p. 191; and see Lord Coulsfield in *Clements* in regard to this principle at 1991 S.L.T. pp. 396-7.

both Lord Reid and Lord Morris of Borth-y-Gest in *Treacy*. Scots law does not now consider it necessary that for the Scottish courts to have jurisdiction in result-crimes the result should occur in Scotland. *Laird* does not, however, represent the view expressed in *Witherington* which, though it is not an appeal court decision in status, should command respect. Moreover, *Clements* is apparently at odds with the analysis based on conduct-crimes being prosecuted where the conduct occurs. It is submitted here that *Clements* was not a case of a result-crime but was a conduct-crime. Viewed in that light therefore *Clements* applies the main act theory and it can therefore only be regretted that *Laird* and *Witherington* were not cited by counsel in *Clements*, since the question of jurisdiction for the Court to resolve always falls to be answered, it is here submitted, by a consideration of whether (1) the common law crime or statutory offence is a result - or conduct-crime; and (2) if it is a result-crime or offence, the harmful effects of the crime or offence occurred in Scotland; and, finally, (3) if the answer to (2) is in the negative, the main act(s) constituting the *spicies facti* of the crime or offence were committed in Scotland.[73]

---

[73]This is an updated version of an article which was first published in the *Juridical Review* in 1987. The author's thanks are due to the publishers of the *Juridical Review*, Messrs W. Green & Son Ltd., Edinburgh, for their kind permission to reproduce the text of the 1987 article where necessary.

6

CRIMINAL EVENTS

Alexander McCall-Smith

Almost four decades ago the Judicial Committee of the Privy Council decided an appeal which was to lodge in the footnotes of edition after edition of criminal law textbooks throughout the Commonwealth. The appeal, *Thabo Meli* v. *R.*,[1] came from what was then Basutoland (now Lesotho), where Thabo Meli and his co-appellants had been convicted of the murder of a victim whom they had thrown over a mountain cliff. There was little in this murder to distinguish it from other crimes of homicide, except for one outstanding fact: the accused thought they had killed the victim by the time they got him to the cliff; in fact, he was still alive, having survived their earlier assault. What killed him was exposure as he lay, injured, among the rocks at the bottom of the cliff. No prosecutor would hesitate to seek a conviction for murder in such circumstances. After all, the accused clearly had the necessary *mens rea* for murder, as demonstrated by the ferocity of their original assault, and the fact that they killed their victim by throwing him over a cliff rather than physically beating him could be considered a classic case of error as to method. Such error in the applicable legal system (Roman-Dutch law), is as irrelevant as it is in Scots law. Yet a cunning defence was to muddy the waters. When the accused

---

[1] [1954] 1 All E.R. 373.

committed the act which led to death (throwing the victim over the cliff) they did not do so with any intent either to do injury or to kill. In their view, the victim was, by that stage, beyond all harm and they were merely tossing a dead body into the void. Nobody would dispute that one cannot murder a dead body, although there is some reason to believe that one might be convicted of attempting to do so.

The Privy Council gave this defence justifiably short shrift, and sustained the conviction of murder. The defence argument, of course, had to be refuted, and this was done by treating the entire sequence of events as one overall event. The fact, then, that there was no intention to harm by the time the victim reached the cliff edge was not considered to affect *mens rea* in relation to the 'extended' event: *mens rea* is satisfied if *at any stage* in the sequence of events leading up to the death, the accused intended to harm or to kill their victim. The attempt by the defence to separate the crime into constituent parts failed, and the murder convictions were upheld.

Thabo Meli found its way into the textbooks on the strength of what it says about the co-incidence of *actus reus* and *mens rea*. It has not been the only case of this sort: in a number of other less well-known decisions much the same issues have been raised. These could be dismissed as curiosities — as examples of last ditch arguments — but they are more than that. From the jurisprudential point of view, they are of some interest as illustrations of a problem which is debated in a rather recondite area of philosophy — the issue of event description (in its most technical manifestations, most technical). More practically, they demonstrate the difficulties that the courts may experience in determining the boundaries of criminal conduct, a matter which in its broader context lies at the very heart of criminal law.

It hardly needs to be repeated that the criminal law punishes offenders for what they do rather that for what they are. In pursuit of this objective, the criminal law identifies very specific acts which are penalised; unless a person's acts conform to a clear *type* of criminal act, there can be no responsibility. This all seems simple enough, and yet it is not. Acts do not take place in isolation. What X does at ten o'clock may only make sense if we know what he did at nine. Then, some acts are preparatory to others. Lifting a telephone receiver and placing a finger in the dial is not the complete act of making a telephone call. How we describe acts may also be important. We can say of Dr Bodkin Adams that in administering large doses of morphine to his patients he was killing them; but he would, and did, say that he was merely deadening pain. Here, as in other areas, language is a malleable tool, and the way in which one describes an event or series of events may depend to a great extent on what end one wants to achieve.

Meli had to be convicted of homicide; any other result would make a nonsense of the law. Yet one would not wish to depart from the principle that the basis of criminal liability is an identifiable, discrete act, accompanied by an appropriate mental element. The *actus reus* of theft is an *amotio* of property. The *actus reus* of murder is the doing of an act which, being either wickedly reckless or intended to kill, causes the death of the victim. In each of these cases, what is done *before* the *actus reus* is merely part of the background, it is not part of the *actus reus itself.* Or is it? The American legal philosopher, Joel Feinberg, has written of the 'accordion effect', the process by which one expands one's notion of an event to take in exactly those features which one wishes to include.[2] The metaphor is useful, and in the rather odd line of cases beginning with *Thabo Meli* the accordion principle can be seen at work. In most cases, it operates to bring within the ambit of a particular event certain occurrences which preceded the 'principal event' (the real *actus reus*); it rarely operates to embrace events which happen later. But this is enough of the theory; the real interest lies in the way in which the courts decided the cases.

---

[2] *Doing and Deserving* (Princeton: Princeton University Press, 1970), p. 134.

Previous events: Ryan v. The Queen; R. v. Pare

The facts in the Australian High Court's decision in *Ryan* v. *The Queen*[3] are quite extraordinary. Ryan, who would appear to have been unduly impressionable, read a magazine story in which the hero robbed a petrol station in order to raise the money to purchase lottery tickets. One of his tickets won, and he then repaid his victim and used the balance to rescue his indigent parents from poverty. Ryan was impressed, and set out to emulate the story. Unfortunately, real life diverted from the script when the owner of the petrol station made a sudden movement while he cowered at the end of Ryan's rifle. Ryan, who had his finger on the trigger, then fired *in reflex action*, killing his victim as a result. The tactic of the defence was to claim that, since the death of the deceased resulted from an involuntary act, there could be no liability for murder on Ryan's part, although even an accidental causing of death in the course of criminal conduct would be manslaughter. This is in accordance with the well-accepted principle, exemplified in *Hill* v. *Baxter*,[4] that reflex acts are not acts in respect of which any criminal responsibility is attributable.

This claim was addressed at considerable length by the High Court, but was ultimately rejected. It was accepted that the movement involved in pulling the trigger might well have been involuntary but this was not in itself enough to relieve Ryan of liability. It was pointed out that the act of killing the victim did not consist merely of the pulling of a trigger. This may well have been the event which finally sealed the fate of the victim, but there was much which preceded it, and all of this was voluntary. The obtaining of the weapon, the shortening of the barrel, the pointing of the gun at the victim; all of these were acts which bore the features of normal, voluntary action. They could each be treated as individual events which happened on the day of the offence, or, and this

---

[3][1966-67] A.L.J.R. 488.
[4][1958] 1 Q.B. 277.

124

was the approach preferred by the majority, these events could be regarded as part of an overall act or event, namely, the killing. So described, it will be seen that most of the constituent parts of the event were voluntary, thus making the event in its entirety a voluntary one. The accordion has therefore been drawn out here and embraced a whole series of acts performed by Ryan during the course of his criminal enterprise.

If the aim is to hold a person in Ryan's position responsible for the death of the victim, then there are several ways in which this result might be achieved. One of them is to adopt the approach which the High Court actually favoured, and to redescribe the event. Another would be to invoke some form of felony murder rule (which was actually applicable according to the New South Wales Crimes Act 1900), although this could be defeated if the felony murder provision required that there be a voluntary act on the part of the accused (it would be different if it merely required that the accused 'caused' the death). In English law, the 'dangerous act' approach could be followed and a conviction for manslaughter achieved.[5] The act of pointing the gun, a voluntary act, was dangerous, and the resulting death was therefore directly attributable to a dangerous act. If the facts of *Ryan* were to be repeated in Scotland, the issue might well be whether the act of pointing the gun were to be judged to amount to wicked recklessness. (The position, though, is far from certain: there is some authority for the view that it would be culpable homicide.)[6] Applying a purely objective test of recklessness, this might be so; but if the accused in such circumstances *did* care about the fate of the person at whom the gun was pointed and did not want to harm him (and this was the case with Ryan, if he were to be believed), then it is difficult to

---

[5] As in *R.* v. *Church* [1966] 1 Q.B. 59.

[6] *H.M. Advocate* v. *Fraser and Rollins* 1920 J.C. 60, *per* Lord Sands at p. 63; see further discussion in G. H. Gordon, *Criminal law* (2nd edn.), Edinburgh 1978, p. 741).

see how he could be said not to care whether his victim lived or died (the classic definition of the wickedly reckless state of mind).

There are further problems with *Ryan*. If a whole string of events is to be gathered together in this way, then it may be necessary to apply some sort of standard of relevance as to which events are to be included. Those identified by the court in *Ryan* were all closely linked with the pursuit of the criminal objective, but cases may arise in which the link between events is considerably more tenuous. In such cases, the temptation to redescribe events may need to be resisted. The Canadian case of *R*. v. *Paré*[7] illustrates this aspect of the problem. Under the Canadian *Criminal Code* a distinction is made between murder and first degree murder. The latter offence, for which more severe punishment is stipulated in the Code, is committed if the death of the victim is caused 'while committing an offence under section 156 [of the Code] (indecent assault).' The policy underlying this distinction is clear enough: sex killings are to be treated as particularly serious, a view which is quite in accordance with public attitudes of understandable abhorrence towards such crimes.

Pare persuaded a boy to accompany him to a secluded spot, where he committed a sexual offence. After the offence had been committed, the victim announced his intention of informing his parents of what had happened, whereupon Pare decided to kill him, presumably to avoid detection. Pare was convicted of first degree murder, but appealed against conviction on the grounds that the murder had been perpetrated by himself 'while committing an offence' under the relevant section; there had been such an offence, but it preceded the killing by a period of time, even if a short one. It was not possible, therefore, to say that the 'while committing' requirement had been satisfied. This argument was rejected, and the court decided to treat the events that happened after the

---

[7] 45 D.L.R. (4th) 546.

committing of the offence as being part of the overall event of killing while committing a sexual offence. The process of event redescription in this case, therefore, involved the same sort of corralling of antecedent events as occurred in *Ryan*. The difference between this case and *Ryan*, though, lies in the fact that Pare's motive in killing his victim was to prevent disclosure of his earlier crime. When he killed the boy, Pare was not doing anything in pursuit of a relevant criminal offence; all acts connected with the commission of the indecent assault had already been committed. To include within the description of an *actus reus* those events which follow its commission is probably to cast the net too widely, even if, as in Pare's case, the accused deserves no sympathy for his crimes. It should not, for example, be murder to shelter a murderer; nor, indeed, should reset be theft.

Describing acts: Timbu Kolian v. The Queen

Event redescription of the sort employed in *Ryan* and *Pare* involves the reassessment of the temporal boundaries of occurrences; in other circumstances the focus may be not so much on temporal as on qualitative aspects. An example of this is *Timbu Kolian* v. *The Queen*,[8] an appeal to the High Court of Australia from Papua New Guinea. The appellant had become involved in a domestic altercation with his wife and had decided to chastise her with a stick, in conditions of darkness. Unknown to him, his wife was carrying their child with her and the blow landed on the child, with fatal results. This is a classic case of *aberratio ictus*, which in Scots law would not have availed the appellant, but this was not the approach adopted by the High Court, which considered the question in terms of sec. 23 of the relevant criminal code. This section is a deceptively straightforward voluntary act provision which states: 'A person is not criminally responsible for an act or omission which occurs independently of the exercise of his will, or for an event which occurs by accident.'

---

[8](1968) 119 C.L.R. 47.

127

It is clear from the judgment that the court was reluctant to hold Timbu Kolian responsible for the death of the child, something which he clearly had not had in contemplation when he struck the fatal blow. Section 23 provided a promising means of avoiding a homicide conviction, and yet could the act of striking the blow be regarded as occurring independently of his will? A willed act, as ordinarily understood in criminal jurisprudence, is one in which the actor consciously wills himself to do something, in contrast with an act, such as a reflex jerking of the knee or a nervous tic, over which the actor has no control. When he picked up the stick and went through the motion of bringing it down on what he thought would be his wife, the appellant can hardly be said to have been acting in an involuntary manner. And there, one might have thought, would the matter stand, with a manslaughter conviction on *aberratio ictus* grounds; the High Court, though, avoided this by deciding, as in *Ryan* and *Pare*, that the act of striking the child could not be divided into individual elements — a physical movement followed by particular consequences. The *actus reus* to which the mental state must relate is not, therefore, the simple act of striking (in the abstract) *but the act of striking a particular victim.*

The adoption of this approach led the court to conclude that the striking of the child was an involuntary act because of the fact that the appellant had not 'willed' that the blow should land on the child. This is somewhat surprising, as criminal jurisprudence has long understood there to be a distinction between 'will' and 'intention'. A willed act may well have unintended consequences, and this is certainly one way of analysing the appellant's conduct in this case. Only by changing the description of the act, and calling it one of 'striking the child' rather than 'wielding a stick' was the court able to avoid this consequence. In *Timbu Kolian* the result of this impressive piece of linguistic legerdemain was to relieve a relatively blameless offender of responsibility for a death which he in no sense wanted; yet there must obviously be limits to the extent to which act redescription may be used to exculpate, or indeed, convict offenders. In particular, act redescription poses problems in the area of *res judicata* and the rule against multiple convictions in respect of the same act. Should a thief be liable to be convicted in respect of possession of stolen property which he himself has stolen? Scots law excludes this,[9] but this is not the case in Canada where a man convicted of theft has been found guilty of being in possession of stolen property after serving a sentence for the theft of that property.[10] In another Canadian case, the issue arose as to whether an accused could be convicted of manslaughter and causing bodily harm in respect of the same act. In the somewhat unusual circumstances of *R* v. *Prince*[11] the accused had, in a single blow to the abdomen of a pregnant woman, stabbed both the woman and her unborn child. The child was born prematurely and died as a result of the stabbing. The accused was initially convicted of causing bodily injury to the mother and then subsequently charged with the manslaughter of the child. On appeal, the court addressed the issue of multiplicity, and ruled that, in cases where a single violent act causes harm to others, the rule against multiplicity was excluded. This then is one area where a single act might properly be described as being a whole series of events. The detonation of a bomb which claims two victims is quite properly described as the murder of A, and the murder of B.

Continuing events: the setting of limits

In both *Thabo Meli* and *Pare* the basis of the charge was a physical act or acts; a very different sort of problem has arisen in possession cases, where the criminal event is for obvious reasons less sharply focused. Possession may result from a positive act on the part of the possessor — such as purchase or acceptance of a gift — but it is not, of course, this positive act of acquisition which the law singles out

---

[9] Hume on *Crimes* (3rd edn.), i, 116.
[10] *Cote* v. *The Queen* 49 D.L.R. (3d) 574.
[11] 33 D.L.R. (4th) 725.

for attention; rather it is the continued exercise of the mental state of control. The criminal 'event' in a drug possession, in fact, is likely to have existed well before that. This seems obvious, and might have been of little interest had it not been for the problem of forgotten possession. Can possession, if established at *time x*, still exist at *time y* if, at the latter point, one of its vital elements (knowledge) is no longer present? Or, put another way, if knowledge is an event — as it must be — does this event span periods during which the mind is otherwise occupied or, more problematically, does it survive its own demise? On Monday, reading his newspaper, X is informed that the new chairman of a bank is Y. On Wednesday, in the course of conversation with a friend he is asked to name the chairman, but his memory fails him. On being told the name, X replies: 'Oh yes, I knew that all along!' But did he? For Sir Robert Megarry V.-C. in his judgment in *Re Montagu's Settlement Trusts*,[12] the answer to a question of this type must be no. 'A person should not be said to have knowledge of a fact he once knew if at the time in question he has genuinely forgotten about it, so that it could not be said to operate on his mind any longer.' If the answer is yes, however, then the 'event' of knowledge embraces periods of forgetfulness and it is perfectly possible to convict people of possession of drugs which they have forgotten they possessed.

The decisions on this question are not altogether consistent, although there has been a general tendency to dismiss the defence of forgotten possession in a fairly perfunctory way. The defence was recognized in *R. v. Russell*,[13] in which the accused had forgotten the presence of a weapon which he had placed under the seat of his car, and it was similarly allowed by the Supreme Court of New Zealand in a drug possession case, *Police v. Rowles*.[14] This judicial acceptance of forgotten possession as a defence is overshadowed by those

---

[12][1987] 2 W.L.R. 1192, at p. 1210.
[13](1984) 81 Cr. App. Rep. 315.
[14][1974] 2 N.Z.L.R. 756.

decisions in which the fact of forgetting is treated as irrelevant. In *R.* v. *Martindale*[15] the Court of Appeal held that possession did not come and go with the fading and revival of memory. A person who put a drug into his wallet and then forgot about it could still be said to be in possession of it two years or more later. To hold otherwise, it was suggested, would result in the unacceptable situation in which a man with a poor memory might be acquitted while one with a good memory might be convicted.

The issue came before the High Court of Justiciary in *Gill* v. *Lockhart*,[16] an appeal against a conviction under the Misuse of Drugs Act 1971 of possession of cannabis resin. The cannabis had been found in the pocket of a golf bag belonging to the appellant, having been put there some years before. The appellant argued that he had forgotten the fact that the cannabis was there, but this argument had been rejected by the sheriff, who took the view that knowledge of the cannabis might have 'gone into abeyance' but did not cease to exist. This was to be endorsed by the Lord Justice-Clerk (Ross), who pointed out the oddness of holding that a person ceases to be in possession of an item the moment it goes out of his mind. Possession, therefore, survives forgetfulness.

One way of testing such a proposition is to measure it against our sense of fairness. In a case where a person is found in possession of a forgotten drug, few people would argue that conviction is unfair, bearing in mind that the accused voluntarily came into possession at an earlier stage. In both *R.* v. *Martindale* and *Gill* v. *Lockhart* the period between the point at which there was knowledge of the drug's existence and the point at which illegal possession was discovered was two to three years. What if this period had been six or seven years, or even more? Of course, the sense of unfairness of convicting in such a case might be attributable to that sense of fairness which underpins notions of prescription, but at least the

---

[15][1986] 1 W.L.R. 1042; approved in *R.* v. *McCalla, The Times,* April 11, 1988.
[16]1987 S.C.C.R. 599.

question should make us wonder just how long a continuing offence can be said to continue. In other words, it may be possible to draw out events fairly far, but there does come a point where even a long drawn-out event must be said to come to an end.

Antecedent liability

Reluctance to hold that events persist or embrace other events points to another solution to this rather puzzling problem in criminal law: an analysis in terms of antecedent liability. Following this approach, the focus of enquiry moves from the damage causing event (an assault, participation in an offence, or whatever) to the events which preceded it. A good illustration of this is afforded by intoxication cases. In *Brennan* v. *H.M. Advocate*,[17] in which the appellant had been convicted of murder, the court expressed the view that voluntary intoxication constituted a form of recklessness, and that since wicked recklessness was one of the forms of *mens rea* for murder, the fact that the accused was intoxicated should not be a defence. In such a case the wrongfulness of the accused's conduct may, therefore, be located at the point at which he becomes intoxicated, rather than at the point at which he performs the act which leads to the death of his victim. There is no need, then, to describe two or more events as being part of one large event.

Coercion cases provide further illustration of this technique. There is a long moral tradition against holding a person liable for those acts which he performs under compulsion, and this principle is recognized in the availability of the criminal defence of coercion, which is fully recognized in Scots law. The problem with the coercion defence, though, is that it may be pled by those whose own conduct has resulted in their being coerced. If A joins a criminal gang, and is then coerced into committing an offence, he may, as in the case of *R.* v. *Sharp*[18] and in a number of other recent decisions,

---

[17] 1977 S.L.T. 151.
[18] [1987] 3 All E.R. 103; also: *R.* v. *Fitzpatrick* [1977] N.I.L.R. 20.

be denied a defence on the grounds that he himself was responsible for exposing himself to the risk of being compelled to commit a crime which he may not wish to commit. In this sort of case, as in intoxication cases such as *Brennan*, a person may be held responsible for something which he may never have envisaged at the time when he took the step which could properly be considered culpable. If A is coerced by one of his fellow gang members into committing a murder in order to save his own life, it may well be that he should be considered to have committed murder, but his crime surely differs considerably from that of one who commits murder at his own instance.

It could be argued, of course, that nothing untoward is happening here, and that all that the criminal law is doing is saying that if you engage in certain forms of behaviour, it is at your own risk. The difficulty with this is that punishment for risk-taking is usually dependent on *foresight* of the risk. In some cases there may well be foresight — in which case there are no grounds for objection to the imposition of liability for the consequences; this is a form of liability for that form of recklessness in which the accused has been aware of the existence of a risk and has acted nonetheless. But what about those situations in which the accused has not adverted to the existence of a risk? According to a controversial, but well-established line of English decisions, this amounts to recklessness.[19] The adoption of this concept of recklessness, however, amounts to a considerable extension in the grounds of liability. This form of recklessness is arguably nothing more than negligence, which is a failure to act in such a way as to avoid causing damage to others. Recklessness is a mental state — the reckless person acts in the knowledge of risk, and his culpability lies in the fact that he does not

---

[19] *R.* v. *Caldwell* [1981] 1 All E.R. 961; *R.* v. *Lawrence* [1981] 1 All E.R. 974; *R.* v. *Pigg* (1982) 74 Cr. App. R. 352. For discussion, see R. A. Duff 'Caldwell and Lawrence: the retreat from subjectivism' (1983) 3 O.J.L.S. 77.

care whether the risk materializes. If harm results, then it is quite appropriate that the reckless actor should be punished, as he has, in a sense, 'adopted' that harm in much the same way as a person who acts intentionally 'adopts' or identifies with the consequence which results from his action. Negligence, by contrast, is not so clearly to be characterised as a state of mind. An objective theory of negligence does not require that there was any awareness on the part of the actor that his behaviour falls below the standard of care expected of him, and the objectively negligent actor may therefore not act with a state of mind which identifies him as being culpable. Subjective theories of negligence, by contrast, require a particular state of mind on the part of the actor. According to these theories, the negligent actor must at least know that he is being careless. This bears some similarities to recklessness, but the real difference must lie in the attitude to the risk. The reckless actor is indifferent to the possibility of harm; the negligent actor may well not want the harm to occur, and is certainly unlikely to be indifferent to it. What really distinguishes the two states, then, is the extent to which the mental state of the actor in each case approaches intentionality. The reckless actor 'as good as wants' the harm to occur; this cannot be said of the negligent actor.

This gives rise to the complex question of whether there should ever be criminal responsibility for negligence as opposed to recklessness properly-so-called. The intuitive answer must be yes: there are, indeed, obvious cases when failures may be held to be culpable. These will usually be cases in which the degree of negligence is high. Indeed, it could be argued that many of the incidents of negligence which give rise to criminal liability could equally well be called recklessness. The contractor who, in order to maximise his profit, instals an electrical system without taking proper precaution is aware of the risk of harm and proceeds in spite of it. Such a person might be prosecuted for culpable homicide on the grounds of negligence, but it is difficult to see the distinction between such behaviour and recklessness. This example is an extreme one, and convincing for that reason. Where the degree of negligence is slighter, it is not so easy to justify criminal liability, mainly because of the possible absence of any state of mind which could amount to *mens rea*. Behaviour which is objectively negligent, but which was not accompanied by any awareness of a risk of harm, should not be punishable by the criminal law unless it is accepted that the reason for punishment is purely a deterrent one. To treat such behaviour as criminal offends a basic principle of the criminal responsibility, namely, that only those who have a blameworthy state of mind should be punished.[20] Negligence liability may, of course, be considered a variety of strict liability, but this, too, would in some cases run counter to the hard-won limitation of strict liability to regulatory offences.

Antecedent liability of the sort discussed above is an example of liability for negligence. In some circumstances, the negligence demonstrated by the accused will be of such a degree that it seems proper to hold him criminally responsible. But that will not always be so. In particular, the negligence shown by the person who becomes intoxicated is hardly of a high order. It is, for example, qualitatively quite different from the negligence shown by the corner-cutting electrician, and it is certainly very different from the recklessness of the person who discharges a firearm in a crowded street knowing, and not caring, that there is a probability that somebody will be harmed. Those who are professionally concerned with the effects of alcohol may be aware of the possibility of homicide being committed by an intoxicated person, but is this knowledge present in the mind of a young person engaged in a drinking bout? If it is not, then the basis of liability can only be objective negligence or possibly recklessness, and this could amount, then, to a form of strict liability. And this leads to the question of

---

[20]The opposite view is held by a number of criminal law commentators. For discussion, see C. T. Sistare, *Responsibility and criminal liability* (Dordrecht, 1989), pp. 133 *et. seq.*

135

whether murder or even culpable homicide or assault should ever be allowed to become strict liability offences by a process of back-door entry.

In both approaches — that of event redescription and that of the imposition of liability for antecedent acts — there are clear dangers. In the case of the event redescription approach the danger is that of making events so general and so broad as to weaken the traditional adherence to the principle of criminal liability being imposed only in respect of discrete, reasonably sharply-defined acts. In the case of liability for antecedent events, the danger is that of sacrificing concepts of foresight and intention which limit liability to those who really do demonstrate *dole* (to resurrect a useful term of Scots law) in relation to the things that they do.

There are several possible responses to this. One is for the courts to say, 'Whatever is said about lack of intention or involuntariness at the time of the commission of the *actus reus*, for policy reasons we do not want to let members of criminal gangs, or those who become dangerously intoxicated, to get away with what they did'. Another approach might be to accept that subjective guilt is the only morally acceptable basis for criminal liability and to allow, for example, a full defence of intoxication, as has happened in Australia, where the half-way house of *Majewski* has now been abandoned.[21] It is also the philosophy underlying German criminal law's approach to offences committed in a state of intoxication, under which what is punished is the act of becoming so intoxicated as to cause damage to persons or property, rather than tying punishment to the consequences of the intoxicated behaviour. This undoubtedly cuts down the arbitrary implications of 'moral luck', the process whereby the extent of liability depends on the consequences that happen to result from wrongful action.

---

[21] *R. v. O'Connor* (1979-80) 29 A.L.R. 449. The Australian approach is discussed by D. O'Connor and P. A. Fairall, *Criminal Defences* (Sydney, 1988), pp. 214 *et seq.*

At the end of the day, the issue might reduce to the simple question of whether, by redescribing events, or by applying antecedent liability, any injustice is done to the accused. None of the accused persons in the actual cases above were morally blameless, but any such judgment of blameworthiness requires reference to some other event in their past, *and that event does not form the gravamen of the charge.* For this reason, there remains something about such cases which makes one want to go back to them and puzzle them out again. They are the hard cases of criminal law, and solutions to hard cases, one must suppose, are rarely going to be easy.

7

HAMESUCKEN AND THE MAJOR PREMISS IN THE LIBEL, 1672-1770: CRIMINAL LAW IN THE AGE OF ENLIGHTENMENT

John W. Cairns

Stallard v. *H.M. Advocate* was one of the last criminal appeals over which Lord Emslie presided as Lord Justice-General of Scotland.[1] The case raised the controversial, if apparently simple, issue of whether or not a husband could be guilty of the rape of his wife, other than art and part, while they were still cohabiting. *H.M. Advocate* v. *D.*[2] and *H.M. Advocate* v. *Paxton*[3] had already determined that, where spouses were living apart, a husband could be guilty of raping his wife. The authority for the traditional view on marital rape is a passage dealing with art and part guilt in the chapter on rape in Hume's *Commentaries*. 'This is true without exception even of the husband of the woman; who, though he cannot himself commit a rape on his own wife, who has surrendered her person to him in that sort, may however be accessory to that crime . . . committed on her by another.'[4] The court suggested in *Stallard*

---

[1] 1989 S.C.C.R. 248.

[2] 1982 S.C.C.R. 182.

[3] 1985 S.L.T. 96.

[4] D. Hume, *Commentaries on the Law of Scotland, Respecting Crimes* (2 vols.; 4th edn., Edinburgh, 1844), i, 306; see also D. Hume, *Commentaries on the Law of Scotland, Respecting the Description and Punishment of Crimes* (2 vols.; Edinburgh, 1797), ii, 10 which has trivial differences in wording. All quotations below will be from the first edition of 1797, unless otherwise noted.

that Hume had adopted this view from Sir Matthew Hale's *Historia placitorum coronae*, where Hale had written: 'But the husband cannot be guilty of a rape committed by himself upon his lawful wife, for by their mutual matrimonial consent and contract the wife hath given up herself in this kind unto her husband, which she cannot retract.'[5] The court did not consider it necessary to decide in *Stallard* whether or not Hume had correctly stated the law of his own day, accepting that, even if Hume's statement ever had been good law in Scotland, it no longer was.[6] The English Court of Appeal, Criminal Division, has recently followed this lead, and rejected the marital rape exemption found in Hale.[7]

Hume acknowledged that he drew on English law in writing his *Commentaries:*

'Let me add, that while I thus disclaim that superstitious admiration of the English Law, which prevails among some persons, and especially, like other superstitions, among the ignorant; and which would set up that system as a standard of perfection, after the likeness whereof we are to reform and new-model our own; yet on a proper occasion, and for a proper purpose, I have been ready to avail myself of the important assistance which its doctrines may often afford me. I have already said, that as a great body of written and practical reason, and recommended by the example of a free and an enlightened people, it has every where, and certainly in our country more than elsewhere, (because the form of our Government, and the general spirit of our jurisprudence are the same with

---

[5] M. Hale, *Historia placitorum coronae. The History of the Pleas of the Crown* (2 vols.; London, 1736), i, 629.

[6] 1989 S.C.C.R. 248, at pp. 253-254.

[7] *R. v. R.*, [1991] 1 All E.R. 747; [1991] 2 All E.R. 257, CA. The husband and wife were no longer living together; but the court pronounced a general principle that husbands could be convicted of the rape of their wives, although pointing out that, had it been decided otherwise, they would have ruled that where a wife had withdrawn from cohabitation, as in this case, so that the marriage was effectively at an end as far as she was concerned, the husband's immunity was lost. At the time of writing the Court of Appeal had given leave to appeal to the House of Lords certifying the point of law as of general public importance. See now [1991] 4 All E.R. 4 81.

that of England), a strong claim to deference and regard. In matters, therefore, which depend on the common feelings of equity and right, and are not determined otherwise by our municipal custom, nor are anywise involved in it, I have made liberal use of the sentiments, and sometimes even of the words of the English writers on law: An obligation, which, as their works cannot properly be quoted as authorities in a book of Scots Law, I beg leave in this place, once for all, to acknowledge.'[8]

It is therefore unsurprising that he may have adopted the doctrine on marital rape found in Hale in the absence of any Scottish authority on the issue. Yet Gane and Stoddart, writing before the decision in *Stallard*, put an obvious and attractive argument on Hume's view of rape in marriage:

'[I]t is not at all clear that the "marital rape exemption" is really a rule of Scots law at all. There is no sign of it prior to Hume, and the other authorities which refer to it merely repeat Hume. Hume himself does not refer to any Scottish authority in support of his view, and it is likely that the rule was adopted by Hume from Hale's *Pleas of the Crown* . . .'[9]

They thus bluntly attack the authority of Hume on the grounds that his statement is one of English law rather than Scots law. Gane and Stoddart were the first to suggest that Hume may have drawn this doctrine from Hale. Certainly it is not found in earlier published treatises on Scots criminal law, and only in Hale of the English authors whom Hume stated he consulted.[10] The sugges-

---

[8]Hume *Commentaries*, i, liv; *cf. Commentaries* (1844), i, 13, in which edition 'common feelings of equity and right' reads 'common feelings of equity and reason'. There are other trivial changes.

[9]C. H. W. Gane and C. N. Stoddard, *A Casebook on Scottish Criminal Law* (2nd edn.; Edinburgh, 1988), p. 671.

[10]Hume, *Commentaries*, i, [lxiv] states that, as well as Hale, he consulted W. Hawkins, *A Treatise of the Pleas of the Crown: Or, A System of the Principal Matters relating to that Subject, digested under their Proper Heads* (2 vols.; 3rd edn.; London, 1739); and W. Blackstone, *Commentaries on the Laws of England* (4 vols.; 1st edn.; Oxford, 1765-69).

tion is plausible, because, though the words used by Hume and Hale are not very close, after the passage quoted above, Hale also went on to discuss when a husband could be indicted for the rape of his wife by assisting another as the actor.[11]

Gane and Stoddart's challenge to the authority of Hume's proposition undoubtedly reflects a traditional view that, since there is no appeal to the House of Lords from the High Court of Justiciary,[12] and since Scots criminal law is primarily common law rather than statutory in basis, it is somehow more 'Scottish' and has been less open to English influence than Scots private law.[13] Indeed, Sheriff Gordon has remarked that 'Scots criminal law has grown up more or less independently of Anglo-American law, and Anglo-American concepts and cases must therefore be treated with care when considering Scots law.'[14] Hume's adoption of a doctrine of English law could thus be stigmatised as somehow illegitimate.

It is undoubtedly correct that to some extent Scots criminal law has developed independently of that of England, and I do not wish here to challenge Sheriff Gordon's view. Instead, I wish to explore the issue raised by Gane and Stoddart (and perhaps implicitly by the court in *Stallard*) of whether demonstration that Hume adopted a doctrine of English law in the absence of Scots authority necessarily impugns the validity of that doctrine as Scots law. I shall do this by examining the law on hamesucken between 1672 and 1770. These two dates are not arbitrary. The first is the year of the creation of the new Court of Justiciary; the second provides a terminus since the previous year had seen the last trial for hamesucken before the High Court of Justiciary until the nineteenth century,

---

[11]Hale, *Pleas of the Crown*, i, 629.

[12]On which, however, see A. J. MacLean, 'The House of Lords and Appeals from the High Court of Justiciary, 1707-1887' (1985) *Juridical Review*, 192-226.

[13]*Cf.* T. B. Smith, 'English Influences on the Law of Scotland', in *Studies Critical and Comparative* (Edinburgh, 1962), pp. 116-136 at pp. 130-131.

[14]G. H. Gordon, *The Criminal Law of Scotland* (2nd edn.; Edinburgh, 1978), p. 3.

when, as I hope to argue elsewhere, the crime of hamesucken gained a new lease of life after the publication of Hume's *Commentaries*. Discussion of hamesucken will allow me to place Hume's account of the marital rape exemption in the more general context of Scots criminal law and practice; furthermore, in one important case on hamesucken, the question of marital rape was considered.

The first section of the paper will be devoted to an account of procedure in criminal trials between these dates, the second will discuss the law of hamesucken as found in treatises and the practice of the Justiciary Court, while the third and fourth will examine one crucial trial in 1752. The final section will return to marital rape, and will offer some tentative conclusions, suggesting that if Hume adopted the marital rape exemption from Hale, he was following the practice, well-established in Scottish criminal law, of drawing on the criminal laws of other countries to explain and develop Scots law. This practice was necessary because the manner of conducting trials and the records of the court tended to leave the law imprecise and without an authoritative judicial statement. It remained vague and inchoate to some extent. Furthermore, criminal law was not viewed as narrowly Scottish: it was legitimate to borrow from the laws of other countries. Scottish criminal law was common law in the sense both of being located in the custom of the courts and in being part of the *ius commune*. Hume's *Commentaries* perhaps marked or continued a turning away from the *ius commune*, and a favouring (if limited in scope) of English law as a source of borrowing; they also continued to some extent an existing traditional approach in these matters.

Procedure in criminal trials 1672-1770

The High Court of Justiciary was established by the Courts Act 1672, c.40. Under this Act, the judges were the Lord Justice-General, Lord Justice-Clerk, and five Lords Commissioners of Justiciary appointed from the Lords of Session. As well as sitting in Edinburgh, the judges went on circuit in twos, once a year under the Act of 1672 and twice a year after 1746.[15] Prosecution was based on a libel which took the form either of an indictment or of criminal letters. The main distinction between the two was that the former could only be used by the Lord Advocate, while the latter could be used by others, such as private individuals.[16] Whether the prosecution was by way of indictment or criminal letters, the libel was in the form of a syllogism, with a major premiss or proposition setting out the crime charged, usually by a *nomen juris*, or if there were none, by a general description, while the minor premiss or proposition named and designed the accused and set out allegations of fact which, if proven, would demonstrate the pannel's guilt of the crime specified in the major premiss. After this came the conclusion, stating that the pannel on conviction should be punished as provided by the law for the crime.[17] It is unnecessary to go through the steps of a criminal prosecution in detail. With lists of witnesses and assizers, the libel was served on the accused who was cited to compear at a stated time at either the High Court or a Circuit Court. When the accused compeared at the trial diet, the libel was read to him or her and he or she was required to plead guilty or not guilty. On the pannel's pleading not guilty, there normally was a debate on the relevancy of the libel. In the later seventeenth century, the procurators for the pannel and the prosecutor normally dictated their objections, replies, duplies, triplies, quadruplies and so on to the clerk who entered them in the record. The Act of 1695, c.6 required that relevancy be debated *viva voce*, to be followed by the giving in of written informations that were entered, recorded, and publicly read to the court, and that could then, if

---

[15]W. Croft Dickinson, 'The High Court of Justiciary', in *An Introduction to Scottish Legal History* (G.C.H. Paton, ed., Stair Society, vol. 20; Edinburgh, 1958), pp. 408-412, at p. 411.

[16]See, *e.g.*, D. Hume, *Commentaries on the Law of Scotland Respecting Trial for Crimes* (2 vols.; Edinburgh, 1800), i, 244-247.

[17]*Ibid.*, i, 247; see also Hume, *Commentaries* (1844), ii, 155.

necessary, be debated *viva voce*. This Act was repealed by the Heritable Jurisdictions (Scotland) Act 1746 (c.43), section 41, which substituted the provision (section. 42) that, after the oral debate on the relevancy, informations could be given in to the court by the procurators for the pursuer and the pannel. On the basis of this debate, the judges pronounced an interlocutor on the relevancy, which could set out in detail which matters were to be proved and which defences considered. After this, the pannel would be put to the cognisance of an assize, that, on the basis of the interlocutor and evidence presented, would either determine the guilt or innocence of the pannel or give a special verdict.[18]

The debate on the relevancy of the libel focussed attention on the definition of the crime set out in the major premiss and on whether or not the averments in the minor premiss, if proved, would constitute that crime. The law on the construction of the major premiss or proposition is set out by Hume in some detail, and it is unnecessary to consider it here.[19] But since much of what follows will revolve around the way in which the major premiss of the libel was phrased, some remarks are appropriate. Alison described it thus:

'The major proposition sets out with the words, "That albeit by the laws of this and of every other well governed realm, theft, especially when accomplished by means of housebreaking, is a crime of an heinous nature, and severely punishable." In cases of murder, it is

---

[18]J. Irvine Smith, 'Criminal Procedure' in [Paton (ed.)], *Introduction to Scottish Legal History*, pp. 426-448, at pp. 439-443; for a good contemporary account of procedure and the steps in a prosecution, see J. Louthian, *The Form of Process before the Court of Justiciary in Scotland* (Edinburgh, 1732); idem, *The Form of Process, before the Court of Justiciary in Scotland. In Two Books* (2nd edn.; Edinburgh, 1752) updates it. Louthian concentrates on the formal steps and styles of documents and records.

[19]Hume, *Trial for Crimes*, i, 263-300; Hume, *Commentaries* (1844), ii, 164-181; see also A. Alison, *Principles of the Criminal Law of Scotland* (2 vols.; Edinburgh, 1832), ii, 228-245.

usual to add the words, "albeit by the laws of God and of this and every other well governed realm, murder is a crime," . . .'[20]

The exact wording or style of the formula of the major premiss varied historically, as Hume explained, glossing the phrase 'and all other well-governed realms':

> 'For it had long ago grown into a fashion, not to be content with referring in this respect to our own laws alone, but to confirm their decision with an appeal to all other high authorities, such as the law of God and nature, or the law and practice of other civilized states, as concurring in the same notions of the offence in question. In times when the authority of the civil and the canon law was higher than it is now, it was not uncommon to call in the aid also of those systems; describing them as 'the *common law*, baith civil and cannon,' in contradistinction to the peculiar and municipal practice of Scotland. Nay, I find, that, in some few instances, the prosecutor had gone the length of setting forth in this part of his libel, the particular texts and authorities of the civil or canon law on which he grounded his proposition, or which might be quoted in support of his conclusion.'[21]

Hume's suggestion that the appeal to the laws of God, of nature, and the common law was a matter of changing fashion in drafting may be presumed to be to some extent correct. None-the-less, he did relate the reference to common law, that is to the civil and canon laws viewed as *ius commune*, to the authority it had once enjoyed in Scotland, thus further suggesting that such allusions to laws other than Scots did have a function in the libel, and were not merely decorative.

Hamesucken in treatises and the practice of the Justiciary Court

Sheriff Gordon has written that until 1887 'to assault a man in his own house after having invaded the house for that purpose

---

[20]Alison, *Criminal Law*, ii, 228.
[21]Hume, *Trial for Crimes*, i, 264; Hume, *Commentaries* (1844), ii, 164 is substantially similar.

constituted the capital crime of hamesucken.'[22] The Criminal Procedure (Scotland) Act of that year (c.35) basically limited the imposition of capital sentences to cases of conviction for murder.[23] As the same act also abolished the need to specify a *nomen juris* in a criminal libel,[24] the crime of hamesucken could reasonably have been expected to vanish, facts which would formerly have been described as amounting to the crime becoming treated as a species of aggravated assault.[25] The recent cases of *H.M. Advocate* v. *Brown*[26] and *McAdam* v. *Ingram*[27] indicate, however, that judges are still willing to use the term 'hamesucken' to describe a particular offence.

Gordon's definition of hamesucken seems clear enough, and certainly encapsulates the essential core of the crime. Yet, down to the publication of Hume's *Commentaries*, there were uncertainties about the nature and punishment of it. Indeed, one of Dirleton's doubts (first published in 1698) had been: 'If Hame-sucken ... be Capital, though no Person be killed?' Sir James Steuart may have answered in 1715 that 'Hame-sucken is thought *capital* though no Person be killed, but in that Case it should be both violent and evident;'[28] it could still be argued, however, in *Macgregor* in 1752[29] and in *Morton Craigieknow* in 1763[30] that the crime was not (or no

---

[22]Gordon, *Criminal Law*, p. 818.

[23]S. 56.

[24]S. 5.

[25]Gordon, *Criminal Law*, p. 818.

[26]1989 G.W.D. 35-1604.

[27]1990 G.W.D. 22-1226. See also 'Hamesucken Charge', *The Scotsman*, 14 July 1978, a reference for which I am indebted to David Sellar.

[28]J. Steuart, *Dirleton's Doubts and Questions in the Law of Scotland, Resolved and Answered* (2nd edn.; Edinburgh, 1762), p. 112.

[29]Books of Adjournal, S[cottish] R[ecord] O[ffice], J.C. 3/28, p. 529, at pp. 562, 569-570 and 618-620 (apart from the case cited in note 30 below, all cases not cited from a published work are cited from the Books of Adjournal and this will not hereafter be noted; not all the volumes are paginated). In quoting from these MS records I have retained the original spelling, use of capitals and punctuation, but have expanded common contractions.

[30]Minute Book of Southern Circuit, SRO, JC. 12/11 (16 Sept. 1763).

longer) capital, while the drafter of one libel in 1703 could be sufficiently uncertain that he wrote in the major premiss:

'Where By the Laws of this and all other well governed realms, The Invading of Her Majesties, peaceable subjects and Leidges violently . . . Speciallie when committed by way of Hamesucken upon any man within his own dwelling house precinct thereof, or entry thereto, are Crimes punishable with the pains of death. Particularly by Caput 9 and 10th Lib: 4th of the Majestie, Which makes the Crime of Hamesucken punishable as that of Ravishment. . . . At least the saids Crimes are severly punishable by the highest degree and pitch of Arbitrary punishment.'[31]

The main difficulty in prosecuting and defending charges of hamesucken arose from the lack of a clear definition of the crime, and the above premiss seems uncertain as to whether the hamesucken should be libelled as an aggravation or as the principal crime, the former only resulting in an 'arbitrary' punishment, that is, one, other than death, in the discretion of the court.

As procurator for the pannel, Sir Robert Colt argued in *Crawford* in 1690 that 'the ffoundations of Hamesucken as to the quality of the cryme Has its very ryse from the Reg[iam] Majest[atem]'.[32] This was a common view through much of the eighteenth century, and it was based on the following passages:

'(4.9) Gif ane man will challenge ane other of Haimsuckin, it is necessare, that he alledge, that his proper house quhere he dwelles, lyes and ryses; daylie and nichtlie, is assailzied.

2. And swa he sall make ane lawfull soyt, because na man may challenge ane other of the crime of haimsuckin, bot in his proper and certaine dwelling house.

---

[31] *Drummond*, SRO, JC. 3/1, p. 545 (29 Nov. 1703).
[32] SRO, JC. 2/17 (10 Mar. 1690).

3. And mairover, he sall follow and persew his crime in the forme, as is vsed, anent the Revising of wemen.

(4.10) It is to wit, that na man sal be heard to accuse ane other of Reif, Revissing of wemen, or of Haimsuckin, except he make any lawfull soyt, in maner foresaid.

2. And gif he delayes be the space of ane nicht, to the effect, he may haue the connsell of his friends; and swa makes not fresh and recent persute; and that be proven against him, the defender sall be quite, and the accuser sall be in the Kings mercie.'[33]

In the case of *Balfour*, Sir James Steuart as Lord Advocate triplied that 'as for the words of the Regiam Majestatem They doe not at all defyne the cryme but only tell whatt Hame is'.[34] This is certainly correct. Though *Regiam* only stated what a person's home was (where he lay and rose, nightly and daily), and how hamesucken should be prosecuted, it was none the less relatively common in the late seventeenth and early eighteenth century to mention these passages specifically in the major premiss of the libel, as in that of 1703 already quoted[35]; they were of limited assistance, however, in explaining the nature of the crime, which it was accordingly necessary to establish from the practice of the courts. To do so, however, presented a number of problems. First, no reports of the decisions of the Justiciary or Circuit Courts were to be systematically published until the 1820s, though Maclaurin and Arnot did publish some selected cases in the later eighteenth century, and the

---

[33]J. Skene, *Regiam Majestatem. The Auld Lavves and Constitutions of Scotland. . . . Quheruneto are adjoined, Twa Treatises, The ane, anent the Order of proces observed before the Lords of Counsell, and Session: The other of Crimes, and Judges in criminall causes* (Edinburgh, 1609), fo. 68v.

[34]SRO, JC. 2/19 (4 June 1694), p. 341 at p. 355.

[35]See, *e.g.*, *Wylie*, SRO, JC. 2/17 (11 July 1687); *Balfour*, SRO, JC 2/19, p. 341 (4 June 1694), *Margaret Johnstoun*, SRO, JC. 3/1, p. 598 (12 June 1708). Louthian, *Form of Process* (1732), p. 11 founds hamesucken as a capital crime on these passages of *Regiam*.

Scots Magazine and newspapers such as the *Caledonian Mercury* could carry extensive report of notable trials.[36] Secondly, though the original records were readily accessible to those advocates who acted as procurators in the Justiciary Court, the form of the official record was limited. It recorded the libel, the debates on the relevancy, and the interlocutor on the relevancy; but it did not include the reasoning of the judges on the procurators' arguments. Thus, there was no recorded judicial ruling on what exactly was the nature of any particular crime. It was necessary to infer it from the libel, the debates, and the interlocutor. This made for a further measure of uncertainty: arguments on past cases tended to focus on whether or not particular earlier libels had been found relevant. Thirdly, procurators in their arguments on the relevancy of the libel necessarily put forward definitions of crimes: these were inevitably geared towards their aims in the debate, and, while plausible definitions, could scarcely be conclusive. The precise nature of individual crimes could thus remain somewhat indeterminate.

In these circumstances, accounts of crimes in legal treatises assumed importance. Thus, in the case of *Macgregor* in 1752, to demonstrate that hamesucken was not obsolete as a capital crime, the Lord Advocate, William Grant of Prestongrange, cited Mackenzie's treatise on criminal law and the short works of Alexander Bayne and William Forbes.[37] The earliest attempt at a doctrinal account of Scots criminal law was by Skene, who wrote that

---

[36] J. Maclaurin, *Arguments, and Decisions, in Remarkable Cases, Before the High Court of Justiciary, and other Supreme Courts, in Scotland* (Edinburgh, 1774); H. Arnot, *A Collection and Abridgement of Celebrated Criminal Trials in Scotland, from A.D. 1536, to 1784. With historical and critical Remarks* (Edinburgh, 1785).

[37] *Macgregor*, SRO, JC. 3/28, p. 529 at p. 570; he is citing G. Mackenzie, *The Laws and Customs of Scotland in Matters Criminal: Wherein is to be seen how the Civil Law, and the Laws and Customs of other Nations do agree with, and supply ours* in *The Works of that Eminent and Learned Lawyer, Sir George Mackenzie of Rosehaugh, Advocate to King Charles II. and King James VII. With Many learned*

'Haymesukin, is quhen ane man searches, and seeks ane other man at his house; or assailzies his house, to slay him, or to doe him any injurie, quhilk crime is punished be death, and confiscation of his moveable gudes, *lib. 4.c.9.*'[38] He wrote essentially the same in his treatise *De verborum significatione,* where he described hamesucken as '[a]ne Dutch word', adding that '*Haim* signifies an house or habitation,' while '*Suchen*'in German meant 'to seike, or search, persew, or follow,' defining the crime thus:

> '[H]ame-suchen, or hame-sucken, is quhen onie person violentlie, without licence, and contrair the Kinges peace, enters within an mans hous, or seiks him at the same, or assailzies his hous (as is written in the best buikes) quhilk crime is punished, as ravishing of wemen . . . quhilk is esteemed an greate crime contrair the common weill, quietnes, and peace of the cuntrie . . .'[39]

Sir George Mackenzie argued that for certainty and the security of the people criminal law ought to be based on statutes.[40] Whether or not *Regiam majestatem* was a statute was hotly debated, but

---

Treatises of his, never before printed (2 vols.; Edinburgh, 1716, 1722), ii, 49-275 at pp. 136-138 (hereinafter this work will be cited as Mackenzie, *Matters Criminal* from this edition); A. Bayne, *Institutions of the Criminal Law of Scotland* (Edinburgh, 1730), pp. 182-186; and W. Forbes, *The Institutes of the Law of Scotland. Volume Second. Comprehending the Criminal Law. In Two Parts.* (Edinburgh, 1730) pp. 139-141.

[38] J. Skene, *Of Crimes, and Iudges in Criminall Causes, Conforme to the Lawes of this Realme,* in *Regiam Majestatem,* fo. 134r (second sequence of foliation). This treatise is almost certainly by Skene.

[39] J. Skene, *De verborum significatione, The Exposition of the Termes and Difficill Wordes, Conteined in the Foure Buikes of Regiam Majestatem* (Edinburgh, 1681), *s.v.* 'Haimsuken' (first published 1597). On the etymology, see further R. V. Colman, 'Hamsocn: its Meaning and Significance in Early English Law' (1981) 25 *American Journal of Legal History,* 95-110. Knud Haakonssen has informed me that the Danish and German words 'hjemsøge' and 'heimsuchen' as well as the literal meaning have the connotation of 'hounding', 'persecuting', 'plaguing' and 'pestering'.

[40] Mackenzie, *Matters Criminal,* pp. 53 and 60-61.

Mackenzie argued that it was 'authentick' *in criminalibus*.[41] He accordingly purported to base his account of hamesucken on *Regiam*, developing the very basic account given by Skene by reference to the practice of the courts. He also pointed out that the prescriptive period for prosecution given in *Regiam* was now obsolete, and that when it was libelled as an aggravation of another crime the punishment was arbitrary *eo casu*.[42] By the second half of the eighteenth century, Erskine could give the following as a standard brief account of the crime:

> 'Haimesucken, from *haime*, home, and *soecken*, to pursue, is the crime of beating or assaulting a person within his own house. A man's house is considered as his sanctuary; and for that reason the violence that is committed there, is deemed an aggravation of the crime, both by Jewish law, . . . and by the Romans . . . . On this ground, the punishment of haimesucken is, by the books of the Majesty, declared to be the same as that of a rape . . .; and the pains of death have been by our constant practice inflicted on the committers of it. . . . The bare aiming a blow, or offering to strike, though no blow be actually given, has been found sufficient to infer this crime.'[43]

In fact, it was exceptional in the eighteenth century for anyone to suffer the death penalty for hamesucken. Furthermore, it is evident that there was considerable scope for argument over the various elements of the crime: What was a house? What type of assault or injury was necessary? What if someone was lured out of his house to be assaulted elsewhere? What if a brawl developed elsewhere and was then continued in a person's house? What if an individual was invited into someone's house and then a fight subsequently ensued in which the householder was assaulted? All of these points arose

---

[41] *Ibid.*, p. 55.

[42] *Ibid.*, pp. 136-138.

[43] J. Erskine, *An Institute of the Law of Scotland. In Four Books. In the Order of Sir George Mackenzie's Institutions of that Law* (2 vols.; Edinburgh, 1773), IV. iv. 51.

and had to be argued before the courts.[44] Furthermore, Erskine might have confidently written that no blow need actually be given, but this was not so certain. Prosecutors were willing to concede that the injury needed to be atrocious, and there was obviously authority for this.[45] And, as we have seen, Sir James Steuart thought hamesucken, to be capital, needed to be 'violent' and 'evident'. Craig, for example, had written that 'Hamesuckin *dicimus de eo, qui quempiam occidendum in domo sua quaerit*'.[46] Even if the intention was not necessarily to pursue someone to compass his or her death, the *de minimis* principle arguably applied. Moreover, although such points frequently arose in debates over the relevancy of the libel, prosecutors commonly restricted the libel for an arbitrary penalty, so the judges did not need specifically to rule in their interlocutor whether the averments in the minor premiss if proven would have amounted to hamesucken.[47] Indeed, in some cases it

---

[44]For some examples, see *Leith*, SRO, JC. 2/17 (15 Nov. 1686) (what is a dwelling-house?); *Crawford*, SRO, JC. 2/17 (10 Mar. 1690) (what is included in a dwelling-house?); *Master of Tarbat*, SRO, JC. 2/18 (18 Aug. 1691) (is it hamesucken to assault soldiers where quartered?); *Balfour*, SRO, JC. 2/19, p. 341 (4 June 1694) (*inter alia*, pannel invited in); *Irvine*, SRO, JC. 3/2, p. 776 and J.C. 3/3, p. 26 (20 Feb. and 2 Mar. 1710) (invasion arose out of earlier tumult); *Phillip*, SRO, JC. 3/9, p. 273 (9 Nov. 1719) (pannel entered peaceably; accidental quarrel subsequently arose); *Thomson and Inglis*, SRO, JC. 3/9, p. 290 (16 Nov. 1719) (quarrel started elsewhere; victim forced subsequently from house); *Home*, SRO, JC. 3/11, p. 630 and JC. 3/12, p.1 (9 and 16 Oct. 1723) (not master of house who was assaulted); *Falconer and Arbuthnott*, SRO, JC. 3/15, p. 264 (22 Jan. 1728) (lured out of house); *Macgregor*, SRO, JC. 3/28, p. 529 and JC. 3/29, p. 1 (13 July 1752) (woman carried out of house in order to be married forcibly).

[45]*Haldane*, SRO, JC. 3/8, p. 543 (28 July 1718) at p. 620 (5 Aug. 1718) (interlocutor rules that attack not sufficiently atrocious to infer hamesucken).

[46]T. Craig, *Jus feudale* (Edinburgh, 1732), II.viii.12 (first published 1655): 'We call it hamesucken when anyone seeks someone in his home with a view to killing him.'

[47]See, *e.g.*: *Morton*, SRO, JC. 3/1, p. 292 (16 Apr. 1701), at p. 294; *Drummond*, SRO, JC. 3/1, p. 545 (29 Nov. 1703) at p. 547; *Irvine* SRO, JC. 3/2, p. 776 and JC. 3/3, p. 26; *Trotter of Mortonhall*, SRO, JC. 3/5, p. 541 (8 Nov. 1714), at p. 542; *Phillip*, SRO, JC. 3/9, p. 273 (9 Nov. 1719), at p. 294; *Thomson and Inglis*,

appears that individuals sought criminal letters libelling hamesucken to secure, not the capital punishment of the pannel, but rather damages as amercement or assythment.[48]

The case of Macgregor

James Macgregor was indicted in 1752 at the instance of the Lord Advocate, William Grant of Prestongrange, in a libel, the major premiss of which read (in part) as follows:

> 'Whereas by the Laws of God, and of this and all other well Governed Realms, Hamesucken, or the violent Entering into any person's house without Licence, or Contrary to the King's peace, or seeking or assaulting him or her there; where he or she was dwelling at the time, and lying and rising nightly and Dailly, Especially when that was done against a woman, or minor, a widow, lately become such, and an Heiress, with Intent to do her a most heinous and attrocious Injury . . . [and various other crimes libelled] are all and Each of them Crimes of the most attrocious, shocking and detestable nature, and most severely punishable. . . .'

Also libelled were forcible abduction, forced marriage, and rape. The libel alleged that Macgregor, along with two of his brothers, Ronald and Robert, and other persons, including Duncan Macgregor, had invaded the house of Edinbelly (in the parish of Balfron) on 8th December 1750, where lived ('lying and rising nightly and daily' in the words of *Regiam*) Jean Key, a young,

---

SRO, JC. 3/9, p. 290 (16 Nov. 1719), at pp. 324-325; *Johnston*, SRO, JC. 3/10, p. 556 (30 Aug. 1721), at p. 558; *Johnston*, SRO, JC. 3/30, p. 129 (9 Dec. 1754), at p. 151 (16 Dec. 1754); *Morton Craigieknow*, SRO, JC. 12/11 (16 Sept. 1763); *Liddel and Jeeves*, SRO, JC. 3/36 (19 June 1769) (no debate on relevancy as libel restricted to an arbitrary punishment).

[48] *Wood*, SRO, JC. 3/2, p. 574 (25 July 1709), esp. at p. 583; *Trotter of Mortonhall*, SRO, JC. 3/5, pp. 541-542 (8 Nov. 1714); *Phlllip*, SRO, JC. 3/9, pp. 273-275 (9 Nov. 1719) (concluding for damages and assythment in the libel) (see comment p. 285, information for the pannel); and *Liddel and Jeeves*, SRO, JC. 3/36 (19 June 1769) (assythment).

widowed heiress, carried her off forcibly, and compelled her to go through a ceremony of marriage with Robert, who had then raped her. Robert was already outlawed for failing to stand trial for murder in 1736.[49] James, Ronald and Robert were sons of Rob Roy, and Robert and Duncan Macgregor were also subsequently to be separately tried for hamesucken arising out of these events, the latter being acquitted and the former convicted and executed (probably the only person executed for hamesucken on a sentence of the Court of Justiciary in the eighteenth century). With these subsequent trials we shall not be concerned.[50]

The libel against Macgregor was read and debated *viva voce* on 13th July, and the court ordered informations to be given in. As was the practice, the first given in and entered in the record was that of the Lord Advocate.[51] I shall concentrate here on the discussion of hamesucken. The procurators for the pannel had argued in the debate 'Impugning the Relevancy of the Lybell, in so far as it Charged the Crime of Hamesucken, and alledging, that, at this Day, that is no longer a distinct Capital Crime by the Law of Scotland; however in former times, it was held or accounted as such'.[52] Grant's argument on hamesucken in his information was intended to counter this claim. He referred to the English law on burglary, citing and quoting from Coke's *Reports*, and pointing out that this crime was a felony punished capitally without benefit of clergy.[53] While this species of crime was 'unknown in the law of

----

[49] SRO, JC. 3/28, pp. 530-537 (13 July 1752).

[50] SRO, JC. 3/29, p. 151 (15 Jan. 1753); JC. 3/29, pp. 250 and 290 (6 Aug. and 24 Dec. 1753). See also (1753) 15 *Scots Magazine*, pp. 49 and 626-627, (1754) 16 *Scots Magazine*, pp. 49-50, and *Caledonian Mercury*, 16 Jan. 1753 and 7 Feb. 1754.

[51] SRO, JC. 3/28, pp. 540-594.

[52] *Ibid.*, p. 562.

[53] *Vaux v. Brooke* IV Co. Rep. 39b. The quotation is not exact from the English version of Coke's *Reports*, and may be a free translation of the text in law French. It is very similar to the definition of burglary in E. Coke, *The Third Part of the Institutes of the Law of England* (4th edn.; London, 1670), p. 63; JC. 3/28, p. 564.

Scotland' it was intended 'for the Security of mankind within their own Dwelling Houses during the night season'. Grant argued:

> 'In like manner the Law of Scotland, and with yet greater Reason for the Security of mens persons within their own Dwelling Houses, where they are lying and Rising nightly and Daily for the Safety and Repose of Mankind at home, and to render it true by peculiar Sanctions which the Civil Law well defines Domus tutissimum cuique refugium ac receptaculum est (L.18.ff. de in jus vocando) hath in ancient times received and established a particular name for the Crime that is Committed by the violation of this asylum, calling it Hamesucken, and making it punishable capitally, even as ravishing of women 4th. Book of the Majesty C.9. where it is not first introduced or enacted, but spoke of as a known thing.'[54]

The analogy may have been suggested by Hale's *Pleas of the Crown*, though it is not mentioned by Grant, as the work would have been familiar to him, having been cited for the pannel in connection with the charge of rape.[55] Hale had written: 'The common genus of offenses, that comes under the name of *Hamsecken*, is that which is usually called house-breaking, which sometimes comes under the common appellation of *burglary*, whether committed in the day or night to the intent to commit felony. . . .'[56] Grant next quoted Skene's definition of hamesucken from his treatise on crimes,[57] and commented that:

> '[I]t is observable that the Definition of the Crime Corresponds with that [of] Burglary, and the Essence of it Consists, not in the actual Completion of the farther Crime intended, let it be murder,

---

[54]SRO, JC. 3/28, p. 564. The citation is to *D*.2.4.18, the Latin meaning: 'His home is to each man his most complete refuge and asylum'.

[55]See, e.g., SRO, JC. 3/28, pp. 597 and 631 citing Hale, *Pleas of the Crown*, i, 635.

[56]Hale, *Pleas of the Crown*, i, 547-548.

[57]Skene, *Of Crimes*, fo. 134r.

or other lesser Injury; but, in assaulting his House, or seeking him there with Intent to do him such Injury. . . .'[58]

Grant next quoted Skene's remarks in his treatise *De verborum significatione*, before writing that '[n]either was this Constitution peculiar to Scotland: The like Law we find Established in other Neighbouring Nations, with whose customs our own, in other Respects, have great affinity.'[59] For these other laws, Grant cited Antonius Matthaeus's treatise *De criminibus*, which he described as an 'approved work', and which indeed was much cited in the Court of Justiciary in this period.[60] He quoted Matthaeus's views on various types of violent intrusion into a person's home, their *tutissimum refugium atque receptaculum*, meriting capital punishment,[61] before adding:

> 'The same Author proceeds to Confirm his opinion from Authoritys, which at the same time prove that the like Law takes Places [sic] in divers other Countrys and States on the Continent, for the Author immediately proceeds as follows, the whole passage being materiall to the present argument, and serving to explain the Nature of this Crime or Species of *vis publica*, to which the Law of Scotland, in Antient Times, gave the particular Name of Hamesucken, which is still retained in our Law Books and Records. . . .'[62]

Grant accordingly quoted a lengthy passage from Matthaeus's work in which the author instanced and discussed a few statutory provisions on capital crimes analogous to the Scots law on hamesucken, and commented:

---

[58]SRO, JC. 3/28, p. 565.

[59]Skene, *De verborum significatione*, s.v. 'Haimsuken'; SRO, JC. 3/28, p. 565.

[60]SRO, JC. 3/28, p. 565; A. Matthaeus, *De criminibus ad lib. XLVII. et XLVIII. dig. commentarius* (4th edn.; Wesel, 1679). This was the most recent edition and the one likely used by Grant.

[61]Matthaeus, *De criminibus*, pp. 465 and 467 (*ad leg. Iul. de vi publica, & privata* (*D*.48.4), cap. 4, *de usu et jure municipali*, ss 2, 3, and 6).

[62]SRO, JC. 3/28, p. 566.

These passages serve, not only to show, that the like Law, and upon the same Reason, is established in other Countrys, but to Explain the sense and meaning of the Law it self, and what kind of Assault, or Injury to the owner of the House, or any of his Family, being Committed by persons who forcibly Entered the House, with Intent to Committ such Injury falls within this Law and subjects the Committer to the punishment thereof; and these are described by the following Expressions, si aliquem ex inhabitantibus male multaverit, which is a Phrase used by Terence and Cicero, and signifies to abuse, to handle, or use one ill vel si eundem expuelerit, verberaverit, capital erit, vim quamcunque personae vel corpori eius illatum, all which exactly corresponds to Sir John Skene's Definition above recited of the Crime of Hamesucken, being to seek another at his house, to slay him or to do him any Injury. And such being the nature of this Crime, can there be any possible Doubt that the particular Injurys, with Intent to Committ which Jean Key was assaulted in her own house, were of a nature sufficiently heinous and Atrocious to come up to the Crime of Hamesucken. . . .'[63]

Grant argued that if Macgregor and his accomplices had boxed Jean Key's ears in her home or beat her in any way short of murder it would have been hamesucken, but all of these would have been lesser injuries than what this hamesucken was committed for, 'which was to rob her, not indeed of Life, but of every thing that is valuable in it, her Liberty, her Chastity, her peace and Content of Mind, her Estimation and Character in the World, and her whole ffortune or Estate.' He argued that even if all the other acts had not occurred, to carry her off 'was a Crime independent of all that ffollowed . . . that would have highly merited the severest Censure of the Law, for the atrocious Hamesucken alone.'[64]

Grant next turned to the argument that hamesucken either was obsolete or the capital punishment of it was. He argued:

---

[63]Matthaeus, De criminibus, p. 467 (the second quotation by Grant is not exact; I have corrected part of it silently); SRO, JC. 3/28, pp. 567-568.
[64]SRO, JC. 3/28, pp. 568-569.

'It may be true, that of latter Times Examples have more rarely occurred of putting the same in Execution, and that hath been plainly owing to the advances of Civility and good manners in this Country; but it ill becomes those, who, in these happier Times in which we Live, take upon them to disgrace and shock the present age by Committing such Barbarities as were more frequent in Times, past, to alledge that the Law is obsolete that was introduced for restraining of such Enormities, as they themselves, by now Committing, demonstrate the necessity that such law should be still in fforce for the Common Safety of Mankind, and in reality the Law is still in Force, although this, like all other penal Laws, lys asleep till the occasion offerrs for exerting its Terrors.'[65]

As already noted, he argued this by citing the works of Mackenzie, Bayne, and Forbes.[66] He also referred to the case of *Haldane* in 1718, where a libel alleging hamesucken resulted in an interlocutor that the facts libelled were not sufficiently atrocious as to infer hamesucken,[67] and argued that this meant 'the Law of Hamesucken stands yet in full force'.[68] He next referred to the curious case of *Campbell and MacKinnon* who were indicted before the Sheriff of Inverness for hamesucken. The indictment was found relevant, they were convicted by a jury, and sentenced to death by the sheriff-depute. The questions then arose, first, of whether the sheriff-depute had jurisdiction to try hamesucken capitally, and secondly, of whether the libel was relevant, as those who had been injured were servants, not the person whom Campbell and MacKinnon intended to injure who had been absent. A bill of suspension was presented to three Lords of Justiciary who did not pass the bill, but sisted execution to 16th July 1725 when the sentence was to have been executed if there had been no further action. The aim obviously was that the full Justiciary Court would hear the case.

---

[65] *Ibid.*, p. 569.
[66] *Ibid.*, p. 570.
[67] *Haldane,* SRO, JC. 3/8, p. 543 (28 July 1718), at pp. 619-620 (5 Aug. 1718).
[68] SRO, JC. 3/28, pp. 571-575.

There was, however, no further application by the suspender, and the Lords decided on 8th June 1725 to act no further. Campbell and MacKinnon were accordingly executed.[69] Grant argued that the Court of Justiciary would not have acted in this way if it had been of the view that hamesucken was no longer capital in Scotland.[70] He ended his discussion of hamesucken thus: 'Upon this head, therefore, the pursuer Concluded that the Lybell was Relevantly laid upon this article of Hamesucken, to Inferr the pains of Law for that Crime, and which pains are Capitall.'[71]

As procurator for Macgregor, Alexander Lockhart gave in an information which addressed the same points.[72] He argued:

> [T]hat however in antient Times, some Instances might have occurred where the Crime of Hamesucken, may have been Capitally punished, yet as this was not Established by any positive Statute to be the Law of Scotland, and as the practice of later years had justly receded from such erroneous precedents, these could not now be resorted to for Establishing a point so directly inconsistent with the first principles of Law and Justice.'

He admitted that since a person's house was his or her asylum, an offence committed against a person in his or her home was highly aggravated, and justly more severely punished, 'but that this

---

[69]I have been unable to trace any details of this case: the proceedings noted by Grant are not entered into the relevant volume of the Books of Adjournal, SRO, JC. 3/12, nor into the relevant Minute Book, SRO, JC. 7/12. I have also been unable to locate any relevant records of the Sheriff Court of Inverness. A similar bill of suspension was presented in 1741 against a death sentence for hamesucken passed by the Sheriff Depute of Ross-shire: see *Caledonian Mercury*, 6 July 1741. The diet in connection with it can be traced being twice continued (on 3 Nov. 1741 and 11 Jan. 1742) but it is not mentioned on the date (13 Jan. 1742) to which it was continued, and it thereafter cannot be traced: SRO, JC. 3/23, p. 680 and Minute Book, JC. 7/23.

[70]SRO, JC. 3/28, pp. 575-576.

[71]*Ibid.*, pp. 576-577.

[72]*Ibid.*, pp. 594-634.

speciality Should so Inflame the Reckoning, as to Convert that Injury into a Capital Crime, was humbly Contested.' He argued that though the Romans venerated the home 'no Instance could be given where any Injury or offence, otherways punishable *poena extraordinaria,* was by that Law subjected to the *ultimum Supplicium*' by virtue of having taken place in a person's home. He continued:

> 'That there is no Statute making this a Capital Crime by the Law of Scotland, was acknowledged; and as no authority could be produced, either from the positive Law of God, or from the Civil Law, which must needs be admitted . . . to be the Fountains and Sources of the Criminall Law of Scotland, so far as not departed from by Municipall positive Constitutions or Invariable Practice; whereby Injurys of this kind should be capitally punished, it remained to be Enquired upon what other Foundation this principle is assumed.'[73]

Lockhart next turned to Grant's arguments from English law and Matthaeus. He argued:

> 'For as to the positive constitutions of other countrys, where something similar to this may possibly have been Enacted, and to which the prosecutor was pleased to resort . . . the Pannel is advised, that though the Laws of Nations in Generall may, with Reason, be Resorted to in cases of Difficulty, where our own Law is defective, it would be of a Dangerous precedent to adopt every peculiar Conceit of other Nations to be the Law of Scotland, especially in regulating the Degree of Punishment, unless these could be supported upon the generall Principles of Equity, and that this must the rather hold, for that the prosecutor, after all the Research into all the Laws of all other Countries, has been able to condescend upon very few, where a Capital Punishment is inflicted for any offence of this kind, not on account of the nature of the Injury it self, but from its being committed against a Person within his own House.'[74]

---

[73] *Ibid.,* pp. 618-619.
[74] *Ibid.,* p. 619.

Lockhart claimed that Grant's admission that the wrong needed to be atrocious underlined the absurdity of his argument, as he could point to no law authorising that distinction.[75] Lockhart next argued that it did not follow from the words of *Regiam* and Skene's annotation on it[76] that hamesucken was to be punished as was rape, but rather was merely to be prosecuted in the same manner, especially since 'these Crimes, [were] of their nature so very different, the one Infinitely more Grievous than the other'. Rape 'by the Laws of all Nations and by the first principles of Justice, is a Crime of so enormous a nature as well merits the punishment of Death,' but this should not extend to crimes of an inferior nature merely because they were committed in a dwelling-house. Furthermore, if this were to have been the case, even the most trivial of injuries if committed in a dwelling-house would have merited death.[77] Lockhart next dealt with the records of the Court of Justiciary arguing that 'for many years past' hamesucken had been prosecuted either as an aggravation of another wrong or only to infer an arbitrary punishment, and claimed that this showed that the crime was in desuetude. He argued that the case of *Haldane* could not be viewed as a judgment of the Court deciding hamesucken to be capital, while that of *Campbell and MacKinnon* was extraordinary and iniquitous, and could not be viewed 'as a precedent of the Court of Justiciary', since the court stayed execution of the sheriff's sentence, but was unable to pronounce on the matter by reason of the failure of anyone to apply to it. Lockhart

---

[75] *Ibid.*, pp. 619-620.

[76] See *Regiam majestatem Scotiae veteres leges et constitutiones, ex archivis publicis, et antiquis libris manuscriptis collectae, recognitae, et notis juris civilis, canonici, Nortmannici auctoritate confirmatis, illustratae, opera & studio Joannis Skenaei, Regiae Majestati a conciliis & archivis publicis* (Edinburgh, 1609), fo. 97r. The annotation to the Latin edition of *Regiam* is similar to the discussion in Skene's treatise *De verborum significatione*.

[77] *Ibid.*, pp. 620-621.

argued that no other case could be found in the Books of Adjournal where the libel in hamesucken had not been restricted to infer an arbitrary punishment. He wrote:

> '[A]nd as the Principles of Justice thus coincide with the later Practice, it would be highly unreasonable to resort to those more ancient Precedents, supported by no positive Law, to revive a practice which probably had taken rise from these ffeuds and animositys, which this Nation in former Times was unhappily engaged in, when every private ffamily was in a State of war, which made it the more necessary to make a man's house his Sanctuary; but as these Times are now long ago happily at an End, and as in Consequence thereof the practice has conformed itself to the Rules and Principles of Justice, it would be highly inexpedient now to revive that antiquated and obsolete Practice, of making every Injury offered to a person within his house a Capital Crime.'[78]

Lockhart's final argument on hamesucken was that the *species facti* charged in the indictment did not amount to hamesucken. He argued that the essence of hamesucken was assault in a person's house *animus injuriandi*, while here the alleged criminal act 'did not proceed from any purpose and Intention to assault and Injure the person, *sed libidinis causa*'. He drew an analogy with the Roman law of theft which required *animus lucri faciendi*, so that, if anyone seized a slave girl, not for gain, but for libidinous purposes, it was not theft. This applied to Macgregor's case, where the forcible entry and abduction were not from a premeditated purpose to injure or assault but to accomplish the intended marriage. He could not therefore be guilty of hamesucken as a separate crime, but at the most as an aggravation of another.[79]

The Lords pronounced an interlocutor on 31st July 1752 to the effect that: 'They found the Crimes charged against the said pannel in the foresaid Indictment jointly and separately Relevant to infer

---

[78] *Ibid.*, pp. 621-625.
[79] *Ibid.*, pp. 625-626. He cited the following text: *D.*47.2.39.

the pains of Law But allowed the pannel to prove all ffacts and Circumstances that may tend either to his Exculpation or Alleviation of his Guilt.' The diet against Macgregor was continued until 3rd August 1752.[80] There was then a lengthy proof lasting two days and two nights.[81] The assize delivered a special verdict on 5th August, unanimously finding it proven that Macgregor with accomplices had entered Jean Key's house and attacked her in order to carry her away. By a majority it was found not proven that she had consented in advance to this abduction. The jury unanimously also found it proven that she had been carried to various places; but, again unanimously, found it proven that she afterwards acquiesced in her condition 'for Alleviation of the pannel's Guilt in the premisses'. Finally, the forcible marriage and rape were unanimously found not proven.[82] The next day counsel argued *viva voce* on the import of this verdict, and the procurators for the defence asked the court for the opportunity to inform upon the debate. This was granted, and the diet was continued to 20th November.[83] The same day as the *viva voce* debate, however, twelve of the jurors attempted to intervene, tendering to the court a declaration that they had believed what they had found proved to alleviate Macgregor's guilt, namely Jean Key's later acquiescence, would have exempted him from capital punishment. Another of the assizers appeared in court, stating that he had refused to sign the declaration, but declaring that he also wished only an arbitrary punishment to be inflicted. The court refused to receive the declaration, and it was not entered into the record of the court.[84]

---

[80]SRO, JC. 3/29, pp. 1-2.

[81]*Ibid.*, pp. 2-84; for the length of the trial, see *Caledonian Mercury*, 3, 4, and 6 Aug. 1752. There is a lengthy account of the case in (1752) 14 *Scots Magazine*, pp. 345-351, and in Maclaurin, *Remarkable Cases*, pp. 137-152.

[82]SRO, JC. 3/29, pp. 84-86.

[83]*Ibid.*, pp. 88-89 (6 Aug. 1752).

[84]See *ibid.*, pp. 98-99 (information for Macgregor) and pp. 122-124 (information for Lord Advocate); for the text of the letter, see (1752) 14 *Scots Magazine*, p. 351.

It is particularly interesting that the assize should have delivered a special verdict. The interlocutor on the relevancy was phrased in such a way that a general verdict of guilty or not guilty would have been possible, and Lockhart and Grant apparently considered it to have been open to the assize simply to acquit.[85] The reason for delivering a special verdict in part seems likely to have been the difficulties faced by the jury and the court in knowing exactly in what the crime of hamesucken consisted. The jury evidently were sympathetic to Macgregor and did not want him to suffer the death penalty for hamesucken, but were none the less conscious that he was culpable in some way.

The informations on the import of the special verdict do not need to be considered here in detail.[86] Lockhart accepted that the court viewed hamesucken as a capital crime (which shows that the judges must have so ruled) and that this could not now be contested. He added:

'[T]hat as the punishment is noways adequate to the offence and as for many years past no one Instance has occurred where an offence of this kind has been capitally punished or sustained relevant to inferr the punishment of Death, but on the Contrary even where the Injuries offered to the person within his own house were extremely attrocious the Indictments have been restricted so as to import only an Arbitrary punishment every alleviating Circumstance should operate to reduce the punishment within reasonable Bounds and to commensurate the same to the Offence.'

Furthermore, the punishment was established by ancient usage rather than statute, while 'neither Law nor practice has determined from what particular ffacts this Crime shall be inferred, so that in every Case it becomes an arbitrary Question from what particular ffacts the Crime of Hamesucken shall be established.'[87] Lockhart

---

[85]SRO, JC. 3/29, pp. 114-115 and 141-142.
[86]*Ibid.*, pp. 91-116, 117-143
[87]*Ibid.*, p. 103.

accordingly argued that the findings in the special verdict did not amount to hamesucken, or that the punishment should be restricted, on the grounds that: the injury was not atrocious; the house was not entered *animo injuriandi*; the jury had not found that the house was where Jean Key lay and rose nightly and daily; she had later acquiesced and such injuries could be remitted; the time passed before prosecution had prescribed the crime; and finally, the jury were justified in finding the acquiescence enough to alleviate the guilt and had not intended to convict of a crime meriting the *ultimum supplicium*.[88]

Grant argued that the verdict showed a clear case of hamesucken. Criticism of the wording of the verdict was not to the point. The jury's finding that she later acquiesced did not alleviate the guilt proven in the first part of the verdict, as by acquiescing one could not mitigate a public wrong. He stated that: 'In support of this answer there seem to be apposite Authorities in the practice of England where Trialls by Jury and Doctrine of Verdicts are more practised and perhaps better understood than with us.' He accordingly cited the English work, *The Complete Juryman*, which was published in the year of the trial, from which he quoted the following passages:

'If the first Part of a Verdict be full to the Issue, either expresly, or by Implication, and the latter Part any Ways contradicts the first Part; the first Part shall be good, and the latter Part void. *Per Dodderidge*J. *James* versus *Harris*, 2 *Bulst*. 56. 2 *Rol. Abr*. 718, *p*. 11, 13, 14. *Cro. Car*. 75. . . If the Jury in a special Verdict find the Issue, all which they find afterwards to the contrary, is Surplusage. 2 *Ld. Raym*. 860, 865.'[89]

---

[88] *Ibid.*, pp. 104-116.
[89] *The Complete Juryman; Or, A Compendium of the Laws relating to Jurors* (London, 1752), pp. 258-259; SRO, JC/29, pp. 132-133.

On this authority, Grant argued that the jury's finding alleviating Macgregor's guilt was surplusage to be ignored. He finally rejected Lockhart's arguments of acquiescence and prescription.[90]

When on 6th August the diet had been continued to 20th November 1752, Macgregor had been committed to the Edinburgh Tolbooth. He did not compear on the required date. It was moved that the magistrates of Edinburgh and the keeper of the Tolbooth should be called. The keeper of the Tolbooth and George Drummond, lately Lord Provost, were present and were interrogated about Macgregor. It was explained that, on a warrant from the Lord Justice-Clerk, Macgregor had been conducted to the Castle because of fears of an attempt to escape; he had none the less escaped from there.[91] The case against Macgregor was continued for some time,[92] but he was not apprehended, and the Lords of Justiciary never pronounced judgment on whether or not Macgregor was guilty of hamesucken, nor passed sentence on him.

The importance of Macgregor

The prosecution of Macgregor for hamesucken is of great interest in a variety of ways. It is noteworthy how both Grant and Lockhart appropriated the language of civility and manners, so crucial in eighteenth-century Scotland, to argue their respective cases: either that there had been so few prosecutions because of the advances in civility, but that when such modern manners were threatened, the old law still existed to preserve them; or that such advances had rendered the law obsolete, as it had been intended for

---

[90]SRO, JC. 3/29, pp. 126-143.

[91]*Ibid.*, pp. 145-146; for an account of his escape, see (1752) 14 *Scots Magazine*, pp. 556-557 and 606, and *Caledonian Mercury,* 20 Nov. 1752.

[92]The last mention I have noted was on 17 June 1754, SRO, JC. 3/29, p. 566 where the case was continued to 12 Aug.; on that date it is not mentioned. I have not searched beyond this.

a society given over to feuding. In this respect, it is telling that Grant commented as follows in the information on the special verdict lodged with the court:

> The Trial of this pannel was in reallity and has justly been treated by the Court as a Case of great Importance. It was brought to vindicate in the due Course of publick Justice one of the most attrocious and scandalous violations of publick peace accompanied with the most grievous wrong to the private party injured, that the present age has seen, or that the most barbarous of the tribe of Macgrigors to which the pannel belongs, noted as they are by the Laws, have in any age committed.'

The threat posed by the Macgregors was located in the wilderness of the Highlands:

> 'The most frequent Enormities committed by the unruly parts of that Tribe have been to prey upon the property of their fellow Subjects that by their Situation have been exposed to their Thefts or Depredations of their Cattle and by the Residence of these people amongst the Rocks Lochs and Woods in the highest parts of the Shires of Stirling and Perth where upon the East hand they were in the Neighbourhood of the Low Country from which to take their Spoils and on the Northward had access through desart uninhabited Countries to the remotest parts of the Highlands to dispose of it.'[93]

The trials of the Macgregors offered an opportunity to be rid of a lawless element in the Highlands, and Grant evidently viewed the prosecutions as an important part of the government's policy of 'civilizing' and pacifying the area in the aftermath of the '45. The threat that the Macgregors posed to polite, lowland Scotland of the Enlightenment required to be extinguished using laws that, deriving from more barbarous times, were well-adapted to dealing with those who were themselves barbarous. Lockhart was undoubtedly

---

[93]SRO, JC. 3/29, p. 118.

correct in his claims that libels or interlocutors had restricted hamesucken to an arbitrary punishment: it cannot but be significant that Grant pursued the Macgregors for the death penalty when the forcible marriage and rape had been found not proven, so that all that remained was the crime of seizing Jean Key in her home and abducting her. Political and social considerations undoubtedly promoted the seeking of the death penalty. It is likewise surely significant that Archibald, Duke of Argyll, presided over the court as Lord Justice-General on 20th November 1752, when it investigated the circumstances in which Macgregor had been able to escape from Edinburgh Castle.[94] Enlightened Scotland with its focus on politeness and modern manners allowed no place for what were seen as relics of more barbarous times.

The arguments of counsel also clearly demonstrated the difficulties with the law on hamesucken in the eighteenth century. What weight was to be given to *Regiam majestatem* as a source of Scots law? What was to be concluded from the records of past cases preserved in the Books of Adjournal? Was the common understanding that hamesucken was capital enough to outweigh the contrary practice in prosecution (and vice versa)? Lockhart attempted to answer these questions by appeal to equity and principles of justice: in the face of a lack of clear statutory definition of the crime and provision for its punishment, justice required that hamesucken should be considered as an aggravation of another crime and its punishment be appropriate to that crime as aggravated, especially when there was no invariable practice to the contrary. It might have been possible to cite similar provisions in the laws of other countries, but they were too few to be of significance, he argued, hardly demonstrating that the law of nations punished hamesucken capitally, and could not be used to introduce into Scots law pernicious principles contrary to justice.

---

[94] *Ibid.*, p. 145; Argyll was in Edinburgh for the election of a representative peer: *Caledonian Mercury*, 20 Nov. 1752.

Society had developed since the time of *Regiam majestatem*, the books of 'which for certain, contain a variety of particulars repugnant to the first Principles of the Law of Scotland'.[95]

Grant's answer to the uncertainty and indeterminacy of the law on hamesucken was apparently different. The major premiss in the indictment against Macgregor was phrased in terms of 'the Laws of God, and of this and all other well Governed Realms'. While in some libels for hamesucken the major premiss referred only to the municipal law,[96] the vast majority of them used the standard formula (or a close variation of it) that 'whereas by the laws of this, and all other well governed realms the crime of hamesucken etc.'.[97] As in Macgregor's indictment, there were occasionally more elaborate allusions to the laws of God, the laws of nature and nations, and the common law (in the sense of civil and canon law) — sometimes

---

[95]SRO, JC. 3/28, p. 620.

[96]See, *e.g.*, *Wylie*, SRO, JC. 2/17 (11 July 1687): 'Notwithstanding be the lawes and acts of parliament off the Kingdome and Constant practique thereof particularlie be the lawes of Reg[iam] Majestat[atem] the Cryme off Hamesucken and the searching and seeking for any [person] or persons in or about their dwelling house to doe them hurt or prejudice is punishable with the panes of death'; *Trotter of Mortonhall,* SRO, JC. 3/5, p. 541 (8 Nov. 1714): 'That where, By the Municiple Law of this Kingdome, The Committers of the Crime of Hamesucken ... As Also, Robbery, Stouthreiff and Oppression . . . are all Crimes of a high nature and severely punishable by death, Confiscation of moveables of otherwise'; *Home,* SRO, JC. 3/11, p. 630 (9 Oct. 1723): 'By the Laws of this Realm, The Crimes of Murder, Hamesucken and violent Invasion of his Majesties Leiges . . . are all Crimes of a high nature and Severly punishable'.

[97]See, *e.g.*, *Drummond,* SRO, JC. 3/1, p. 545 (29 Nov. 1703); *Forbes,* SRO, JC. 3/1, p. 687 (18 Dec. 1704); *Muirhead,* SRO, JC. 3/2, p. 385 (14 Apr. 1708); *Wood,* SRO, JC. 3/2, p. 574 (25 July 1709); *Irvine,* SRO, JC. 3/2, p. 776 (20 Feb. 1710); *Seton and Porteous,* SRO, JC. 3/7, p. 340 (16 July 1716); *Thomson and Inglis,* SRO, JC. 3/9, p. 290 (16 Nov. 1719); *Anstruther,* SRO, JC. 3/9, p. 428 (25 Mar. 1720); *Johnston,* SRO, JC, 3/10, p. 556 (30 Aug. 1721); *Torrance and Baillie,* SRO, JC. 3/13, pp. 340-341 (8 Mar. 1726); *Arbuthnott and Falconer,* SRO, JC. 3/15, p. 265 (22 Jan. 1728).

all together.[98] Such references in the major premiss to laws other than that of Scotland legitimated drawing on them to explain Scots law. Grant quoted Craig's view that when there were no statutes or customs in Scotland recourse was to be had to the laws of neighbouring nations,[99] and argued:

'This last principle does more specially hold and take place in the Criminal Law of Scotland, where by the long received and accustomed Form of the Libells, the major proposition Contains an averment, as the said Lybell against the Pannel did, that the Crimes Charged were such, and, punishable by the Laws of God, and the Laws of this, and other well Governed Realms. And from the Records of the Court of Justiciary, called the Books of Adjournal, it appeared that such hath been the Constant Practice, not only in the Lybels, but in the Arguments of the Council on the Relevancy either of the Lybell or Defence, that frequent appeals are made to Texts of the Holy Scripture, or the opinions of foreign Lawiers, or the Decisions of fforeign Courts in similar Cases; and the Reasonableness of such usage and appeal consists in this, that Crimes are offences against Common Humanity, and are equally such in all Civilized Nations, and depend not upon peculiar Constitutions, in such manner as the Laws Concerning private Right and publick Government may do, and which are therefore more various in different Countrys. . . .'[100]

Lockhart commented that 'the prosecutor was pleased to resort [to foreign laws], by reason that criminal lybels do for ordinary referr to the Laws of all other well governed Realms'.[101] Grant thus argued that the statements of Matthaeus could be used, not only to show

---

[98] *Master of Tarbat*, SRO, JC. 2/18 (18 Aug. 1691); *Keith*, SRO, JC. 2/18 (11 Jan. 1692); *Balfour*, SRO, JC. 2/19, p. 341 (4 June 1694); *Munro*, SRO, JC. 3/1, p. 155 (9 Dec. 1700); *Morton*, SRO, JC. 3/1, p. 292 (16 Apr. 1701); *Haldane*, SRO, JC. 3/8, p. 543 (28 July 1718); *Johnston*, SRO, JC. 3/30, p. 128 (9 Dec. 1754); *Liddel and Jeeves*, SRO, JC. 3/36 (19 June 1769).

[99] Craig, *Jus feudale*, I.viii.15.

[100] SRO, JC. 3/28, pp. 582-583; see also p. 585.

[101] *Ibid.*, p. 619.

that other countries had similar provisions, but also to explain Scots law. This was not an exceptional argument. In the information for the pannels in *Thomson and Inglis*, for example, it had been claimed on etymological grounds, presumably relying on Skene, that the Scots laws on hamesucken had flowed from those of Germany, and one of the passages of Matthaeus used by Grant was drawn on to explain the law.[102] Though used for 'German' law, Matthaeus was still a civilian writer, and the passages cited by the Scots lawyers on hamesucken, occurred, after all, in a commentary on *D.48.4*; and Lockhart, for example, argued, as was not unusual, that the positive law of God and Roman law were the sources of Scots law except where varied by statute or practice. Grant, however, went beyond this, citing English law to argue that hamesucken was capital, and later using an English work and case law to explain special verdicts. Underlying his argument from English law was a view that the basis of Scots criminal law was ultimately moral, founded on the laws of God and of nature and nations, so that English law could accordingly be used to support an argument that hamesucken was a capital crime, since, if it had similar provisions in similar situations, the view of Scots law being argued for could be seen to be, at the very least, not contrary to the law of nations.

Grant did not use the language of the law of nature and nations; Lockhart did to some extent with his allusions to principles of justice and equity and the laws of nations. None the less, though in many ways very different, both their arguments at some level rely on it. This, of course, is scarcely surprising in eighteenth-century Scotland where moral philosophy had come to be defined in terms of the natural law of Grotius and Pufendorf (especially of the

---

[102]SRO, JC. 3/9, p. 290 (16 Nov. 1719) at p.313; Matthaeus, *De criminibus*, pp. 467-468 (cap. 4 s 6 on *D.48.4*).

latter).[103] And there were examples of reliance on natural law in Scotland going back at least to the time of Craig. We have already noted that the major premiss of the libel sometimes referred to the law of nature and nations to found the crime, and it is possible to find Pufendorf cited by procurators in their informations, while the style given by Louthian in 1732 for an information for the pannel included argument from the laws of nature, of God, and of other nations.[104] Thus, while of primary significance were Scottish statutes and practice, the law of nature and nations was regarded as underpinning Scots criminal law, legitimating reference to the laws of other countries to explain obscurities and supply deficiencies. Further study would be required, however, to know whether this was a tendency reinforced after natural law became such a popular study in the later seventeenth and early eighteenth centuries, and how it related to arguments on the development of the law made with reference to the historical source (or alleged historical source) of the law, typically taken to be in that of Rome. It does show, however, that the subtitle given by Mackenzie to his work on criminal law — 'Wherein is to be seen how the Civil Law, and the

---

[103]See now, above all, K. Haakonssen, 'Natural Law and Moral Realism: The Scottish Synthesis', in M. A. Stewart (ed.), *Studies in the Philosophy of the Scottish Enlightenment* (Oxford, 1990), pp. 61-85. See also *idem*, 'Natural Law and the Scottish Enlightenment' (1985) 4 *Man and Nature*, 47-80; *idem*, 'Hugo Grotius and the History of Political Thought' (1985) 13 *Political Theory*, 239-265; and J. Moore and M. Silverthorne, 'Natural Sociability and Natural Rights in the Moral Philosophy of Gerschom Carmichael', in V. Hope (ed.), *Philosophers of the Scottish Enlightenment* (Edinburgh, 1984), pp. 1-12; *eidem*, 'Gershom Carmichael and the Natural Jurisprudence Tradition in Eighteenth-Century Scotland' in I. Hont and M. Ignatieff (edd.), *Wealth and Virtue: The Shaping of Political Economy in the Scottish Enlightenment* (Cambridge, 1983), pp. 73-87.

[104]*Trotter of Mortonhall*, SRO, JC. 3/5, p. 541 (8 Nov. 1714) at p. 549, citing S. Pufendorf, *De jure naturae et gentium libri octo* (Lund, 1672, and many subsequent edns.), II.v.4 and 16 (the passages concern self-defence and defence of property: I consulted the edition, Amsterdam, 1688, at pp. 186-187 and 198-199); Louthian, *Form of Process*, pp. 139-184.

Laws and Customs of other Nations do agree with, and supply ours'
— is of some importance, and not a mere scholarly puff.[105]

Marital rape

Lockhart argued that neither law nor practice had determined
from what facts hamesucken would be inferred, so that in each case
it became an arbitrary question; if perhaps exaggerated, this claim
was certainly not unfounded.[106] There were a number of causes of
this indeterminacy of the law. *Regiam majestatem* was an unsatisfactory and suspect source from which to derive the crime: it really
only dealt with the nature of 'home' and the mode of prosecution.
It was not always easy to infer practice from the Books of Adjournal
because of their nature as a record: there were no authoritative
judicial definitions of the law; judicial views had to be deduced
from interlocutors on the relevancy of libels which had commonly
been restricted by prosecutors so that judges did not have to rule on
the question of whether or not the *species facti* averred amounted to
capital hamesucken.

An argument on one area of Scots criminal law focussing on one
case is not a sufficient basis from which to extrapolate to the law as
a whole; it does provide enough evidence, however, to suggest that
Scots criminal law may have suffered more generally from problems
of uncertainty, and at least one well-informed contemporary
commentator was of this view, while it is also possible to find
arguments to this effect in other cases.[107] Turning to the area of law
at issue in *Stallard*, William Forbes, for instance, felt able to define
the crime of rape as including that of a man by a woman. He

---

[105]See note 37 *supra*.

[106]SRO, JC. 3/29, p. 103.

[107]H. Arnot, *The History of Edinburgh* (Edinburgh and London, 1779), p. 486;
H.M. Advocate v. *Gray et al.* conveniently reported in (1751) 13 *Scots Magazine*,
pp. 353-355 (I am grateful to Roger Emerson for bringing the latter to my
attention).

explained: 'for that as there are weak faint harted and effeminate men, and stout harted masculine women; nothing hinders a woman to force a man to ly with her by the same power that she carries him away'.[108] One can see here some influence of the Roman crime of *raptus*, though Forbes stressed that 'there is no Rape without carnal Commerce'.[109] In the face of such conflicts over definitions and scope of crimes, the solution adopted by procurators for the pannel and the prosecution was to argue from analogous laws in other countries and from natural law: a solution suggested by the form of the major premiss of the libel and validated by the natural-law thinking of Scots lawyers in this period. The reference to the laws of other well-governed realms was therefore not an empty formula devoid of significance. In so far as Scots criminal law was vague and inchoate, secreted in the practice of the courts, it could be elaborated from the laws and doctrinal writings of other states considered as the law of nations.

It was perhaps this indeterminacy of Scots criminal law which ensured the outstanding success of Hume's treatise. For the first time lawyers had access to a comprehensive and fully argued account of crimes, defining them, explaining their nature, and discussing them on the basis of the records of the Justiciary Court. Hume himself eschewed overt philosophising about the basis of Scots law, and he had little sympathy for natural law of the speculative and rationalist type.[110] Yet, he regarded English law 'as a great body of written and practical reason', on which, in 'matters ... which depend on the common feelings of equity and right', he considered himself able to draw to expound Scots law where 'not

---

[108]G[lasgow] U[niversity] L[ibrary], MS Gen. 1249, pp. 414-415 (this is part of his unpublished 'Great Body', GUL, MSS Gen. 1246-1252); Forbes, *Institute*, ii, 125.

[109]Forbes, *Institute*, ii, 125.

[110]See the remarks in J. W. Cairns, 'John Millar's Lectures on Scots Criminal Law' (1988) 8 *Oxford Journal of Legal Studies*, 364-400 at pp. 395-400.

determined otherwise by our municipal custom'.[111] In doing so, Hume was following the well-established practice of Scots advocates when they acted as procurators in the Court of Justiciary.

If Hume adopted from Hale the doctrine that husbands could not be guilty of the rape of their wives other than art and part, he had done nothing unusual: indeed, eighteenth-century Scots criminal law presupposed and upheld such borrowing. Furthermore, he was probably only making articulate a doctrine on rape already accepted in the common understanding of the legal profession in Scotland. Thus, between 1736 and 1745, Forbes added the following passage to his manuscript treatise on Scots law: 'A Husband cannot be guilty of a Rape committed by him upon his Lawful wife, for by their mutual matrimonial consent the wife hath given up herself in this kind to her Husband.' He went on to discuss the situation of a husband aiding and abetting another to rape his wife. His authority for this was Hale's *Historia placitorum coronae*, and the passages are virtual quotations from Hale.[112] Though Forbes did draw comparisons with English law, he none-the-less appears from the context to have accepted this as Scots Law. It is therefore unsurprising to find Lockhart arguing in the debate *viva voce* on the relevancy in *Macgregor* (where one of the offences libelled was rape), 'that no man can be guilty of a Rape on the Body of his own wife.'[113] Grant conceded:

'It may be true that the Husband, who is Lawfully such with the Consent of [the] wife, cannot committ a Rape upon her Body, because he is intitled to the Enjoyment of it, and seldom would have to Employ fforce to be allowed the exercise of his Right; but if that should happen it would be no Crime in him. . . .'[114]

---

[111]Hume, *Commentaries*, i, p. liv.
[112]GUL, MS Gen. 1249, p. 415; Hale, *Pleas of the Crown*, i, 629.
[113]SRO, JC. 3/28, p. 562 (the quotation is from Grant's information where he is recapitulating Lockhart's *viva voce* arguments).
[114]*Ibid.*, p. 578.

It is possible that Hale suggested this to Lockhart and Grant, since the former cited him on rape (but not on this point which he did not argue in his information);[115] it seems obvious, however, that neither man doubted the correctness of the proposition. Though these statements were not authoritative, they would have been known to Hume who had read *Macgregor*, and would have indicated to him that Hale (if he was following him in this respect) either expressed what was already Scots law or, at least, established a principle at one with Scots law. It would in any case be difficult to accept that this doctrine was contrary to the mores of Hume's day.

Yet, it may be that Hume's *Commentaries* in one respect marked a change or confirmed one that had already taken place. Writing in 1730, Alexander Bayne had contrasted the private with the criminal law of Scotland. Though based on the civil (Roman) and feudal laws the former had developed — he argued — and become 'accommodated to the particular Genius and Manners of our Country'. Criminal Law was different. It was concerned with 'the *Peace* and *Order* of the Community', but fewer rules were needed than in private law, and it was less necessary 'to accommodate them to our particular Constitution, since the Nature of Man remaining the same in all Times and Places, Crimes affect all States and Kingdoms almost in the same manner'. Roman criminal law accordingly had needed 'small Alteration to make it ours', and 'being thus fit for our Use, as it stood in the Body of the *Roman* Laws, superseded the Necessity of reducing it into a peculiar System of our own.'[116] Grant had likewise argued in *Macgregor* that, in contrast to matters of private right, 'Crimes [were] offences against

---

[115]See, *e.g.*, *ibid.* pp. 597 and 631, citing Hale, *Pleas of the Crown*, i, 635. He did not need to argue the point on marital rape because Grant conceded it.

[116]Bayne, *Criminal Law*, pp. 5-7.

Common Humanity, and [were] equally such in all Civilized Nations, and depend[ed] not upon peculiar Constitutions', so that:

> '[W]hen the Neighbouring Customs are thus settled by the Statutes or Edicts formed on generall Principles, which are for the Common Interest and Utility of Mankind, it would altogether defeat Craig's Rule, for having Recourse to the Laws of other well Governed Nations, quoties jure proprio et consuetudine destituimur, if every foreign Law was to be rejected, merely because they were so much wiser than we, as to Enact it by positive authority.'[117]

Such views of criminal law supported the use, for example, of Matthaeus's commentary on the *libri terribiles* to understand and interpret Scots law. In contrast, Hume wrote in 1797:

> If I have . . . paid but little regard to the compilations of Justinian; still less have I thought it material to detain the reader on every occasion, with a scrutiny into the sentiments of the numerous modern commentators on them in modern times. Not that I mean to speak of their works as useless or nugatory in themselves; but that it were absurd to look into any of them for an exhibition of the practice of Scotland, which the foreign authors could know nothing about.'[118]

The years since the publication of Bayne's work had seen a revolution in thought about law in Scotland, carried out, not least, by Hume's teacher John Millar, in which the historical development of law and its relationship to different types of society and forms of government had come to be ever more stressed.[119] The passage from Hume's *Commentaries* quoted at the beginning of this essay emphasised that English criminal law was eminently

---

[117]SRO, JC. 3/28, pp. 582-583, 585.

[118]Hume, *Commentaries*, i, p. lx.

[119]Cairns, 'John Millar's Lectures'; *idem*, 'Rhetoric, Language, and Roman Law: Legal Education and Improvement in Eighteenth-Century Scotland' (1991) 9 *Law and History Review*, 31-58.

suitable for transplanting — to use Alan Watson's term[120] — 'because the form of our Government, and the general spirit of our jurisprudence are the same with that of England'.[121] Influenced by enlightenment thought on law in Scotland, Hume thus perceived the works of English lawyers to be the best to which to resort 'for confirmation of what equity and reason dictate';[122] English criminal law was that 'of a free and enlightened people'.[123] The natural-law thinking of men such as Grant and Lockhart had become the more historical, perhaps sociological, natural jurisprudence associated with Adam Smith and John Millar. No longer could someone such as Bayne argue as easily that humanity was everywhere the same as regards crimes. The result of this greater sensitivity was that England was now the 'well governed realm' (in the terms of the major premiss of the libel), the law of which was the appropriate source to which to turn to develop and elucidate indeterminate Scottish criminal law. A tendency to look to England would only have been reinforced by the now generally accepted view that English and Scots law had had a common mediaeval origin; while this recognition can be traced back to Craig,[124] it had been made popular by the writings of eighteenth-century scholars such as Kames.[125] It could no longer be simply assumed that Scots criminal law could be much the same as Roman law.

---

[120]A. Watson, *Legal Transplants: An Approach to Comparative Law* (Edinburgh, 1974).

[121]Hume, *Commentaries*, i, p. liv.

[122]*Ibid.*, i, p. lxi.

[123]*Ibid.*, i, p. liv.

[124]See, *e.g.*, B. P. Levack, *The Formation of the British State: England, Scotland, and the Union 1603-1707* (Oxford, 1987), pp. 77-78; J. W. Cairns, T. D. Fergus, and H.L. MacQueen, 'Legal Humanism in Renaissance Scotland' (1990) 11 *Journal of Legal History*, 40-69 at pp. 56-57.

[125]See, *e.g.*, H. Home, Lord Kames, *Historical Law-Tracts* (2nd edn.; Edinburgh, 1761), p. xiv.

H.M. Advocate v. *D.*[126] and *H.M. Advocate* v. *Paxton*[127] showed that 'the general spirit of our jurisprudence' — in Hume's phrase redolent of Montesquieu — was no longer in favour of the marital rape exemption. Even if it had been appropriate for Scots law in 1797, it no longer was in the 1980s. In *Stallard*,[128] the Lord Justice-General and the Lords Commissioners of Justiciary laid it to rest.[129]

---

[126] 1982 S.C.C.R. 182.

[127] 1985 S.L.T. 96.

[128] 1989 S.C.C.R. 248.

[129] I am grateful to Beverley Brown, Roger Emerson, Hector MacQueen, David Sellar, and Alan Watson for comments on earlier drafts.

8

CONTROVERSIAL ASPECTS OF THE LAW OF RAPE: AN ANGLO-SCOTTISH COMPARISON

Pamela R. Ferguson

Introduction

Among his many notable judgments, Lord Emslie's decision in the case of *Stallard* v. *H.M. Advocate*,[1] that the marital rape exemption no longer applied in Scots law, is arguably one of the most important. English law has now followed his approach in the recent case of *R.* v. *R.*[2] Despite this, there remain certain fundamental differences in the approach of the two legal systems to the crime of rape. It is not possible to provide a full exposition of the law of rape in these two countries, in a paper such as this. Rather, the paper attempts to compare the definitions in Scots and English law, and to highlight some of the more controversial aspects of this area of the law. In particular, the *mens rea* of rape, marital rape, and problems of evidence are explored.

Traditionally, Scots law has regarded rape as an aggravated form of assault.[3] It was defined by Hume as requiring 'carnal knowledge

---

[1] 1989 S.L.T. 469; 1989 S.C.C.R. 248.

[2] The decision of the Court of Appeal is reported at [1991] 2 All E.R. 257, CA. The decision of the House of Lords is reported at [1991] 4 All E.R. 481.

[3] In his *Commentaries on the Law of Scotland Respecting Crimes* Hume stated that 'it is not as a lustful, but as a malicious and injurious act, that rape is the object of the vengeance of the law' (4th edn.), i, 305. See also the dictum of Lord Emslie in *Stallard* v. *H.M. Advocate* 1989 S.L.T. 469, at p. 473: 'rape has always been essentially a crime of violence and indeed no more than an aggravated assault.'

of the woman's person, by penetration of her privy parts, or entry of her body', which is achieved 'against her will, and by force'.[4]

A definition which perhaps reflects the present law more accurately is that offered by Sheriff Gordon. He refers to 'the carnal knowledge of a female by a male person obtained by overcoming her will.'[5] This description makes it clear that the victim of rape may be a female child, rather than a woman,[6] and that there is no minimum age requirement for the perpetrator.[7] Gordon's omission of a reference to the 'forcible' nature of the intercourse is in accordance with the current approach of the courts; there need not be actual violence done to the complainer to effect intercourse, threats of violence will suffice.[8]

In England, rape is now a statutory offence, by virtue of sec. 1(1) of the Sexual Offences Act 1956. This simply provides that it is an offence 'for a man to rape a woman'. The 1956 Act gives no definition of 'rape'; this is contained in sec. 1(1)(*a*) of the Sexual Offences (Amendment) Act 1976, which states that: 'a man commits rape if he has unlawful sexual intercourse with a woman who at the time of the intercourse does not consent to it'.

English law was formerly the same as Scots law in using the term 'carnal knowledge', but this was changed to 'sexual intercourse' by the 1956 Act. 'Carnal' simply means 'sexual', and one might suppose that both 'carnal knowledge' and 'sexual intercourse' would cover a variety of sexual conduct. In fact, the accused's conduct may only amount to 'rape' if he has achieved penile

---

[4]Hume, i, 301-302.

[5]Gordon, *The Criminal Law of Scotland* (2nd edn.), para. 33-01.

[6]Hume gives examples of rapes committed on pupils; in the case of *Robert Fulton, Junior* (1841) 2 Swin. 564, the victim was a girl aged five. At the trials of *William Ripley* and *William Currie* the complainers were aged six, and nine, respectively.

[7]See the case of *Robert Fulton, Junior* (n. 6, *supra*) in which a successful conviction was obtained against a boy of 13 years and 10 months.

[8]See pp. 188-189, *infra*.

penetration *per vaginam*. In both Scots and English law forced anal or oral intercourse with a woman is not rape.[9]

In both countries, the perpetrator of rape requires to be male, but a female may be found guilty as accessory.[10] In contrast to the Scottish position, there is an irrefutable presumption in English law that a boy who is under the age of fourteen is not capable of committing rape.[11] This presumption has been described as 'an absurd rule, capable of producing injustice'.[12] As Glanville Williams has pointed out, puberty may be attained before a boy reaches his fourteenth birthday. More importantly, since rape requires penetration, but not fertilisation '[i]t is an ability to have an erection, not an ability to emit semen, that is physically necessary for the crime'.[13] A boy under the age of fourteen may, instead, be convicted of indecent assault. Where the indecent assault has involved sexual intercourse it is difficult to understand why the presumption against rape should not be rebutted. Its abolition was recommended over a decade ago by the Criminal Law Revision Committee[14] and it is submitted that English law ought to be brought into line with Scots law on this point.

---

[9]In Scots law anal or oral intercourse which is engaged in without the consent of the complainer constitutes indecent assault. Oral intercourse with a female without her consent is a form of sexual assault in English law also, and anal intercourse is the offence of buggery under English law, even where the woman consents. The Scottish crime of sodomy is probably limited to acts of anal intercourse between males. See Gordon, para. 34-01.

[10]See the case of *Charles Matthews and Margaret Goldsmith*, High Court, December 1910 (unreported) for the Scottish position, and *R.* v. *Ram and Ram* (1893) 17 Cox C.C. 609, for the English authority.

[11]See Hale, *Pleas of the Crown*, vol. 1, p. 630, and the case of *R.* v. *Groombridge* [1892] 2 Q.B. 600.

[12]Smith and Hogan, *Criminal Law*, (5th edn.), at p. 412.

[13]Williams, *Textbook of Criminal Law* (2nd edn.), at p. 237. Note also that English law has recognised paternity in boys under 14; see *L.* v. *K.* [1985] Fam. 144.

[14]See the Criminal Law Revision Committee Report on Sexual Offences, 1984, (15th Report) Cmnd. 9213, para. 2.48.

In both jurisdictions rape is restricted to penile penetration by a male person, of a female person, *per vaginam*. It follows from the English case of *R. v. Tan*[15] that a person who has undergone a 'sex-change' procedure, and who has the genitalia of a woman at the time of complaint, could not be the subject of a rape charge.[16] This would apply even where an accused was unaware of the fact that his victim was not 'female' in the eyes of the law. It seems likely that the Scottish Courts would follow English law in this area. Were a case to arise in either country in which a transsexual had been assaulted in this way, the accused could be charged with indecent assault.[17]

Lack of consent, or overcoming the will

As already noted, the English law of rape is defined as intercourse with a woman who 'does not consent to it'. It is frequently suggested that the Scots law requirement of 'overcoming the complainer's will' is equivalent to this. In the majority of cases, of course, the two will be synonymous, the 'overcoming of the will' being evidenced by the complainer's testimony that she was 'not consenting'. It is submitted, however, that equating the Scots law definition with a lack of consent can, in certain situations, be

---

[15][1983] Q.B. 1053.

[16]In the *Tan* case, one of the accused was a person who had been born male but had undergone a 'sex-change' operation and had female sexual organs at the time of the trial. The accused were charged with 'keeping a disorderly house', and the court held that the sex of the 'sex-change' accused was male. *Tan's* case follows the earlier, civil law case of *Corbett v. Corbett* [1971] P. 83 in which it was held that there could not be a valid marriage between a man and a person who had been born male but who had undergone a sex-change operation. It seems, therefore, that the *legal* sex of a person is determined at the time of birth and cannot be altered by any medical or surgical procedure.

[17]A full discussion of the law relating to 'transexuals' is outwith the scope of this paper, and it is suggested that the position of a transexual 'rape-victim' is but one aspect of the law which requires attention. (See also the recent decision of the Court of Human Rights in *Cossey* (Application No. 10843/84) *The Times,* October 17, 1990.)

misleading[18]. If one were to focus on 'lack of consent', one might imagine that a man who has intercourse with a sleeping woman commits rape, since the complainer does not consent to his actings. However, as the Scots law of rape requires *the overcoming of the will*, intercourse with a sleeping woman is not rape, on the basis that a woman who is asleep arguable has no 'will' to overcome. This was the approach taken in the case of *H.M. Advocate* v. *Charles Sweenie*[19] in which Lord Deas opined that he could: 'see no difficulty in holding, that the wickedly and feloniously invading, by stealth . . . the bed of a woman while asleep, and having carnal knowledge of her person without her consciousness *or consent*, is an offence of an aggravated kind . . .'[20] — hence the learned judge recognised that the act was clearly committed 'without consent'. However, he considered that the 'more difficult question' was 'whether the offence be the crime of rape? The prosecutor defines rape to be carnal knowledge of a woman without her consent . . . I cannot concur in this view.'[21] The indictment was therefore held to be irrelevant in so far as it libelled a charge of rape. The remainder of the libel was found to disclose a relevant crime, which has since been referred to as 'clandestine injury to women',[22] a form of indecent assault.

It follows from this insistence on the overcoming of the complainer's will that it is not 'rape' in Scotland to have intercourse with

---

[18]Compare P. W. Ferguson, '*Crimes Against the Person*', at para. 4-08, where he argues: 'Since the absence of consent is the essence of the crime of rape, it is not rape for a man to have intercourse with a sleeping woman', yet later in the same paragraph states, in relation to the *Charles Sweenie* case, that 'since the victim was asleep and could neither give nor withhold her consent, the correct view should have been that the crime was rape.'

[19](1858) 3 Irv. 109.

[20]At p. 146, emphasis added.

[21]At p. 146.

[22]See Macdonald (5th edn.), p. 120.

a woman who has rendered herself so drunk as to no longer have any 'will' in the matter. Hence in the case of *H.M. Advocate* v. *Grainger and Rae*[23] Lord Anderson said:

> 'Just as a sleeping woman is temporarily in a state of unconsciousness wherein she is incapable of exercising her will power, so here it seems to me that the woman was in the same temporary condition of unconsciousness by reason of intoxication . . . what is said to have been done by the accused, although not rape, is a criminal offence — the crime of inflicting clandestine injury on a woman . . . But the crime must be indicted as such, and not as rape.'[24]

This approach was followed in the case of *Sweeney and Another* v. *X*[25] and more recently in *Quinn* v. *H.M. Advocate.*[26] Hume suggested that the position was quite different where the accused was responsible for the woman's intoxicated state. A conviction for rape: 'ought to be given where the woman has been overpowered and stupified, or laid asleep, by means of drugs or potions *administered to her*, and is abused in this state of insensibility. For this is as great a violence to her person and constitution, as if she were bound with cords or stunned with blows, or were in any other masterful way disabled from resisting.'[27]

This situation differs from the sleeping or self-intoxicated woman, since an accused who deliberately sets out to render the complainer drunk is, indeed, aiming to 'overcome her will'. Hume's approach was followed in *H.M. Advocate* v. *Logan*[28] in which Lord Justice-Clerk Aitchison directed the jury as follows:

---

[23] 1932 J.C. 40.
[24] *Ibid.*, p. 41.
[25] 1982 S.C.C.R. 509.
[26] 1990 S.C.C.R. 254.
[27] Hume, i, 303, emphasis added.
[28] 1936 J.C. 100. See also the case of *Duncan McMillan* (9th January 1833), mentioned in *William Fraser* (1847) Ark. 280, at p. 293, as being a case in which the accused was charged with rape by plying the complainer with drink.

'If you thought that the Crown had proved that the woman was plied with drink . . . in order to overcome her resistance, you could find a verdict of guilty of rape; but if the position was that the woman was not given the drink for the purpose of overcoming her or making her incapable of resistance, but had taken it of her own free will, and it had not been given to her for a criminal purpose, and she became insensible, and advantage was then taken of her in her insensible condition, then, in the eye of the law, the crime would not be rape but indecent assault only.'[29]

It is now a statutory offence to administer 'any drug, matter or thing' to a female with intent to 'stupefy or overpower' her, for the purposes of sexual intercourse.[30]

In *Logan's* case Lord Aitchison put forward one possible reason for the decision in *Charles Sweenie* that the charge could not be rape, but only indecent assault. He suggests that the judges in the *Sweenie* case 'were very unwilling to extend the definition of rape so as to bring any new class of crime within the category of a capital offence.'[31] Certainly, there are *dicta* in *Sweenie* to this effect.[32] However, another plausible explanation for the reluctance of the judges is that they feared that the crime would be susceptible to abuse. Hence Lord Deas opined:

'Where the woman has been drugged by herself or another . . . or even where she falls into a faint, there are still likely to occur other facts and circumstances . . . by which her story may be corroborated or contradicted. But when her story is that her person was penetrated in her sleep . . . *the danger is imminent that, through malice, or to save her character in the fear of discovery, she may successfully make a charge . . .*'[33]

---

[29] 1936 J.C., pp. 101-102.
[30] Sec. 2 (1) (*c*) of the Sexual Offences (Scotland) Act 1976.
[31] 1936 J.C. at p. 102.
[32] See the judgments of Lords Cowan and Deas at pp. 143 and 150.
[33] At p. 150.

If the judges in the *Charles Sweenie* case were indeed influenced mainly by their reluctance to extend the parameters of a capital crime, the abolition of capital punishment makes the continuation of this distinction difficult to justify. It would be particularly difficult to explain to a complainer that her attacker could be charged with rape if he had plied her with drink, but that if she got herself drunk, he could only be charged with indecent assault.

As already noted, English law defines rape in terms of consent. It has been suggested that the tests 'was the act against the complainer's will?' and 'was the act without her consent?' are different, since only the latter 'emphasises that it is not necessary for the Crown to prove a positive dissent by the woman; it is enough that she did not assent.'[34] It follows from this emphasis on consent that a man who has intercourse with a sleeping or heavily intoxicated woman *is* guilty of rape under English law. This is illustrated by the cases of *R.* v. *Young*[35] and *R.* v. *Camplin*,[36] respectively.

A comparison of Scots and English law in relation to intercourse with sleeping or self-intoxicated women does suggest that the crime of rape is defined more narrowly north of the Border. The Criminal Law Revision Committee in its Report on Sexual Offences considered whether rape should be redefined in English law.[37] It is interesting to note its conclusion: 'To return to a test which asked whether the intercourse was against the woman's will would *narrow* the definition of rape.'[38]

---

[34]See Smith and Hogan, *Criminal Law* (5th edn.), at p. 408.

[35](1878) 14 Cox C.C. 114. See also *R.* v. *Mayers* (1872) 12 Cox C.C. 311 and *R.* v. *Fletcher* (1859) Bell C.C. 63.

[36](1845) 1 Den. 89.

[37]Criminal Law Revision Committee, Fifteenth Report. *Sexual Offences.* Cmnd. 9213, (1984).

[38]*Ibid.*, pp. 11-12.

By force or threats of violence

As already noted, one element of the crime of rape specifically required by Hume's definition was that the intercourse be obtained 'by force'. Hume made it clear that in his day a woman was required to resist to the 'uttermost'. He stated that the resistance must 'be continued to the last; so that it is by main force only and terror that the violation is accomplished'.[39] This was based on the view that rape was 'a fate worse than death', a notion which is stressed in many of the older judgments. Hence in the case of *Charles Sweenie* Lord Deas referred to the possibility of a woman being 'deprived of her virtue, rather than have yielded which, she would have yielded her life . . .'[40] In the same case, Lord Ardmillan stated that 'force — actual or constructive — is an essential element in the crime of rape . . .' but that — 'any mode of overpowering the will, without actual personal violence, such as the use of threats, or drugs, is force in the estimation of the law . . . any degree of force is sufficient in law to constitute the crime of rape, if it is sufficient in fact to overcome the opposing will of the woman.'[41]

Although it is necessary in every case to show that the complainer's will to resist was overcome, Gordon has suggested that 'the important matter is not the amount of resistance put up, but whether the woman remained an unwilling party throughout, and the degree of violence or resistance is important only as evidence of this.'[42] This approach was followed by the High Court in *Barbour* v. *H.M. Advocate*.[43] In a passage which closely resembles Gordon's statement Lord Stewart directed the jury that the 'significance of resistance is only as evidence of unwillingness'.[44]

---

[39]Hume, i, 302.
[40](1858) 3 Irv. 109, at p. 145.
[41]*Ibid.*, p. 137.
[42]Gordon, para. 33-09.
[43]1982 S.C.C.R. 195.
[44]*Ibid.*, p. 198.

In Scotland, threats of violence may be used to overcome the woman's resistance[45] and these threats may be directed at her or at a third party.[46] It seems that Scots law requires that such threats be of imminent harm.[47] It is also a statutory offence to procure a woman to have sexual intercourse by the use of threats.[48]

As regards English law, Williams has argued that: 'Common sense suggests that a person who submits to an act only because he believes that otherwise he will be over-powered and have it done to him anyway does not consent in law, even though the force necessary to overpower him will be small and non-injurious.'[49] Procuring a woman to have sexual intercourse by threats or intimidation is a statutory offence,[50] but in one unreported case it was held that threats directed at a woman's boyfriend could not serve to vitiate her consent.[51] The Criminal Law Revision Committee has recommended that legislation should specify what types of threat will be capable of nullifying the complainant's purported consent.[52] It suggested that only threats which were capable of immediate execution should be considered to be sufficient for this purpose.[53] Enactment of this proposal would bring English law into line with Scottish practice.

Mens rea

One of the most controversial cases concerning the *mens rea* of rape

---

[45]Hume, i, 302.

[46]See the unreported case of *Paul Macdonald* (June 1969, Glasgow High Court, cited by Gordon) in which the threats were directed at the woman's young child.

[47]Gordon, para. 33-10.

[48]See sec. 2 (1) of the Sexual Offences (Scotland) Act 1976.

[49]Williams, *Textbook of Criminal Law*, (2nd edn.), p. 552.

[50]By sec. 2 (1) of the Sexual Offences Act 1956.

[51]See (1981) 131 New L.J. 791.

[52]Criminal Law Revision Committee, *Sexual Offences*, Cmnd. 9213

[53]*Ibid.*, at para. 2.29.

in English law is *Director of Public Prosecutions* v. *Morgan.*[54] Three
of the accused had intercourse with the complainant, without her
consent. They alleged that her husband had told them that she
would be a willing participant, and that they should ignore her signs
of protest as this was simply his wife's way of expressing enjoyment.
The House of Lords was required to consider the effect of an
accused's mistaken belief that the complainant was consenting.
The court held that an accused who believed that the woman
consented to his behaviour was entitled to be acquitted, even where
this belief was not based on reasonable grounds.

This principle was adopted in Scotland by Lord Emslie in the
case of *Meek and Others* v. *H.M. Advocate.*[55] Both *Morgan* and *Meek*
have been criticised.[56] The approach of the courts in these two cases
did not accord with the usual criminal law rules which were current
at that time, concerning mistaken beliefs held by an accused. One
may, for example, consider the law on self-defence. Where an
accused acted under a mistaken belief that he was about to be
attacked by a third party, he could only plead self-defence if he
believed that he was in danger of imminent attack, *and* this belief
was based on reasonable grounds.[57]

The justification for the *Morgan* and *Meek* decisions is that, in
a charge of rape, one's belief as to whether or not a woman consents

---

[54][1976] A.C. 182. While any critique of the *Morgan* approach necessarily
involves some consideration of 'recklessness', a full discussion of this aspect of the
mens rea of rape is outwith the scope of the present paper. (See *Director of Public
Prosecutions* v. *Caldwell* [1982] A.C. 341; *R.* v. *Pigg* [1982] 2 All E.R. 591, and *R.*
v. *Satnam* (1984) 78 Cr. App. R. 149.)

[55]1982 S.C.C.R. 613.

[56]See Temkin, *Rape and the Criminal Process*, at p. 79.

[57]This is still the Scottish position — see *Owens* v. *H.M. Advocate* 1946 J.C.
119. English law had been similar (see *Lavin* v. *Albert* [1982] A.C. 546, and *R.* v.
Rose (1884) 15 Cox C.C. 540), but now appears to be applying the *Morgan*
approach, to self-defence. See *Beckford* v. *R.* [1988] A.C. 130, and *R.* v. *Williams*
(1984) 78 Cr. App. R. 276.

or is willing is not a 'defence' but an integral part of the *mens rea* of the crime. It is therefore for the *Crown* to establish that the accused was aware of a lack of consent. As was stated in the *Morgan* case:

> 'Once one has accepted . . . that the prohibited act in rape is non-consensual sexual intercourse, and that the guilty state of mind is an intention to commit it, it seems to me to follow as a matter of inexorable logic that there is no room either for a 'defence' of honest belief or mistake, or of a defence of honest and reasonable belief or mistake. Either the prosecution proves that the accused had the requisite intent, or it does not. In the former case it succeeds, and in the latter it fails. Since honest belief clearly negatives intent, the reasonableness or otherwise of that belief can only be evidence for or against the view that the belief and therefore the intent was actually held.'[58]

The outcry in England which followed this case led to the setting up of the Heilbron Committee[59] which emphasised that the direction in *Morgan* should only be given to the jury in extreme circumstances. Similarly in Scotland the case of *Meek* itself, while holding that the direction sought by counsel was good in law, decided that in the circumstances of that particular case a direction to the jury along those lines was not required. This was also the position in the recent case of *Quinn* v. *H.M. Advocate*.[60] One of the accused appealed against his conviction for rape on the grounds that 'the trial judge should have directed the jury that they could only convict if they were satisfied that *reasonable* grounds did not exist for genuine belief on the part of the appellant that the complainer was consenting.'[61] Standing the *Meek* decision, such a belief in consent need not, of course, be based on reasonable grounds, so long as genuinely held. No comment on this aspect of

---

[58][1976] A.C. 182, *per* Lord Hailsham of St Marylebone at p. 214.
[59]Report of the Advisory Group on the Law of Rape, Cmnd. 6352, 1975.
[60]1990 S.C.C.R. 254.
[61]*Ibid.*, p. 263, emphasis added.

the direction being sought was made, on appeal. The Court held, however, that the evidence in the case had presented the jury with a straight-forward choice between violence and consent, hence there was no room for any 'half-way house' which such a direction would have suggested.

In England, juries are now directed to take the reasonableness of the accused's belief into account in testing its veracity: 'If at a trial for a rape offence the jury has to consider whether a man believed that a woman was consenting to sexual intercourse, the presence or absence of reasonable grounds for such a belief is a matter to which the jury is to have regard . . . in considering whether he so believed.'[62] It is submitted that it will be a rare case indeed in which the jury accept that the accused genuinely believed that the complainer was a consenting party, find that he had no reasonable basis whatever for this belief, and yet be prepared to acquit him.

The *Morgan* ruling has, however, led to a number of acquittals simply because the trial judge had failed to direct the jury in accordance with that decision.[63]

The approach of the courts in *Morgan* and *Meek* may be justifiable from a jurisprudential perspective. Nevertheless, it is submitted that the criminal law *ought* to penalise an accused who has intercourse against the will of a woman, where his belief in her consent or willingness is not a reasonable one. Where the evidence of the accused is that he gave no thought to the matter of the woman's willingness/consent, or that it never at any stage occurred to him that the complainer was not willing, but he now accepts that the woman was in fact resisting his advances, then, in my submission, he may be a fit subject for the criminal law. If a woman

---

[62]Sec. 1 (2) of the Sexual Offences (Amendment) Act 1976, which followed the recommendation of the Heilbron Committee that the *mens rea* requirement for rape be spelled out in the legislation.

[63]See, for example, *R.* v. *Steele* (1976) 65 Cr. app. R. 22 and *R.* v. *Satnam* (1983) 78 Cr. App. Rep. 149.

struggles or otherwise indicates her dissent, then the law ought to require a man to act *reasonably*. As a minimum, he should be expected to make some inquiry into her state of mind. If he persists in intercourse in the fact of apparent resistance or protests by the woman, his conduct should be denounced by the criminal law.

A critic might argue that it is unfair to punish an accused who genuinely believed that the woman had been consenting. Let us, however, consider the circumstances of a *Morgan*-type case, and postulate that the court is confronted with evidence from the complainant that she had made clear her lack of consent, and that her evidence is accepted by the accused, at the trial.[64] Let us further suppose that the accused maintain that they had persisted at their attempts at intercourse in the belief that the complainant's protests were not authentic. It is submitted that the law ought to require this belief to be based on reasonable grounds. It is difficult to see how such beliefs could be considered reasonable. In the *Morgan* case the accused alleged that they had been told by the complainant's husband that his wife would be willing, and that they should disregard her protests, since this was simply her way of heightening her own pleasure. It is submitted that one should never engage in sexual intercourse with someone who is giving clear signs of resistance, and may certainly not base one's beliefs as to a woman's state of mind on information supplied by a third party.

In short, where a woman offers resistance or otherwise appears to be dissenting, a reasonable man would entertain some doubts as to her willingness, and should then be expected to clarify the position. He could do that simply by *asking* her.

It may be counter-argued that asking will not necessarily give a definitive answer since a woman may express her dissent yet be willing for the man's advances to continue. This approach reflects

---

[64]In fact, the accused in *Morgan* did not accept the evidence of the complainant, but maintained that any signs of resistance offered by her had not been genuine.

the commonly held attitude that women who say 'No' sometimes mean 'Yes'. The accused in *Morgan* decided that the complainant was not genuinely objecting; in the circumstances they could only have reached that conclusion if they believed that some women pretend to resist sexual advances while secretly enjoying them. It is conceded that a woman may affect reluctance, either due to shyness, or even coyness, but this will be evident only at the initial stages of the intercourse. If her opposition is maintained at the point of penetration then it is ridiculous to suppose that her 'No' really means 'Yes'.

In this context, references to the 'reasonable man' and the requirement of 'reasonable belief' may create a misleading impression if it conjures up the image of a completely rational being, who gives due consideration to all potential consequences before embarking on any course of action. A man who persists in intercourse with a woman despite obvious signs of dissent on her part does not simply act 'unreasonably' in the sense that he has failed to evaluate the situation in a logical fashion. Rather, he has failed to display even the most basic sense of decency and consideration for others; by his conduct, he treats the complainer as a 'thing', rather than as a person.

The Heilbron Committee approved the reasoning of the House of Lords in *Morgan*, and concluded that the definition of rape should *not* be extended 'to include conduct which, however deplorable, does not in justice or in common sense justify branding the accused as a guilty man.'[65] Perhaps a man who has intercourse with a woman in the mistaken, but unreasonable, belief that she is consenting does not deserve to be branded as a *rapist*, since he does not intend to have intercourse against the woman's will. But a man who has intercourse with a woman who appears to be resisting takes a risk that she is not, in fact, consenting. The criminal law ought to

---

[65]Cmnd. 6352, at para. 76.

make clear its disapproval of such 'deplorable' conduct. Any signs of dissent by a woman should put a duty of inquiry on a man, and if he persists in intercourse in the face of apparent resistance, he should be penalised by the criminal law.

It is submitted, therefore, that the Law Commissions ought to give consideration to the introduction of a statutory offence, criminalising such behaviour. As Lord Cross of Chelsea stated in the *Morgan* case: 'it can be argued with force that it is only fair to the woman and not in the least unfair to the man that he should be under a duty to take reasonable care to ascertain that she is consenting to the intercourse and be at risk of prosecution if he fails to take such care.'[66]

Marital rape

In both England and Scotland, it was for a long time accepted that the law provided one exception to the usual rule that intercourse without the complainer's consent/against her will was rape. If the accused and complainer were married to one another at the time of the incident the former was immune from prosecution, due to the so-called 'marital rape exemption'.

In Scotland, Hume referred to this exemption in his discussion of art and part liability for rape. He stated that: 'Those who [assist in the rape] are all involved in the same guilt as the actor. This is true without exception even of the husband of the woman; who, *though he cannot himself commit a rape on his own wife*, who has surrendered her person to him in that sort, may however be accessory to that crime . . . committed on her by another.'[67] This approach was reiterated by Alison, Burnett and Macdonald.[68] Gordon noted that there were in fact no recorded cases in which the matter had arisen,

---

[66][1976] A.C. 182, at p. 203.
[67]Hume i, 305-306, emphasis added.
[68]See Alison, i, 215; Burnett, at p. 102; and Macdonald (5th edn.), at p. 119.

and questioned whether Hume's view was still valid.[69] Although the issue of the marital rape exemption had not been directly confronted in any case prior to 1982, its validity seems to have been accepted.[70]

Two cases in the 1980s chipped away at the exemption in Scotland. In *H.M. Advocate* v. *Duffy*[71] the accused and his wife, the complainer were living apart at the time of the alleged incident. There was, however, no judicial separation in force. A plea was taken to the relevancy of an indictment, charging the husband with rape. This plea was repelled by Lord Robertson, who stated: 'I do not think it can be affirmed as a matter of principle that the law of Scotland today is that a husband in no circumstances can be guilty of the crime of rape upon his wife.'[72] The sole reason suggested by Hume for this exemption was that a wife had 'surrendered her person to [her husband] in that sort'.[73] The ruling in the case of *Duffy* was based on the premise that Hume's exemption was still valid, but that it was limited to the situation where a husband and wife were living together.

Duffy's case was followed in *H.M. Advocate* v. *Paxton*[74] in which evidence led from the complainer at the trial revealed that she and the accused had been married to one another at the time of the alleged incident. The couple had been living apart for only a few weeks, and it was not a formal separation. Defence counsel argued

---

[69]Gordon, para. 33-12.

[70]In the case of *Charles Sweenie* (1858) 3 Irv. 109, the indictment referred to 'invading by stealth the bed of a *married woman*, and having carnal connection with her when asleep without her knowledge and consent, *by a man not her husband*' (emphasis added). Also, in the case of *William Fraser* (1847) Ark. 280, at p. 292, in which the accused pretended to be the victim's husband, it was conceded by the Crown that the woman could not 'in any proper sense be said to have a will in the matter. To her husband it was her duty to yield her person'.

[71]1983 S.L.T. 7; *sub. nom. H.M. Advocate* v. *D.*, 1982 S.C.C.R. 182.

[72]1983 S.L.T. 7, at p. 9.

[73]Hume, i, 306.

[74]1984 J.C. 105; 1984 S.C.C.R. 311; 1985 S.L.T. 96.

that this fell short of the type of separation which was required in order to overcome the implied consent presumed by the marital rape exemption. In refusing this submission Lord Cameron stated that: 'where it is admitted that the parties are *de facto* separated, not living at bed and board, and the wife has withdrawn herself from the society of her husband . . . then that is the plainest possible notice that the implication of 'surrender of her person in that sort' by the wife is not to be accepted.'[75]

Hence *Duffy* and *Paxton* limited the scope of the husband's immunity. It should be noted, however, that Hume's statement that a woman 'surrendered her person' by marriage was accepted in both cases. Neither judgment attacked this notion, but merely held that evidence of separation could show that a wife had revoked this implied consent. Thus in *Paxton* it was stated that a wife's 'surrender' on marriage was a 'voluntary but not irrevocable act' which could be 'recalled' by her.[76] It was not until the case of *Stallard* v. *H.M. Advocate* in 1989 that the whole basis of the exemption was called into question by the Scottish courts.[77]

In the *Stallard* case, the indictment charged the accused with, *inter alia*, the rape of his wife, and specifically libelled that the couple were married to one another, and still cohabiting together at the date of the alleged incident. Lord Mayfield held that the reason given by Hume for the husband's immunity was no longer applicable. His approach was confirmed, on appeal, by Lord Emslie who stated that there was no 'no justification for the supposed immunity of a husband'.[78] This was based on the changed position of women in society since the time of Hume. According to Lord Emslie:

---

[75] 1984 J.C., at p. 107.

[76] 1984 J.C., at p. 107. According to Lord Cameron, at p. 106, it was also noticeable that the Crown 'did not seek in this case to traverse the general proposition advanced by Hume'.

[77] 1989 S.L.T. 469; 1989 S.C.C.R. 248.

[78] 1989 S.L.T., at p. 473.

'the status of women, and the status of a married woman, in our law have changed quite dramatically. A husband and wife are now for all practical purposes equal partners in marriage . . . A wife is not obliged to obey her husband in all things nor to suffer excessive sexual demands on the part of her husband . . . A live system of law will always have regard to changing circumstances to test the justification for any exception to the application of a general rule. Nowadays it cannot seriously be maintained that by marriage a wife submits herself irrevocably to sexual intercourse in all circumstances.'[79]

This is in accordance with the view which had been expressed by Gordon, in 1978. In discussing a man's privilege from prosecution for the rape of his wife Sheriff Gordon argued thus: 'The common law must take contemporary attitudes and *mores* into account and contemporary *mores* manifestly do not recognise any such privilege.'[80]

The reasons put forward by counsel for the accused for upholding the law as suggested by Hume were that the abrogation of the exemption would actually take away a number of 'basic rights' from women. These were stated to include 'the right to forgive'; 'the right to tolerate and decide whether the marriage should survive or not'; and 'the right to change her mind'.[81] These arguments have been criticised.[82] Certainly, the Criminal Appeal Court was: 'not impressed . . . by counsel for the appellant's warning of the dire consequences which, he foresaw, would flow from a refusal of this appeal.'[83]

In Scotland, therefore, the fact that the accused and complainer were married to one another at the date of the alleged offence will

---

[79] *Ibid.*

[80] Gordon, para. 33-12.

[81] See 1989 S.L.T. at p. 472.

[82] See 'Recognising Marital Rape', L. Farmer, 154 SCOLAG 102 and 'Marital Rape', T. H. Jones, 1989 S.L.T. (News) 279-282.

[83] 1989 S.L.T., at p. 474.

not bar a prosecution for rape. Such cases are, however, notoriously difficult to prove[84] and in *Duffy, Paxton* and *Stallard*, the accused were acquitted of rape.[85]

The law on 'marital rape' in England was in a more confused state until the recent *R. v. R.* case.[86] Traditionally, the law was similar to that suggested by Hume. In Hale's *Pleas of the Crown* it was stated that: 'the husband cannot be guilty of a rape committed by himself on his lawful wife, for by their mutual matrimonial consent and contract the wife hath given up herself in this kind to her husband, which she cannot retract.'[87] This wording is similar to that employed by Hume, and indeed it has been suggested that Hume simply adopted Hale's approach in this area of the law.[88]

Prior to *R.*'s case it seemed that the husband generally lost his immunity from prosecution only if a court order was in force at the time of the alleged rape. The first case to decide this was *R. v. Clarke*.[89] It had also been held that the wife's implied consent to intercourse with her husband could be taken to be revoked if she had obtained a decree nisi of divorce[90] or an injunction which restrained her husband from molesting her. In the latter situation, it was enough that the husband had given a court undertaking not to molest his wife.[91] In general, however, the fact that a woman had commenced proceedings to obtain a divorce petition would not

---

[84]See *infra* regarding evidential problems in rape trials.

[85]The accused in *Duffy* was found 'not guilty'. 'Not proven' verdicts were returned in the cases of *Paxton* and *Stallard.*

[86]See [1991] 4 All E.R. 481, HL, and [1991]2 A11 E.R.257, CA.

[87]1778 ed., vol. i, at p. 629.

[88]See the judgment of Lord Emslie in *Stallard* v. *H.M. Advocate* 1989 S.L.T., at p. 472, where he states that it is 'likely that the view expressed by Hume . . . was taken from Hale's *Historia Placitorum Coronae*'.

[89](1949) 33 Cr. App. R. 216.

[90]*R. v. O'Brien* [1974] 3 All E.R. 663.

[91]*R. v. Steele* (1976) 65 Cr. App. R. 22 (CA).

have been sufficient.[92] Even the effect of a personal protection order obtained by a wife against her husband was less than clear.

In the case of *R. v. Sharples*[93] the complainant had obtained such an order, prohibiting her husband from using or threatening to use violence against her. It was alleged that the husband thereafter had intercourse with the complainant without her consent. Despite the personal protection order, the court held that the marital exemption still applied; his Honour Judge Fawcus held that the mere fact that the husband was precluded from using violence against his wife did not necessarily mean that the wife's implied consent to intercourse had been revoked. This seems to have been on the basis that a woman could continue to have sexual intercourse with her husband despite the fact that such a personal protection order was in force. Certainly, such an order is not intended to prohibit sexual relations between spouses. It is respectfully submitted, however, that the learned judge erred in the *Sharples* case by assuming that an act of intercourse in these circumstances could in no circumstances be 'violent'.

Prior to the *R* case, the notion that a wife could withdraw her implied consent simply by living apart from her husband, as in *Duffy* and *Paxton*, had received little acceptance by the English courts. One reason for this was that it was felt that since the wife's consent was implied by law it could only be withdrawn by the law itself, and not by any extra-legal action on the part of either spouse.[94] Further erosion of the marital rape exemption had occurred in the case of *R. v. Kowalski*[95] which held that it provided no immunity to a husband who forced his wife to engage in oral

---

[92]See *R. v. Miller* [1954] 2 Q.B. 282, in which there had been a partial hearing of the divorce petition prior to the incident which formed the subject-matter of the charge.

[93][1990] Crim. L. R. 198.

[94]See *R. v. Clarke* (1949) 33 Cr. App. R. 216.

[95][1988] Crim. L. R. 124.

sex.[96] We have already noted that a narrow definition of rape can cause certain categories of anti-social behaviour to be excluded from within its ambit; this is apparent from the fact that the Scottish definition does not extend to acts of non-consensual intercourse with a sleeping or self-intoxicated woman. It is somewhat ironic, therefore, to note that the restriction of rape to 'penile penetration *per vaginam*' operated to the *dis*advantage of the accused in the *Kowalski* case.

These attempts at circumscribing the marital rape exemption in English law have been rendered obsolete by the decision of the House of Lords in *R. v. R.* The complainant had returned to live with her parents having been advised by her husband, the accused, that he intended to seek a divorce. This was to be based on the wife's refusal to have intercourse. The complainant herself then sought legal advice as to how she could obtain a divorce. Three weeks later the accused broke into her parent's home and attempted to have sexual intercourse with her, without her consent.

It was held by Owen J. at first instance that the cessation of cohabitation in the marital home by the wife, accompanied by her clear indication that her consent to sexual intercourse had been withdrawn, had revoked any consent implied by marriage and removed the husband's immunity to a charge of rape. The accused then pleaded guilty to a charge of attempted rape and assault occasioning actual bodily harm.[97] Owen J.'s decision was limited to cases in which the parties were actually living apart at the time of the incident, hence his judgment seemed to move English law closer to the position of Scots law at the time of the *Duffy* and *Paxton* cases. A more radical approach was, however, taken when the case reached the Court of Appeal. It held that the marital rape exemption, as propounded by Hale, was: 'an anachronistic and

---

[96]The accused was convicted of indecent assault.
[97]He was sentenced to three years imprisonment.

offensive common law fiction which no longer represents the position of a wife in present day society and should no longer be applied.'[98]

It had been felt by many authors that it was not within the power of the courts to abolish the exemption. The Sexual Offences Act 1976 refers to rape as 'unlawful' intercourse, and it had been suggested that the inclusion of this word by the legislature must have been intended to embody the marital rape exemption into the statute.[99] This approach had itself been criticised[100] and found no favour with the House of Lords. Much confusion had surrounded the meaning of 'unlawful' as used in the 1976 Act. Recent Crown Court judgments had varied from that of *R.* v. *C.*[101] in which Simon Brown J. had held that Hale's position was no longer the law, to that of *R.* v. *J.*[102] in which Rougier J. had ruled that the use of the word 'unlawful' in the 1976 Act had: 'precluded any up-to-date declaration of the state of the common law on this subject. The matter has now become one of statutory interpretation and remains so.'[103]

The debate has now been settled by the House of Lords. Lord Keith of Kinkell held that : 'it was clearly unlawful to have sexual intercourse with any woman without her consent and. . . the use of the word [unlawful] in the subsection added nothing.'[104] In his view, the word should be treated as 'mere surplusage' in the enactment.

---

[98]See [1991] 2 All E.R. 257 and (1991) 141 New L.J. 383.

[99]See *R.* v. *Sharples* [1990] Crim. L.R. 198; *R.* v. *Chapman* [1959] 1 Q.B. 100; *R.* v. *Jones* [1973] Crim. L. R. 710. Note also the opinion of Lord Emslie in *Stallard* 1989 S.L.T., at p. 473, where he states that English law 'proceeds upon a definition of rape which was, in 1976, incorporated in statute, *viz.* sec. 1 of the Sexual Offences (Amendment) Act 1976. As we understand that definition it is not enough that a man has intercourse against a woman's will. The intercourse must also be unlawful. It is no doubt for that reason that any change or development of the law of England is likely to require the intervention of Parliament.'

[100]See Brooks 'Marital Consent in Rape,' [1989] Crim. L.R. 877.

[101][1991] 1 All E.R. 755.

[102][1991] 1 All E.R. 759.

[103][1991] 1 All E.R., at p. 764.

[104][1991] 4 All E.R. 481.

Prior to the *R. v. R.* case the Law Commission had published a Working Paper on marital rape, which recommended the statutory abolition of the husbands' immunity.[105]

It is suggested that the decision of the House of Lords should be reinforced by legislation. This would make it clear that the immunity was also abrogated in respect of certain related statutory offences, such as secs. 2, 3 and 4 of the Sexual Offences Act 1956. Without legislative reform, it will be left to the courts to decide, on a case by case basis, whether the word 'unlawful' in each of these sections is 'mere surplusage'. In conclusion, both Scots and English law, have now recognised that: 'a rapist remains a rapist subject to the criminal law, irrespective of his relationship with his victim.'[106]

Evidence of sexual history

Hume highlighted the unfairness of allowing evidence of a complainer's 'bad character' to be led at a rape trial:

> 'it is *robbery* to take a single penny from any one by force, be he a rich man or a beggar. It is *murder* where a man is killed, whether he be sane or insane, in health or on a deathbed, an honest citizen or a convicted felon. And just so it is rape, to know a woman carnally by force, *of what condition or quality soever she be.*'[107]

Recent legislation in Scotland has circumscribed the extent to which the complainer's sexual character can be made an issue at the trial. Section 141A of the Criminal Procedure (Scotland) Act 1975 now prohibits the leading of evidence or the asking of questions by the defence which suggest that the complainer is not of good character in relation to sexual matters, or that she is or has been a prostitute, or has associated with prostitutes. Also banned is any

---

[105]The Law Commission, Working Paper No. 116, '*Rape Within Marriage*', (1990), para. 4.2, p. 83.

[106]*R. v. R.*, [1991] 2 All E.R. 257 *per* Lord Chief Justice Lane at p. 266.

[107]Hume, i, 305, emphasis added.

evidence of her sexual experiences with persons, not forming part of the subject matter of the charge. However, sec. 141B allows the judge to admit such evidence in limited circumstances, such as where the evidence is relevant to a defence of incrimination, or is of sexual behaviour which allegedly occurred on the same occasion as that which is libelled in the indictment. Furthermore, the judge may allow the defence to lead such evidence where it would be 'contrary to the interests of justice to exclude it'.[108]

Under English law, sec. 2 of the Sexual Offences (Amendment) Act 1976 provides that evidence of a complainant's sexual history is restricted to any prior sexual dealings she has or may have had with the accused. Other evidence of the complainant's past sexual experiences can only be admitted with the leave of the court, and a judge should not permit such evidence unless he is satisfied that a refusal to do so would be 'unfair to the defendant'.[109]

It has been suggested that, in practice, English courts have too readily held that evidence of a complainant's sexual history ought to be admitted.[110] This may also be the case in Scotland. Certainly, the wording of the legislation leaves a wide discretion to both Scots and English judges, alike. It is submitted that the courts should be protective of a complainer's rights and allow such evidence to be admitted only in very exceptional circumstances.

Examination of reported cases suggests that, in practice, many rape trials seem to focus on the actions and intentions of the complainer, rather than on those of the accused. It is the latter who is on trial; it is his *mens rea* which is at issue. One would therefore expect any questions suggested by the bench for the jury to consider to concentrate on the intentions of the accused — did he, for instance, intend to have intercourse with the complainer without

---

[108]These sections were added by the Law Reform (Miscellaneous Provisions) (Scotland) Act 1985, sec. 36.

[109]Sec. 2(2) of the 1976 Act.

[110]See Temkin, *Rape and the Legal Process*, pp. 121-122.

her consent or against her will? Did he know that the woman was not a willing participant?

In any criminal trial the jury requires to examine closely the testimony of a complainer and to assess his or her credibility and reliability as a witness. Particularly close scrutiny of the complainer's evidence is bound to occur in a rape trial where the jury is often confronted with two conflicting versions of the incident. Be that as it may, the questions posed to the jury should reflect the issues which are central to the trial, hence should be framed in terms of the *mens rea* of the *accused*. In many rape cases the emphasis seems to have shifted, such that the jury is asked to decide on the 'willingness' or otherwise of the complainer, and how far she manifested to the accused her opposition to his conduct.

An extreme example is provided by the case of *R. v. Stapleton*.[111] The accused had intercourse with the complainant, having broken into her flat in the middle of the night. The case centered on the extent to which the complainant had made clear that she was not consenting to the intercourse. In fact, she testified that she was so terrified at discovering the accused, a stranger to her, standing by her bed in the middle of the night, that she had been unable to offer much resistance. The accused was acquitted. It is arguable that such a verdict might have been less likely had the jury been directed to concentrate more on the intentions of the *accused* — why had he broken into this woman's flat, and entered her bedroom? What possible reason did he have for believing that a woman, whom he had not met before, and into whose home he had trespassed, would be willing to engage in sexual intercourse with him?

In *R. v. Olugboja*[112] the Court of Appeal stated that the attention of the jury ought to have been focussed upon: 'the state of mind *of the victim* immediately before the act of sexual intercourse, having regard to all the relevant circumstances, and in particular the events

---

[111] Unreported, but see Toner, *The Facts of Rape*, Ch. 1.
[112] [1981] 3 All E.R. 443.

leading up to the act, and her reaction to them showing their impact on *her mind.*'[113]

Finally, in the recent Scottish case of *Quinn* v. *H.M. Advocate*[114] Lord Cameron of Lochbroom directed the jury as follows: 'At the end of the day, ladies and gentlemen, the question for you is, looking at the whole circumstances, are you satisfied beyond reasonable doubt that she was an unwilling party and that she made clear her unwillingness? If you take that view then you would be entitled to convict of rape.'[115]

It is clear that many complainers in rape trials find the experience of giving evidence to be a traumatic one. Studies suggest that in many cases the complainer feels as if *she* is the person on trial.[116] The bench could help to reduce such fears by ensuring that it frames its questions to the jury in an appropriate manner, that is, in a way which reflects the fact that it is the acts and intentions of the *accused* which are at issue.

Corroboration

In Scotland, the vast majority of crimes require to be proved by corroborated evidence, that is, there must be evidence from two sources which prove that the act was committed, and that the accused was the person who committed it:

> 'by the law of Scotland no person can be convicted of a crime or a statutory offence, except where the legislature otherwise directs, unless there is evidence of at least two witnesses implicating the person accused with the commission of the crime or offence with which he is charged.'[117]

---

[113][1981] 3 All E.R., at p. 449, emphasis added.

[114]1990 S.C.C.R., 254.

[115]1990 S.C.C.R., at p. 255.

[116]See Chambers and Millar, *Prosecuting Sexual Assaults*, (1986), Scottish Office Research Unit, at pp. 90-91.

[117]*Morton* v. *H.M. Advocate* 1938 S.L.T. 27, at p. 29.

Rape cases are notoriously difficult to prove; the complainer is often the only Crown witness who is able to speak to the incident., although her allegation of intercourse may be corroborated by forensic medical evidence.[118] Usually, however, the accused will admit to this, but contend that the complainer was a willing participant. In such circumstances, there may be little evidence to support the complainer's version of events. Corroboration of the complainer's account can be provided by evidence from third parties, testifying as to her state of distress following the incident. This form of corroboration is not confined to sexual offences,[119] but it has been crucial in several rape cases.[120]

Although there is no general corroboration requirement at common law in England it is sometimes required for proof of a particular statutory offence. Sections 2, 3 and 4 of the Sexual Offences Act 1956 specify that no one is to be convicted under the provisions of these sections without corroborated evidence. Furthermore, a jury requires to be reminded of the danger of relying on the testimony of a single witness where that witness is an accomplice, a child, or a complainant in a sexual offence.[121] In relation to the third category: 'Though corroboration of the evidence of the prosecutrix is not essential in law, it is, in practice always looked for and it is the established practice to warn the jury against the danger of acting upon her uncorroborated testimony.'[122]

It is competent for an English jury in a rape trial to convict the accused even if it can find no corroboration of the complainant's testimony, so long as it has been given a proper corroboration

---

[118]The advent of D.N.A. fingerprinting techniques means that in many cases the accused will be unable to deny that he had intercourse with the complainer.

[119]See, e.g., Horne v. H.M. Advocate 1991 S.C.C.R. 248.

[120]See Yates v. H.M. Advocate 1990 J.C. 378 (Note); 1977 S.L.T. (Notes) 42; Gracey v. H.M. Advocate 1987 S.L.T. 749 and compare the recent case of Moore v. H.M. Advocate 1990 J.C. 371; 1990 S.C.C.R. 586.

[121]See Archbold, Criminal Pleadings, Evidence and Practice, at para. 16-2.

[122]Archbold, op. cit., at para. 20-351.

warning.[123] However, it has been held that this warning must be given, even where the issue at the trial was one of identification. In *R.* v. *Birchall*[124] the accused did not dispute that the complainant had been the victim of a rape attack; his defence was that he had not been its perpetrator. Despite this, it was held on appeal that the jury ought to have been warned of the dangers of accepting the complainant's uncorroborated testimony that she had been raped.

The reasoning behind the corroboration warning in respect of all three types of witnesses was explained in the case of *Director of Public Prosecutions* v. *Hester*:[125] 'the danger sought to be obviated by the common law rule in each of these three categories of witness is that the story told by the witness may be inaccurate for reasons not applicable to other competent witnesses: whether the risk be of deliberate inaccuracy, as in the case of accomplices, or unintentional inaccuracy as in the case of children and some complainants in cases of sexual offences.'[126]

It is not easy to understand why the evidence of an adult witness in a sexual offence case should be considered more likely to be 'unintentionally inaccurate' than that of any other witness. One cannot help but suspect that the original reason behind the corroboration requirement for sexual offence complainants was a fear that they, like criminal accomplices, may be guilty of '*deliberate* inaccuracies'. Although there is no particular form of words which are required to be used by the judge it has been suggested that: 'the jury should be warned in plain language that it is dangerous to convict on the evidence of the complainant alone, because experience has shown that female complainants have told false stories for various reasons, and sometimes for no reason at all.'[127]

---

[123]See *R.* v. *Henry and Manning* (1969) 53 Cr. App. R. 150, CA.
[124](1986) 82 Cr. App. R. 208, CA.
[125](1973) Cr. App. R. 212, HL.
[126]At p. 244.
[127]Archbold, *op. cit.*, at para. 16-21.

Recent appeals such as those of the 'Guildford Four' and 'Birmingham Six' have caused the English law of evidence in criminal trials to be subjected to fierce criticism, particularly over its reliance on uncorroborated confessions. It may be that England will decide to follow Scottish procedure and require corroboration for most criminal charges. As the law is at present, however, it is invidious to require a 'corroboration warning' where a complainant is giving evidence in a sexual assault case, but not for other crimes. In the view of the present author, the complainant in a rape or other sexual assault case should be treated no differently from any other adult witness. It is submitted, therefore, that the English 'corroboration warning' should no longer be applied to such cases.

Conclusion

The recent changes to Scots and English law in relation to marital rape are to be welcomed, as finally dispensing with the fiction that a woman gives a blanket consent to sexual intercourse with her husband by the act of marriage. These developments notwithstanding, other aspects of the law could benefit from reform. For example, the presumption in English law that a boy under the age of fourteen cannot be found guilty of rape should be abolished, and the 'corroboration warning' should cease to be required in cases involving adult complainants of sexual assaults.

In Scotland, it is submitted that rape should be redefined to include any act of intercourse engaged in without the complainer's consent. Hence, intercourse with a sleeping woman, or one who is under the influence of alcohol, should be regarded as rape, even where the latter's intoxication is self-induced. Such behaviour on the part of a woman may be undesirable, or even foolhardy, in the circumstances, but this does not at all diminish the liability of the accused.

In both countries, it is submitted that the attention of the jury in a rape trials should on the actings and intentions of the accused, be directed to rather than on the complainer's mental state. The latter's position at the trial would be further ameliorated by a tightening up of the rules relating to sexual history evidence.

Perhaps the most important aspect which requires to be considered in both Scots and English law concerns the *mens rea* of the accused. It is submitted that the law ought to require an accused to have a reasonable belief in the woman's consent or willingness. The *Stallard* and *R. v. R.* cases suggest that the law now recognises that a woman is entitled to refuse to engage in sexual intercourse with a man, irrespective of any prior intimacy which may have existed between them. Each act of intercourse should therefore be treated separately, notwithstanding any relationship which exists between the parties. It should follow from this that a man ought not to engage in intercourse with a woman unless he is confident of her willing participation.*

---

* I would like to thank Colin Reid, University of Dundee, for his helpful comments on an earlier draft of this paper.

9

SOMETHING TO DECLARE: A DEFENCE OF THE DECLARATORY POWER OF THE HIGH COURT OF JUSTICIARY

Scott Crichton Styles

Unlike the English criminal courts,[1] the High Court of Justiciary explicitly retains the 'declaratory power' to create new crimes, a power which has been almost universally criticised by academics and legal theorists,[2] but has nevertheless been continually upheld. Part of the fascination with the issue stems from the fact that it is at once a very practical matter, and yet also one which raises fundamental questions as to the nature and scope of the criminal law and the proper function of the courts within the criminal justice system. The contention of this essay is that far from being 'a threadbare nineteenth century garment which the court could well afford to discard',[3] it is a serviceable robe fulfilling a useful and necessary function within our judicial system.

---

[1] See *Knuller (Publishing, Printing and Promotions) Ltd and Others* v. *D.P.P.* [1973] A.C. 434. This is the overt 'official' position; the reality appears to be rather different, but that is a subject for a separate argument.

[2] See W. A. Elliot, '*Nulla poena sine lege*', 1956 J.R. 22; Gane and Stoddart, *Casebook on Scottish Criminal Law* (2nd edn.), pp. 7-27; Gordon, 'Crimes Without Laws', 1966 J.R. 214; Gordon, *Criminal Law* (2nd edn.), paras. 1-15 to 1-43 (Gordon is not entirely condemnatory, see para. 1-16); I. A. Willock, 'The Declaratory Power: an Untenable Position,' 1989 *SCOLAG* 152. There has been at least one theorist who has given a qualified approval: Timothy H. Jones, 'Common Law and Criminal Law; the Scottish Example' [1990] Crim. L.R. 292.

[3] Willock, *op. cit.*, p. 154.

While many critics disparage the value of the declaratory power, few deny its existence. The argument is not, therefore, whether the declaratory power exists, but whether it ought to do so. One recent critic, Willock, has attempted to show that the declaratory power no longer exists, arguing that it has fallen into desuetude. This argument can be swiftly disposed of on the ground that the doctrine of desuetude has no pertinence in these circumstances: desuetude in the strict sense is a fate befalling only certain ancient pre-union Scots statutes,[4] with no application to either case law or the courts. Older cases may, of course, be overruled by more recent ones, and may also be subject to the maxim *cessante ratione cessat ipsa lex*,[5] which might loosely be described as desuetude. In considering the declaratory power, however, we are considering not a case, nor even, as Willock asserts, a 'practice', but an 'inherent power'[6] of the court, and court powers are not subject to desuetude. Willock cites no authority for his radical proposition that the powers of the Court of Justiciary, or indeed any other court, atrophy with time. His one analogical example, the 1966 Practice Statement issued by the House of Lords stating that it would no longer be bound by its prior decisions, fails to convince on three grounds: first, the Lords were concerned with a practice and not a power; secondly, the prior practice was changed not by the operation of desuetude but by a specific declaration of the court; thirdly, the very fact that the Lords were about to abolish a rule they had followed since 1898 showed that the 'inherent power' had subsisted despite explicit renunciation in several reported decisions.

Given that the declaratory power does still exist, we can consider the normative question of whether it ought to. The objections to the declaratory power are threefold: the law-maker argument; the

---

[4]Stair, I, i, 16.
[5]See *Beith's Trs.* v. *Beith* 1950 S.C. 66, at p. 70; *Douglas-Hamilton* v. *Duke and Duchess of Hamilton's Trustees* 1961 S.L.T. 305, at p. 309.
[6]Hume, i, 12.

law-form argument; and the law-morals (positivist) argument. The law-maker argument states that is is inappropriate for a court to make criminal law as this is, or should be, the sole prerogative of the legislature. the law-form argument states that a statute is a better type of law than a decision by a judge. (The law-maker and law-form arguments are two aspects of the alleged 'principle of legality' *nullum crimen sine lege*). The law-morals argument is the belief that the declaratory power fails adequately to distinguish law from morality.

Law-maker argument: The usurpation of the role of parliament

The first meaning of *nulla poena sine lege* is that Parliament is the only legitimate source of new criminal law and, therefore, for a court to make criminal law usurps the role which properly belongs only to Parliament. This argument is but one aspect of a long-standing debate on the validity and appropriateness of judicial legislation. Any discussion of the declaratory power must be seen in this wider context. Hostility to judicial legislation appears to have originated in the late eighteenth century. In Revolutionary France, and also in various radical movements in Britain, it was taken for granted that judges were part of the *ancien regime*. But in Britain, the main origins of this view can be traced back to Jeremy Bentham, who considered law-making to be the sole prerogative of the legislature.[8] In *Greenhuff*[9] it is notable that the sole dissenting

---

[7]For historical accounts of the origin of the maxim see Jerome Hall, *'Nulla poena sine lege'*, 47 *Yale Law Journal* 167; Jennings, *Law and the Constutition* (5th edn.), p. 51; Glasser in (1942) 24 J. Comp. Leg 29. The hostility of theorists to judge-made law could not develop earlier, at least in Europe, given the inadequacy of central government and the legislature.

[8]See an interesting discussion in G. Postema, *Bentham and the Common Law*, ch. 8.3.

[9](1838) 2 Swin. 236. Out of the six judges in *Greenhuff* four, Lord Justice-Clerk Boyle, Lords Meadowbank, Mackenzie and medwyn, were Tories, and two, Lords Moncrieff and Cockburn, were Whigs.

opinion was delivered by Lord Cockburn, who was a leading whig and was almost certainly influenced, either directly or indirectly, by the writings of Bentham.[10]

Despite, or perhaps because of, its radical origins, hostility to judicial legislation became widespread, particularly among the British judiciary. As a former Lord Chief Justice of England, Lord Goddard, commented regarding the ability of the Court of Appeal to create new crimes: 'it is surely now the province of the legislature and not of the judiciary to create new criminal offences'.

This tendency to deny the existence, or at least the legitimacy, of judicial legislation, was probably at its strongest in the earlier half of the present century but since then has rapidly lost ground. Today, acceptance of the existence, inevitably and even desirability of judicial legislation is widespread: 'It is idle to debate whether . . . . the court is making law . . . it depends on what you mean by "make" and "law" in this context'.[12]

Even if one accepts that judicial law-making is inevitable, there is still a widespread belief that something about judge-made law makes it unsuitable for the creation of criminal law in particular, and something about legislature-made law makes it distinctly fit for

---

[10]A view which according to Elliot has 'come into its own and to represent the modern outlook on this question;' *op. cit.* p. 32.

[11]*Newland* [1954] 1 QB 158, 167.

[12]*Stock* v. *Frank Jones (Tipton) Ltd* [1978] I.C.R. 347, *per* Lord Simon of Glaisdale at p. 353. Another judge, Lord Radcliffe, has also written: 'there was never a more sterile controversy than that upon the question of whether a judge makes law. How can he help it?' *Not in Feather Beds* and a standard modern jurisprudence text states: 'the general consensus is that, within certain narrow and clearly defined limits, new law is created by the judiciary. Attention centres primarily not on the fact of judicial legislation but rather on the ways in which this occurs . . .' Lloyd and Freeman, *An Introduction to Jurisprudence* p. 1129. For a contrasting view on the inevitability of judicial legislation see Roland Dworkin, *Taking Rights Seriously* and Rolf Sartorious, *Individual Conduct and Social Norms.* 13. *Director of Public Prosecutions* v. *Lynch* [1975] A.C. 653, *per* Lord Kilbrandon, at p. 700.

that purpose: 'It will not do to claim that judges have the duty — call it the privilege — of seeing to it that the common law expands and contracts to meet what the judges conceive to be the requirement of modern society. Modern society rightly prefers to exercise that function itself, and this it conveniently does through those who represent it in Parliament.'[13]

The modern essence of the law-maker argument is that the democratic nature of Parliament gives it a unique authority in the matter of the creation of criminal law. As Willock says: 'Members of parliament, collectively and individually, are to some degree accountable for their decisions. Judges are not.'[14] It seems, therefore, that the key justification for a parliamentary monopoly in criminal law-making is that M.P.s are accountable.

This accountability can take two forms. First, there is 'electoral accountability', *i.e.* as M.P.s are elected officials they may lose their seats if they displease the electorate. Secondly, there is 'responsiveness to public opinion', *i.e.* the notion that M.P.s listen to and take account of public opinion on criminal law matters. On closer examination, neither of these arguments is particularly strong.

At first sight it may seem obvious that an M.P. is electorally accountable for his actions in a way an appointed judge is not. It is clearly a fact that many M.P.s lose their seats at election time, whilst judges are almost irremoveable from office and only retire at 75. However, it is questionable just how much more accountable an individual M.P. is to the people than an unelected judge[15] with regard to their respective roles in the formation of the criminal law.

---

[13] *Director of Public Prosecutions* v. *Lynch* [1975] A.C. 653 *per* Lord Kilbrandon at p.700.

[14] 1989 *SCOLAG* at p. 153.

[15] It is of course perfectly possible to have an elected judiciary as commonly happens in the U.S. It is not inevitable that the legislature should be the only branch of the state appointed democratically.

First, it is widely recognised that the electorate votes for a party[16] rather than for an individual candidate;[17] secondly, when deciding which party to support, people tend to cast their vote on economic issues, not on matters of the criminal law;[18] thirdly, if democracy means 'majority rule', it is now widely recognised that the present British electoral system of first past the post fails to achieve this.[19] In the present British political system, the alleged accountability of M.P.s for their actions in developing, or failing to develop, the criminal law is at most symbolic, and in reality a myth.

If we consider the responsiveness to public opinion as an element of democratic accountability, in reality M.P.s are not particularly accountable; nor are judges as unresponsive as might be thought. Accountability implies that the official in question be identified for his actions. Unfortunately, this is very difficult to apply to M.P.s because of the way they are bound by the party whip on the vast majority of issues, and also on account of the fact that each M.P. holds only one vote out of 650; it is difficult to hold an individual accountable for his or her actions in the midst of the parliamentary crowd. As a consequence of these two factors very few citizens either

---

[16]Nor is the selection of party candidates very democratic, residing as it does in the hand of a tiny number of party activists. It is estimated that less than 2 per cent of the electorate even belong to a political party.

[17]And this is appropriate given the very limited freedom of action enjoyed by M.P.s in the Commons under our present system of strict party whips.

[18]This is but one aspect of the more general problem faced by any representative form of democracy, *viz.* that whilst the voters may be concerned about many issues, they have only one vote to cast and that only every four years or so.

[19]For example in the 1987 general election the first past the post system resulted in the party with 42.2 per cent of vote getting 376 parliamentary seats. The complete figures are:

Party	% of votes cast	No. of Seats	% of seats
Conservative	42.2	376	57.8
Labour	30.8	229	35.2
Alliance	22.6	22	3.4
Other	23.0	23	3.5

(Source, A. H. Birch, *The British System of Government*, 8th edn. p. 85.)

know or care how their M.P. voted on any given issue, including the criminal law. In contrast, judges sit in court either alone or in benches of three to five, and therefore cannot hide behind a party whip nor evade their individual responsibility for a decision. If Parliament makes a criminal law decision which is unpopular with the people, this will generally be communicated through opinion polls, the press and constituency mail. Only the last of these three methods does not apply to judges. In practice, adverse press criticism is the most important form of accountability to which M.P.s are subject and, for the reasons outlined above, judges are even more exposed to this than M.P.s. If a democratic decision is one which is in accord with public opinion, then, whilst judges may sometimes ignore this, so, likewise, will M.P.s.[20]

When we turn to consideration of the actual use of the declaratory power it can be argued that the Justiciary Court has satisfied the test of responsiveness to public opinion. In every case[21] where the declaratory power has been used it has outlawed behaviour which the public probably thought was already illegal or ought to be so. For example, in the case of *Khaliq*, public support for the court's decision was overwhelming.[22] If democracy means actions in accord with the will of the people, then the way the declaratory power has been exercised would appear to satisfy that criterion. Where courts are exercising their powers in accordance with the will of the people that is just as democratic a decision as one taken

---

[20]For example the majority of the British population have consistently indicated that they favour a return of the death penalty but M.P.s have consistently ignored this.

[21]*Charles Sweenie* (1858) 3 Irv. 109; *Kerr* v. *Hill* 1936 J.C. 71; *Strathern* v. *Seaforth* 1926 J.C. 100; *H.M. Advocate* v. *Martin and Others* 1956 J.C. 1; *Khaliq* v. *H.M. Advocate* 1984 J.C. 23; 1984 S.L.T. 137; 1983 S.C.C.R. 483.

[22]As doubtless, did most of the public in England who probably were surprised and disappointed that the English courts seemed unable to deal with the menace of selling glue sniffing kits to children, England having to wait until Parliament could find the time to pass an appropriate act.

by Parliament. This is not to argue that the Justiciary Court is always, or even often, responsive to public opinion, but merely to describe the way the declaratory power has operated in Scotland. Lord Hailsham once described the modern political system as an 'elected dictatorship'. Perhaps, in a sense, we might equally describe the exercise of the declaratory power by the Justiciary Court as an 'unelected democracy'.

Although the essence of the argument against judicial legislation is the accountability of Parliament, as opposed to the courts, there are two subsidiary law-maker arguments which must be considered: the argument from silence, and the progress argument.

Argument from silence

It is commonly said that if Parliament has not seen fit to make an act illegal, then that is to be taken as tacit parliamentary approval of the behaviour in question: 'It might well be that the legislator has deliberately refrained from penalising certain types of conduct while bringing others within the scope of the criminal law.'[23]

This is an extremely dubious proposition given that the real reason Parliament fails to declare certain harmful behaviour criminal tends to be out of ignorance or lack of time. Furthermore, the argument from silence cuts both ways, with regard both to the existence of the declaratory power and the way it has been exercised.

---

[23]Gane and Stoddard, *Caseboook of Criminal Law* (2nd edn.) p. 9. This was also, for example, the opinion of the 1879 Royal Commission on a draft criminal code for England: 'In bygone ages, when legislation was scanty and rare, the powers [to create new crimes] referred to may have been useful and even necessary; but that is not the case at the present day. Parliament is regular in its sittings and active in its labours; and if the protection of society requires the enactment of additional penal laws, Parliament will soon supply them. If Parliament is not disposed to provide punishments for acts which are upon any ground objectionable or dangerous, the presumption is that they belong to that class of misconduct against which the moral feeling and good sense of the community are best protection' quoted in Glanville Williams, *Crimninal law* (2nd edn.), pp. 595-596.

The fact that Parliament has failed to pass an act stripping the Justiciary Court of the declaratory power must be taken as an indication that Parliament is content to allow that jurisdiction to continue. Likewise, the failure of Parliament, subsequent to *Greenhuff*, to decriminalise any behaviour proscribed by the exercise of the declaratory power, must be deemed to indicate tacit parliamentary approval of the court's decision. Where Parliament has disapproved of the decision of the court it has passed appropriate statutes legalising the behaviour in question. Thus the use of the declaratory power by the court in *James Taylor*,[23a] to outlaw 'combinations of workmen' was reversed by statute in 1825.[24]

The progress argument

The progress argument is one which was strongly put by Lord Cockburn in the first two paragraphs of his opinion in *Greenhuff*, and is the belief that judicial law-making is 'appropriate, if at all, to a formative stage in criminal law, which in Scotland is long past'.[25] This is truly a 'whig version' of history (the notion that the history of Britain is one of progress through time) and it has possibly enjoyed even wider popularity than the argument from silence.[26] There is no need for any explicit refutation of the progress argument, because to have any substance it must rest on some premise other than the mere passage of time, *i.e.* there must be something relevantly different about law-making today from law-making in 1838. Suffice to say that the increased frequency with which Parliament meets in the late twentieth century as opposed to the

---

[23a] (1808) Burnett App. 100

[24] 6 Geo. 4, c. 129, sec. 4.

[25] Willock, p. 153.

[26] 'It is the writer's personal opinion that the declaratory power as described by Hume, though indespensible to the development of the law at a certain stage, should not, even in exceptional circumstances, be invoked today,' T. B. Smith, *A Short Commentary on the Law of Scotland*, p. 125; see also Elliot, *op. cit.*, p. 27.

early nineteenth century does not, of itself, provide much substance for the belief that Parliament is well equipped for the task of dealing with the development of new crimes. This is particularly the case for Scotland, a country whose legislature is composed of members with little interest in Scottish matters of any sort.[27] If the Court of Justiciary lacked the declaratory power then the possibility that some harmful and widely condemned behaviour might arise, which Parliament was slow to check, is all too real.

The law-form argument

The second meaning of *nullum crimen sine lege* is the law-form argument which reasons that a statute is a better legal vehicle than a judicial decision; that there is something in the nature of a statute which makes it an inherently better way of expounding the law, especially criminal law, than the written opinion of a judge. The law-form argument has tended to be discussed in the same context as the law-maker argument, but the two are conceptually quite distinct. There is nothing inherently democratic or even 'parliamentary' about legislation: a monarch, dictator or committee can have the power to issue statutes (using the broad meaning of the term). The law-form argument is rather that, even without the existence of a democratic legislature, legislation is superior to case-law as a form of criminal law, in two vital essentials: it is clear, more certain, and fairer because it is non-retroactive. We will look at each of these arguments in turn.

The apparent certainty of statutes

Perhaps the most appealing meaning of the principle of legality is the idea that the criminal law should be clear and that illegal acts should be precisely defined. As Gordon says: 'each crime should be

---

[27]Elliot, p. 29, observed that one of the explicit reasons why the court chose to exercise the declaratory power was that 'If their Lordships could not innovate upon the common law a new statute would probably require to be passed with all the delays notoriously attendant upon purely Scottish legislation'.

capable of fairly precise definition so that its application to any particular set of facts can be clearly seen. A man contemplating a course of action is entitled to notice that it is criminal; otherwise it is unfair to punish him for having broken the law.'[28]

Whilst the 'certainty principle' does not automatically entail a statute rather than a precedent, it has also been commonly held that a statute is inherently a more precise document than a judicial opinion: 'the rules which Parliament enacts., though never entirely free from doubt, are made on purpose *with as much clarity as can be achieved,* while those made by judges have to be deduced from judgments drawn up to justify a single decision.'[29]

Unfortunately, however, there is nothing inherently clearer about a statute than a precedent. One obvious point is that much will depend on the actual wording chosen by the draftsmen or judge in question: there are many clear opinions and equally many, if not more, opaque statutes,[30] but the fundamental point is that certainty can never be achieved: ambiguity is an inevitable part of the operation of any legal system.

The idea that all law, statute and precedent, is inherently ambiguous, is most closely associated in modern academic circles with the writings of H. L. A. Hart,[31] but the basic insight is probably as old as the law itself, and it has always been clear, to practising lawyers at least on one level, that no statute can ever be free from ambiguity. For example, Lord Denning, arguably the least philo-sophical of judges, wrote: 'The truth is that the law is uncertain. It does not cover all the situations that may arise. Time and again

---

[28] *Criminal Law,* p. 24.

[29] Willock, p. 153, my italics.

[30] It cannot be denied that there is much that is unsatisfactory in the wording of modern U.K. statutes, see M. Zander, *The Law Making Process,* ch. 1 for general discussion of the problem of the wording of modern statutes.

[31] See especially, *The Concept of Law,* ch. 8.

practitioners are faced with new situations, where the decision may go either way.'[32]

Unfortunately this fact has not been as clear to certain theorists as to practitioners, and hence there has from time to time been a demand for clear and certain statutes in preference to the allegedly less clear common law. The most extreme exponent of the belief that statutes could be made clear and certain in their application was probably Bentham: 'A law is complete [that is completely expressed] when the act it prohibits . . . and the punishment for it . . . are so expressed as that, granting the act so described to have been done, no supposition can be framed, on which, according to the Will of the Legislator, the punishment in question shall not take place.'[33]

It is interesting to contrast this idealism with the more realistic approach found in Hume: 'all statutes are liable to be partial and defective in their description of new offences; and thus the transgressor finds the means of eluding the sanction, and the law itself fall into contempt.'[34]

The most lucid explanation for this uncertainty was given by Hart in a well-known passage, which is worth quoting at length: 'Whichever device, precedent or legislation, is chosen for the communication of standards of behaviour, these, however smoothly they work over the great mass of ordinary cases, will, at some point where their application is in question, prove indeterminate; they will have what has been termed an *open texture*. So far we have presented this, in the case of legislation, as a general feature of human language; uncertainty at the borderline is the price to be paid for the use of general classifying terms in any form of

---

[32] *The Reform of Equity* in C. J. Hanson (ed.) *Law, Reform and Law-making* quoted in Zander, at p. 312.

[33] UC lxx(a), 8, quoted in Postema, p. 428. For discussion of Bentham's views generally see Postema, ch. 12.

[34] *Commentaries*, i, 12.

communication concerning matters of fact. Natural languages like English are when so used irreducibly open-textured. It is, however, important to appreciate why, apart from this dependence on language as it actually is, with its characteristics of open-texture, we should not cherish, even as an ideal, the conception of a rule so detailed that the question whether it is applied or not to a particular case was always settled in advance, and never involved, at the point of actual application, a fresh choice between open alternatives. Put shortly, the reason is that we are men, not gods. It is a feature of the human predicament (and so of the legislative one) that we labour under two connected handicaps whenever we seek to regulate, unambiguously and in advance, some sphere of conduct by means of general standards to be used without further official direction on particular occasions. The first handicap is our relative ignorance of fact: the second is our relative indeterminacy of aim.'[35]

The open-texturedness of the criminal common law was explicitly recognised by Lord Justice-General Emslie in *Khaliq:* 'It would be a mistake to imagine that the criminal common law of Scotland countenances any precise and exact categorisation of the forms of conduct which amount to crime.'[36]

Once the open-textured nature of law is accepted it can be seen that legislation, contrary to what Bentham thought, has no intrinsic advantage over judicial decision as a law-form. Both statute and decision suffer from an irreducible amount of uncertainty as to their meaning.

Retrospectivity

Even if one accepts that legislation is inherently no more precise than precedent, one might still hold that it is a more apt criminal law-form because, unlike precedent, it is prospective in effect. The

---

[35] *The Concept of Law,* pp. 124-125.
[36] *Khaliq* 1984 J.C., at p. 31, citing with approval Lord Justice-General Clyde in *McLaughlan* v. *Boyd* 1934 J.C. 19, at p. 22.

declaratory power in particular is held to be unacceptable because it is so clearly violates the presumption against the retrospective effect of criminal law. At first sight the non-retrospectivity principle seems very convincing. What could be more unfair than to punish people for behaviour which was not criminal when it was committed? Retrospectivity in criminal law is often seen as one of the grossest of procedural sins and has been condemned by the European Convention on Human Rights, art. 7 (1): 'No-one shall be held guilty of any criminal offence on account of any act or omission which did not constitute a criminal offence under national or international law at the time it was committed. Nor shall a heavier penalty be imposed than the one that was applicable at the time the criminal offence was committed.'[37]

Willock,[38] following Gane and Stoddart, argues that the declaratory power violates the European Convention but fails to consider the effect of art. 7 (2), which specifically preserves the retrospective operation of the criminal law provided it is in accordance with general principles: 'This article shall not prejudice the trial and punishment of any person for any act or omission which, at the time it was committed, was criminal according to the general principles of law recognised by civilised nations.'

A classic exposition of the retrospective argument was given by the leading English authority on criminal law, Glanville Williams: 'The citizen must be able to ascertain beforehand how he stands with regard to the criminal law; otherwise to punish him for breach of that law is purposeless cruelty.'[39]

---

[37] See also the Universal Declaration of Human Rights 1948, art. 11(2): 'No-one shall be held guilty of any penal offence on account of any act or omission which did not constitute a penal offence at the time when it was committed. Nor shall a heavier penalty be imposed than the one that was applicable at the time the penal offence was committed.'
[38] In 1957 *SCOLAG* at p. 154.
[39] *Criminal Law*, p. 575.

224

The answer to these criticisms is simply to acknowledge that any exercise of judicial power is retrospective but to deny that this is necessarily unfair. All case law is retrospective because one only knows for certain that one has committed a criminal offence when the court pronounces its verdict; up until that point the issue remains open.[40] This is a fact recognised by the common law doctrine that all precedents operate retrospectively, and one of which Bentham, for one, was well aware. Indeed, Bentham thought that this feature of case-law was yet another reason why statute should be the only valid law-form.[41] Common-law was, in his view, fit only for animals. Yet, once this inherent retrospectivity is acknowledged, it can be seen that it cannot be used as an objection to the declaratory power *per se*; it also highlights the lack of importance in the distinction which has been drawn, from the time of *Greenhuff* onward,[42] between 'extreme' and 'moderate' uses of the declaratory power,[43] or between the declaratory power generally and other types of judicial decision. The jurists have tended to argue that, while the extreme form of the declaratory power is completely indefensible, moderate use may be less objectionable (although some have condemned its exercise in any form). Once the inherent ambiguity and retrospectivity of all judicial decision-making is

---

[40]That all judicial decisions are retrospective is put well by Hall: 'In a sense, to be sure, all case law — and that includes jurisprudence interpretative of statutes or codes — operates retrospectively. For only fictitiously can it be said that all acts found to be criminal upon trial were criminal when committed. The fact is that it is the subsequent decision which reaches back into time and places the authoritative stamp of criminality upon the prior conduct:' *Nulla Poena Sine Lege*, p. 171.

[41]'When your dog does anything you want to break him of, you wait till he does it and then beat him for it': Browning, *Works of Jeremy Bentham*, v. 235 (quoted in Dinwiddy, p. 57).

[42]See Lord Cockburn's opinion in *Greenhuff*, also T. B. Smith *op. cit.*, pp. 126-129; Elliot's entire article and especially pp. 32-36; also Willock's entire article.

[43]The extreme form of the declaratory power is the overt creation of new crimes, the moderate form is the extension of old crimes to novel behaviour.

acknowledged, however, it can be seen that the distinction between moderate and extreme forms of the declaratory power, or between the declaratory power and other types of judicial decisions, is more apparent than real.

The only difference between the extreme use of the declaratory power to create new crimes and its moderate use, to cover new ways of committing old crimes, is that of the method chosen to justify the reasoning of the court: both arise out of the inherently open-textured nature of law. Likewise, moderate use of the power shades imperceptibly into the 'reasoning by analogy' which is so fundamental a conceptual tool for any judge in making his decisions.

An example of what one might call 'covert' operation of the declaratory power is the recent series of cases criminalising marital rape.[44] Because the marital rape issue has always been posed in terms of 'removing an exemption' the courts did not acknowledge that what they were in fact doing was creating a new crime or, more precisely, a new way of committing an old crime: *viz.* a husband became liable to punishment for having intercourse with his wife against her will. This is a clear, and perfectly correct, use of the declaratory power even although it has not generally been acknowledged as such.

The declaratory power is simply an open admission of something the courts do covertly every day of their existence: apply the law retrospectively. The open-textured nature of language and our ignorance of fact and purpose make this inevitable. Whether a given set of circumstances will come under a prior statute or precedent is simply a matter of degree, and there is always room for doubt. In this context the principle of legality can be seen as unworkable. There is therefore no particular reason for condemning the declaratory power, as opposed to any other exercise of

---

[44] *H.M. Advocate* v. *Duffy* 1983 S.L.T. 7, 1982 S.C.C.R. 182; *H.M. Advocate* v. *Paxton* 1984 J.C. 105, 1985 S.L.T. 96, 1984 S.C.C.R. 311; *Stallard* v. *H.M. Advocate* 1989 S.C.C.R. 248.

judicial power, for conflicting with the principle of legality. For although the declarctory power is incompatible with *nullum crimen*, this is a defect shared by all case law. As all judge-made law suffers from the defect of retrospectivity, we must choose between it and pure legislative law as advocated by Bentham. We know the latter is a factual impossibility and thus that the principle of legality must be wrong; we are compelled to choose case law because statue law cannot survive without courts to enforce it.

It can also be noted that, in common law jurisdictions at least, there has been very little concern with prior notification of the law to the public, unlike *nullum crimen, ignorantia juris non excusat* is undoubtedly a fundamental principle of our legal system, but if it is lack of forewarning that makes the enforcement of the criminal law unfair then ignorance, for whatever reason, should always be a complete defence. Our system does not accept ignorance as an excuse, indeed it is difficult to see how it could do given the vast amount of law produced by Parliament and the courts at present.

Positivist argument

Perhaps the most fundamental of the objections against the use of the declaratory power is that its use entails a confusion of law with morality. Ever since the early positivists, Hume, Bentham and Austin, most jurists have been at pains to distinguish law from morality and also to hold that we cannot derive the former from the later. It cannot be denied that the opinions of several of the judges in *Greenhuff* are heavily influenced by natural law. Lord Meadowbank, for example, talks of 'The inherent power of the court to repress whatever are, by the law of God, and the laws of morality, *mala in se.*'

This is an approach which has been heavily criticised: 'Some (judges) considered the test of relevancy to be whether the acts libelled offended against the laws of God or morality, others

---

[45]See below, also Gordon, *Criminal Law*, para. 1-16.

whether they were *mala in se. But these are not really legal tests.*'[46]

Elliot clearly believes that the courts should restrict themselves to the application of 'legal tests'. He does not make clear what principles are 'legal' ones, but presumably he is working with some positivistic conception of law as being contained solely in statutes and precedents. The courts themselves have been heavily influenced by the positivist separation between law and morals. In *Khaliq*, for example, the trial judge Lord Avonside said: 'I do not sit as a judge of morals and my task is confined to a judgment in law, and that alone, on the validity of the indictment before me.'[47]

The division of legal tests from moral tests is too simplistic and unworkable. First, statutes and precedents themselves contain explicit and implicit moral concepts: harm, public interest, morals, *etc.* Secondly, as we have seen, judicial legislation is an inevitability, and just like legislators judges base their decisions on a variety of factors. In coming to their decisions judges will inevitably have to consider a variety of factors other than purely legal concepts. The notion that judges ought, or even can, work solely with legal concepts belongs to an earlier age. It is now widely recognised that judges quite naturally will, to some extent, reflect the general values of their time, age, class, temperament, *etc.* This is partially because of the inevitable open-texture of the law already discussed, and partially because legal concepts alone will seldom, if ever, be enough to guide a court in coming to a decision: the facts, and the attitude of the court towards those facts, will always be relevant. Law is not a self-contained logical system but a decision procedure for the conduct of our lives in society. This is especially true in the case of the criminal law, where the moral notion of 'wrongful' and the legal notion of 'criminal' behaviour are so intimately intertwined. It is difficult to see how society could survive without holding certain

---

[46]Elliot, 1965 J.R. 22 at 32.
[47]1984 J.C. 24, at p. 25.

behaviour to be inherently wrongful, and also officially proscribed as criminal; even so staunch a positivist as Hart recognises a 'minimum content of natural law'.[48] Given that the Court of Justiciary does indeed have the power to define or refine crimes, the only real issue for debate is what criteria the court should employ when exercising that function. It is submitted that the correct test of whether or not behaviour is criminal should be the twin stage test laid down by Lord Medwyn in *Greenhuff*: 'when any new offence, which is itself a wrong, and is hurtful to the persons and properties of others . . . though altogether unknown in former times, it will become through the force of our common law, the object of punishment'.[49]

Lord Mackenzie applies a similar test in slightly different language; he talks of acts being 'grossly immoral and mischievous' and this formulation found favour in subsequent cases, like the opinion of Lord Justice-Clerk Inglis in *Balantyne*.[50] Lord Medwyn's wording is to be preferred because of the less emotive meaning of 'wrongful' as compared to 'immoral' (a term which for many people refer primarily to the condemnation of sexual mores) and because the meaning of 'mischief' has changed since the nineteenth century and now refers to trial behaviour. Under Lord Medwyn's criteria, the mere wrongfulness of an act is not of itself enough to justify its being criminalised; it must also be harmful. It may be objected that wrong and harm are vague concepts, but, whilst this must be admitted, it is difficult to see how society could function without them. For present purposes an act is 'wrong' or 'immoral' if it is condemned by the community, whilst an act is harmful if it

---

[48] *Concept of Law*, pp. 189-195.

[49] *Greenhuff* (1838) 2 Swin., at p. 270. Lord Medwyn's formulation is similar to that laid down by Alison: 'by the common law every new crime, as it successively becomes the objects of punishment, provided it be in itself wrong, and hurtful to the person or property of others,' *Criminal Law*, i. 624.

[50] (1857) 3 Irv. 352, at p. 359.

violates the interests of others or of oneself.[51] By insisting on the wrongness[52] of the act test, we ensure that the court does apply its powers to situations where there is no public support for its actions, and by insisting on the harm test we can rule out the application of the declaratory power to cases of alleged sexual immorality where, although there may be widespread public condemnation, no harm is committed.

It is submitted that, provided the courts restrict themselves to exercising the declaratory power in cases which fall within both these categories, then the declaratory power will continue to play a useful and important part in our legal system. However, far from being a defect, it appears to me to be a virtue of the Scots law that it continues to give morality a central place in the criminal law.

Conclusion

The distinguishing feature of the declaratory power as exercised in Scotland, as opposed to the other judicial techniques employed in Scotland and elsewhere, lies mainly in its open acknowledgment of the realities of judicial decision-making. The alleged defects of the declaratory power — its usurpation of parliament's function; its uncertain operation and retrospective effect, and its reliance on non-legal reasoning — are the features of any exercise of the judicial function. Whether or not we continue to employ the explicit concept of the declaratory power, judicial decision-making will continue to manifest these features because they are an inevitable

---

[51]The law has always adopted a paternalistic rather than a *laissez fair* approach to consensual harm, see for example *H.M. Advocate* v. *Rutherford* 1947 J.C. 1; *Smart* v. *H.M. Advocate* 1975 J.C. 30; 1975 S.L.T. 65.

[52]As one commentator has observed 'when one is talking about immorality as a *necessary* condition for invocation of the criminal sanction, the inquiry should simply be whether there exists any significant body of dissent from the proposition that the conduct in question is criminal? . . . the criminal sanction should ordinarily be limited to conduct that is viewed, without significant social dissent as immoral.' H. Packer, *The Limits of the Criminal Sanction* (1968), pp. 263-264.

part of the operation of any modern judicial system. That courts and jurists have over the past 200 years tried so vehemently to play down these aspects of judge-made law does not make them any less real. In fact, the declaratory power is to be commended for its honesty and openness and its frank admission of the creative power of the courts, rather than such judicial fictions as that judges only find the law; they do not make it. This frankness can only help to promote the sense of accountability for their decisions which it is essential that judges should feel in a democracy.

10

THE WAR CRIMES ACT 1991[1]

Mark R. Poustie and Michael G. J. Upton

'My objection to the bill is a simple one. The bill damages a great institution and that institution is the rule of law in Britain.'[2]

Introduction

In the Parliamentary session of 1989-1990 the government introduced into Parliament 'a bill to confer jurisdiction on the United Kingdom courts in respect of certain grave violations of the laws and customs of war committed in German-held territory during the Second World War'.[3] The measure attracted a considerable degree of controversy, and finally achieved the distinction of being the first government bill to be rejected twice by the House of Lords since the Parliament Act 1949. The Act received the royal assent on 9th May 1991 having been enacted under the procedures of the Parliament Acts.

The Act went so far as to raise a constitutional issue because it is the most extraordinary and contentious piece of criminal legislation to have been brought forward in many years. Whatever its merits, it may be welcomed for the opportunity it provides to reconsider a number of basic concepts in our criminal law which it affects.

---

[1]The authors would like to thank Lord Campbell of Alloway Q.C. for his help in advising them of parliamentary developments and Professor Robert Black, Q.C., for his helpful comments on a draft of this paper. However, the authors alone are responsible for any errors it contains.

[2]Lord Goodman, 519 H.L. Deb. (June 4, 1990), col. 1098.

[3]War Crimes Act 1991, preamble.

The Act's origins lie in the British government's undertaking during the Second World War to prosecute Nazi war criminals when the war ended. In pursuance of that undertaking, Britain assisted in the work of the United Nations War Crimes Commission and the International Military Tribunal at Nuremburg, as well as conducting trials in the British zone of Germany. However, in 1948 a decision was taken, of which Parliament was informed at the time, to wind up the investigations and to prosecute no further in Germany, notwithstanding that the greater number of suspects remained at large, and to transfer responsibility for prosecutions in the British occupied zone to the Federal Republic of Germany.

During those same years, some 120,000 eastern European refugees were permitted to settle in Britain. The immigrants were screened to exclude known war criminals, but this process was flawed by a lack of information about those who had offended in areas subsequently to the east of the Iron Curtain. It was not until the thawing of the Cold War in the 1980s that substantial evidence came to light which suggested that there were former war criminals resident in this country. In October 1986, the Simon Wiesenthal Centre passed to the government a list of alleged Nazi offenders thought to be in the United Kingdom; this was followed by a further list obtained from the Soviet Embassy by Scottish Television. As a result, the Home Secretary took up the matter. In February 1988 the government commissioned two former senior prosecutors[4] to report on the allegations and 'to consider in the light of the likely probative value in court proceedings in the U.K. of the relevant documentary material and of the evidence of potential witnesses, whether the law of the United Kingdom should be amended in order to make it possible to prosecute for war crimes'.[5]

---

[4]William Chalmers, Esq., C.B., M.C., former Crown Agent in Scotland and Sir Thomas Hetherington, K.C.B., C.B.E., T.D., Q.C., former Director of Public Prosecutions in England.

[5] *War Crimes* Cm. 744 (1989), p. ii, hereinafter cited as 'the report'.

Their report was published in July 1989. Its authors had considered the cases of 301 persons, the details of whom were not published but were presented to the Home Secretary. They concluded that in three cases consideration should be given to prosecuting, and that 78 other cases should be investigated further. They recommended that legislation be passed to give the courts jurisdiction over the offences in question; furthermore, that the law of evidence be changed; in particular 'to allow a witness outside the United Kingdom to give evidence through a live television link...[as] the Criminal Justice Act 1988 provides for English courts and that recorded statements of persons now dead should be admissible as evidence'. In addition, recommendations were made to render admissible '(i) video recordings of evidence taken abroad by letters of request' and '(ii) documents held in archives if authenticated by the archivist,' and that consideration be given to altering procedure for taking evidence on commission.[6]

Many arguments were led in favour of the reform, but the overriding one was that the Act would allow the prosecution of anyone resident in our country who took an active part in the Nazi atrocities; in crimes 'of a magnitude and horror which it is hard to comprehend ... premeditated acts of cold-blooded mass murder which were perpetrated upon defenceless civilians'.[7] There can be little disagreement with a presumption in favour of legislation which allows for the prosecution of crimes which 'cry out for punishment'.[8]

What then are the objections? Very many were levelled, but only those on which lawyers can claim some special authority will be discussed here. There are criticisms of the Act itself, that it involves firstly, extraterritorial jurisdiction; secondly, retrospection; and,

---

[6]Report, paras. 9.31-9.42.

[7]Earl Ferrers 513 H.L. Deb. (December 4, 1989), col. 604.

[8]Lord Irvine of Lairg, 519 H.L. Deb. (June 4, 1990), col. 1088; *cf.* Mr Roy Hattersley, 163 H.C. Deb. (December 12, 1989), col. 892.

thirdly, selectivity. These are discussed in the following part of this paper. Furthermore there are concerns about procedural and evidential aspects of prosecutions which may be taken under the Act to which the third part of this paper is addressed.

The Act

The heart of the Act is in section 1, which provides, *inter alia*:

'1. - (1) Subject to the provisions of the section, proceedings for murder, manslaughter or culpable homicide may be brought against a person in the United Kingdom irrespective of his nationality at the time of the alleged offence if that offence —

(a) was committed during the period beginning with 1st September 1939 and ending with 5th June 1945 in a place which at the time was part of Germany or under German occupation; and

(b) constituted a violation of the laws and customs of war.

(2) No proceedings shall by virtue of this section be brought against any person unless he was on 8th March 1990,[9] or has subsequently become, a British citizen or resident in the United Kingdom, the Isle of Man or any of the Channel Islands'.

Extraterritoriality

The principle of criminal jurisdiction in Scotland is that of *forum delicti*: jurisdiction is restricted to crimes committed in Scotland except where statute provides otherwise.[10] The War Crimes Act

---

[9]The date of the Bill's introduction into Parliament.

[10]Renton and Brown *Criminal Procedure* (5th edn., Edinburgh, 1983), para. 1-07; Captain Bruce's Case, (Privy Council, 29th March 1622); Alison *Practice of the Criminal Law* (Edinburgh, 1823), pp. 70-83; Anderson *The Criminal Law of Scotland* (Edinburgh, 1904), p. 261ff.; Macdonald *A Practical Treatise on the Criminal Law of Scotland* (5th edn., Edinburgh, 1948), p. 190; Report, paras. 6.25, 6.29-6.32. This contrasts most obviously with the continental principle of the *forum originis*, or jurisdiction according to nationality; *cf.* Gordon *The Criminal Law of Scotland* (2nd edn., Edinburgh, 1978), para. 3-39.

provides otherwise by granting jurisdiction over offences committed in Germany and German-occupied territory. However, it is only one of a number of statutory exceptions to the rule.[11] The subject is characterised by piecemeal legislation, and at least six different guiding principles can be gleaned from the statutory exceptions:[12]

(1) jurisdiction founded on a recognition of the unity of the United Kingdom;[13]

(2) jurisdiction founded on the notional extension of British territory, either by assuming jurisdiction over areas of the surrounding seas, or by treating British ships and aircraft as if they were parts of Scotland;[14]

(3) jurisdiction founded on the fact of crimes committed abroad taking effect in Scotland;[15]

(4) jurisdiction founded on the need to protect British citizens and others overseas in circumstances where there might otherwise be a

---

[11] *Cf.* Renton and Brown, *op. cit.*, paras. 1-08-1-20.

[12] Although some measures are justified by more than one of these principles.

[13] *E.g.*, the law on theft in the Criminal Procedure (Scotland) Act 1975, secs. 7 and 292.

[14] *E.g.* the Herring Fishery (Scotland) Act 1889 (*cf. Mortensen* v. *Peters* (1906) 8 F. (J.) 93); the Wireless Telegraphy Act 1949; the Merchant Shipping Acts 1894 to 1988 (*cf.* Anderson, *op. cit.*, p. 218); and the Civil Aviation Act 1982.

[15] In some cases, this may be regarded as hardly an exception, as 'with one, who standing on the English side of the border, discharges a gun at a man on the Scotch side; . . . no reasonable doubt can be entertained of the competence of trying him in this country, where his crime has taken its destined effect', Alison, *op. cit.*, p. 75; cf. Mackenzie, *Criminal Law* (Edinburgh, 1699), ii, 2, p. 179; Macdonald, *op. cit.*, p. 191; Gordon, *op. cit.*, para. 3-40. Further extensions of this idea may be seen in the Representation of the People Act 1983, sec. 178(1); the Official Secrets Act 1911, sec. 10(1), and in the common law jurisdiction over treason committed abroad; Macdonald, *op. cit.*, p. 190; Alison, *op. cit.*, pp. 70-71; *cf.* supplying goods to the enemy; Macdonald, *op. cit.*, pp. 191-192; *cf.* also the Nuclear Material (Offences) Act 1983.

legal vacuum in which no state had jurisdiction;[16]

(5) the *forum originis, i.e.*, jurisdiction founded on the British nationality or allegiance of the offender;[17] and finally,

(6) jurisdiction founded purely on the magnitude of certain offences, particularly those touching on the basic principles of humanity.[18]

The Act is an extension of this last principle.[19] It is notable that here Hume was prepared to argue for the existence of a common law exception to the *forum delicti* principle 'in the case of those monstrous deeds . . . that are a matter of deep and general concernment to all civilized communities, as affecting their own tranquillity and welfare . . . whereof the actors, as foes of all sovereigns and of the human race, ought equally to be denied a refuge', but it is clear that he had in mind in particular only the executioners of Louis XVI.[20] Today the main example under this heading is the statute with which the Act is most closely comparable, the Geneva Conventions Act 1957. This enacts the Geneva Conventions of 1949, and, makes it a crime for anyone anywhere in time of war to commit serious offences against wounded

---

[16]*E.g.* the common law jurisdiction over piracy; Anderson, *op. cit.*, p. 218; Macdonald, *op. cit.*, p. 192; Renton and Brown, *op. cit.*, para. 1-08; Hume *Commentaries* (Edinburgh, 1797), vol. 1, pp. 480-483; *cf.* the Suppression of Terrorism Act 1978; the Foreign Jurisdiction Act 1890 (*cf.* Anderson, *op. cit.* p. 217); the Internationally Protected Persons Act 1978 (*cf.* Hume, *op. cit.*, vol. 2, pp. 56-57); and the Taking of Hostages Act 1982.

[17]*E.g.*, treason, (see note 15 above); murder and culpable homicide by British citizens and offences by Crown servants abroad under the Criminal Procedure (Scotland) Act 1975, s. 6; and offences by British merchant seamen abroad under the Merchant Shipping Acts (see note 14 above).

[18]*E.g.*, the Internationally Protected Persons Act 1978; the Suppression of Terrorism Act 1978; the Genocide Act 1969; and the Criminal Justice Act 1988, sec. 134.

[19]As implied by the report, paras. 6.30-6.31.

[20]Hume, *op. cit.*, vol. 2, pp. 56-57.

servicemen, prisoners of war, and civilians in occupied territories,[21] but, of course, only since 1957. The Act must therefore be considered together with these other statutory exceptions.

The principal argument in favour of the *forum delicti* is that used by Alison: 'Our courts . . . are not instituted to administer justice over the whole world,'[22] and the same argument has been raised against the Act: 'otherwise British justice would be claiming jurisdiction over the whole of mankind'.[23] Such criticism is not strictly fair, since the Act does not provide for extraditing war criminals from abroad to stand trial here; rather, it enacts the *forum domicilii*.[24]

Hume also defended the freedom of foreign offenders taking refuge in Scotland: 'not only was his deed no disturbance of the peace or good order of Scotland[25] but the man himself, at the time of his offence, was one who stood in no sort of relation to the society . . . of this country';[26] moreover, 'his crime was not an evil example

---

[21]Sec. 1(1).

[22]See Alison, *op. cit.*, p. 73. For a systematic discussion of the sources of jurisdiction, see pp. 70-83.

[23] *The Times*, editorial, 20th March 1990.

[24]It may alternatively be seen as an example of the *forum deprehensionis* (*cf.* Codex Iustinianus, in vol. 2 *Corpus Iuris Civilis*, (ed. Krueger, Berlin, 1896), at pp. 128-129, C.3, 15, *ubi de criminibus agi oportet*. This was used by the Israeli courts as an authority for their assumption of jurisdiction over Eichmann, see: *Attorney General of Israel* v. *Eichmann* (1961) 36 I.L.R. 5 & 277; Alison, *op. cit.*, p. 77), but only if that concept is taken to be a necessary condition of trial, *i.e.*, you cannot try someone until you have caught him, in which case it applies to all our criminal law, in contrast to systems which permit trial in absence. Properly, the concept of *forum deprehensionis* is, rather, a sufficient condition of trial, and means jurisdiction purely on the ground of apprehension, of which the Act would not be an example, because it applies only to British citizens and residents and would not catch a temporary visitor.

[25] *Cf.* Lord Campbell of Alloway's argument against the Bill: 'there is no extant threat to destabilize society', 513 H.L. Deb. (December 4, 1989), col. 620.

[26]Hume, *op. cit.*, vol. 2, p. 56; cf. Alison, *op. cit.*, p. 77; Hume and Alison both extended the argument to cast doubt even upon the propriety of extradition; Hume, p. 56; Alison, pp. 72-77.

to the people of this country'.[27] This last argument is less persuasive in view of modern communications, and in any period of history there is a clear danger of domestic law coming into disrepute if anyone can openly boast of having committed murder or atrocity abroad.[28] However, Hume's other arguments are founded firmly in a tradition which goes back to the mediaeval concept of personal fealty and obedience in return for protection from a territorial lord. Thus, the king's title to prosecute was for a breach of the king's peace; conversely, the foreigner who respected the local law was, with the native, entitled to his protection.[29] While this may be contrasted with modern ideas of international community, the *forum delicti* was bolstered by principles of international comity[30] which are echoed in the modern argument that the creation of extraterritorial jurisdictions is an example of the arrogance of parliamentary sovereignty.

However, if chauvinism is in issue, it is clearly less satisfactory to take the opposing view, that what happens to other people in far-away countries is of no concern to us. 'Humanity does not recognise national boundaries'.[31] Underlying this is a recognition that, in principle, the place where a serious crime is committed is immaterial to moral culpability.[32] To this argument of principle may be

---

[27]Hume, *ibid.*

[28]*Cf.* Lord Mishcon, 519 H.L. Deb. (June 4, 1990), col. 1201.

[29]*Cf.* Alison, *op. cit.*, pp. 72, 77, 82.

[30]*Cf.* Lord Campbell of Alloway's argument that extraterritoriality 'is contrary to international usage and custom', 519 H.L. Deb. (June 4, 1990), col. 1086. It may be noted that from 1948 to 1988 it was the policy of H.M. Government that the proper place for war crimes prosecutions was in the appropriate *forum delicti.*

[31]Lord Fitt, 519 H.L. Deb. (June 4, 1990), col. 1194.

[32]Such a proposition is more doubtful in the case of minor offences, the need for which may be dictated by the peculiar circumstances of a particular country. However, it cannot be pretended that the distinction between major and minor offences is easy to draw, even if it is argued to correspond with the supposed distinction between *mala in se* and *mala prohibita*, *cf.* Gordon, *op. cit.*, paras. 1-07-1-09.

added one of policy, that to prosecute for offences *extra territorium* helps to foster a sense that the world is one moral community.[33]

It would be facile to conclude that the principle of *forum delicti* represents historical insularity in contrast to a new international comity. There are practical arguments of some force in favour of *forum delicti*. Instead, a more helpful conclusion to draw is that the starting point from which to evaluate the competing arguments is a recognition that jurisdiction raises a very basic question; that of the definition of the moral community to which our criminal law relates. To define that community is of special difficulty because it is a question to which justice or fairness give no direct answers. Political borders, and hence legal jurisdictions, are the products of practice, not of moral imperatives. The law is framed to enforce such imperatives within a given community. Accordingly, it contains no guidance on whether or not to redefine the community, and positive lawyers can do no more than identify a problem for the legislature. It is because the legislature is lamentably uninterested in consistency that the statute law in this field is a mess of unsystematic legislation, which has hardly been aggravated by the War Crimes Act. The statute merely highlights the need for rational codification informed by a settled principle. In the light of recent moves towards the codification of English criminal law, that may not be a naive aspiration. Whatever that principle, the object of the legislature should be to make it as simple for the ordinary citizen to understand as the rule expressed by *forum delicti*.[34]

---

[33] *Cf.* Lord Jakobovits, 513 H.L. Deb. (December 4, 1989), col. 615.

[34] It is of interest to note that allegations about war crimes have already raised the question of extraterritorial jurisdiction in civil law, with the granting of an apparently unprecedented worldwide interdict in *Gecas* v. *Ashford Press Publishing*, 26th September 1988 (unreported), *The Scotsman*, 27th September and 12th October 1988; *cf. Gecas* v. *Zuroff*, 17th October 1988 (unreported), *The Scotsman*, 18th October 1988; *cf.* Wilson Finnie, 'War Crimes', 1990 J.R. 61 at p. 62; David Williamson, 'Why Choose the Court of Session?' unpublished paper, Court of Session Practice and Procedure Seminar, 6th February 1989 (Law Society of

Retrospection

'It is hardly credible that any government department would promote or that Parliament would pass retrospective criminal legislation,' remarked Lord Reid in 1974.[35] Indeed, while the content of 'the rule of law' is as controversial as any other department of ethics, that it entails the absence of retrospective penal laws is commonly cited as the most obvious of truths: *nullum crimen sine lege*.[36] No such criminal legislation has been passed in Britain in modern times.[37]

The charge that the Act is an exception to this rule is therefore a serious one.[38] Although not retrospective in the sense of creating

---

Scotland), p. 4 at pp. 7-8. The question of penalties for breach of such an interdict overseas emphasises the inconsistency between this civil jurisdiction and the common law criminal jurisdiction.

[35] *Waddington* v. *Miah* [1974] 2 All E.R. 377, at p. 379.

[36] *E.g.* the Declaration of Delhi 1959, on the content of the rule of law (International Commission of Jurists) (1959) 2 Journal of the I.C.J., pp. 7-43; 'The Rule of Law in a Free Society', Report of International Congress of Jurists (New Delhi, 1959); *cf.* O. Hood Phillips, *Constitutional and Administrative Law* (7th edn., London, 1987), p. 35; Wade and Bradley, *Constitutional and Administrative Law*, (10th edn., London, 1985), p. 101. It was pointed out in the House of Lords that even the Third Reich — at least on occasion — accepted this principle: Lord Campbell of Alloway 513 H.L. Deb. (December 4, 1989), col. 620.

[37] Parliament has, however, legislated retrospectively in non-criminal fields, often controversially; *e.g.*, the Indemnity Act 1920; the War Charges (Validity) Act 1925; the Enemy Property Act 1953; War Damage Act 1965; the Northern Ireland Act 1972; the Education (Scotland) Act 1973; the National Health Service (Invalid Direction) Act 1980; *cf.* Wade and Bradley, *op. cit.*, p. 67. Moreover, while the Genocide Act 1969 is not retrospective, it provides that the retrospective effect of a foreign law against genocide shall not be a defence in proceedings for extradition in the British courts; sec. 2(3). On this point see also L. C. Green, 'Canadian Law, War Crimes and Crimes against Humanity', (1988) 59 B.Y.I.L. 217, at pp. 219, 225.

[38] *Cf.* Lord Watson, 519 H.L. Deb. (June 4, 1990), col. 1170; Mr Edward Heath, 188 H. C. Deb. (March 18, 1991), col. 1170; Mr Robert Maclennan *ibid.*, col. 50; Lord Hailsham of St Marylebone, 528 H.L. Deb. (April 30, 1991), col. 638; Lord Ackner, *ibid.*, col. 672; Lord Wilberforce, *ibid.*, col. 677; Lord Blake, *ibid.*, col. 688.

offences that did not exist at the time, it is said to be retrospective in effect because it extends the jurisdiction of the courts over acts of murder and culpable homicide to cover (1) persons[39] who and (2) places[40] which were not subject to that jurisdiction at the time of those acts.[41]

The government were naturally anxious to rebut this criticism. To do so they adopted the argument of the report, and it is one that is relevant and worth examining. It is suggested in the wording of art. 7 (1) of the European Convention on Human Rights, which provides that: 'No one shall be held guilty of any criminal offence on account of any act or omission which did not constitute a criminal offence under national *or international law* at the time when it was committed' (emphasis added).

The argument is that the Act is not retrospective because it outlaws only acts which were at the time already crimes at international law.[42] If that were not enough, art. 7 (2) further provides that:

---

[39] *I.e.*, to take jurisdiction over persons who were not British citizens at the time; *cf.* note 40 below.

[40] In this the position is different in England, where there was at the time jurisdiction over murder and manslaughter committed abroad by British citizens, under the Offences against the Person Act 1861. In Scotland equivalent jurisdiction (over British citizens only) was not established until 1949, by the Criminal Justice (Scotland) Act of that year (*cf.* the report, para. 6.2). Accordingly, in English law any retrospection lay solely in the extension of jurisdiction to include foreigners. That the Act represents a wider reform in Scotland was ignored by virtually every person speaking in its favour in the original parliamentary debates; *e.g.*, Lord Morris of Kenwood, 519 H.L. Deb. (June 4, 1990), col. 1121; Viscount Tonypandy, *ibid.*, col. 1147; Earl Ferrers, *ibid.*, col. 1082; Sir Bernard Braine, 163 H.C. Deb. (December 12, 1989), col. 881; Mr Merlyn Rees, *ibid.*, col. 884; the Home Secretary (Mr David Waddington), *ibid.*, col. 888, 890; Mr Roy Hattersley, *ibid.*, col. 893; Mr John Wheeler, *ibid.*, col. 907.

[41] It was also argued in Parliament that the Bill was retrospective in its application to the law of evidence; Lord Hailsham of St Marylebone, 513 H.L. Deb. (December 4, 1989), col. 629-630; an analogous argument was rejected in *Rodway* v. *R.* (1990) 92 A.L.R. 385, Federal Court of Australia.

[42] The report, paras. 6.35-6.44; *cf.*, Earl Ferrers, 513 H.L. Deb. (December 4, 1989), col. 606-607; the Home Secretary (Mr David Waddington), 163 H.C. Deb. (December 12, 1989), col. 888-889; the Minister of State for the Home

'This article shall not prejudice the trial and punishment of any person for any act or omission which, at the time it was committed, was criminal according to *the general principles of law recognised by civilised nations*[43] (emphasis added).

In the light of art. 7, the report was concerned to establish the position of war crimes under international law when the Second World War began. For this, there were two principal sources; customary international law and the 4th Hague Convention of 1907 (on the laws and customs of war on land). The relevance of the latter is, however, limited for the following reasons. First, it is arguable that it bound only the contracting states (which included Germany), rather than individuals;[44] moreover, it had no application to events taking place in peacetime or under an occupation which had not been resisted militarily, nor to the mistreatment by a state of its own citizens;[45] and finally, the Hague Convention expressly disapplied itself to conflicts other than those 'between contracting powers, and then only if all the belligerents are parties to the Convention'.[46] Following the view of the International Military Tribunal at Nuremburg, the report's authors accepted that, consequently, only customary international law governed

---

Office (Mr John Patten, 188 H.C. Deb. (March 18, 1991), col. 51; Lord Waddington, 528 H.L. Deb. (April 30, 1991), col. 620; Lord Donaldson of Lymington, 519 H.L. Deb. (June 4, 1990), col. 1173; Lord Lloyd of Hampstead, *ibid.*, col. 1167; Mr Alistair Darling, H.C. Deb. (March 18, 1991), col. 102; Lord Glenamara, 528 H.L. Deb. (April 30, 1991), col. 649; Lord Mackie of Benshie, 528 H.L. Deb. (April 30, 1991), col. 652; Eva Steiner, 'Prosecuting War Criminals in England and France', [1991] Crim.L.R. 180, at p. 186.

[43] *Cf.* the report, para. 5.38; Steiner, *op. cit.*, p. 187.

[44] *Cf.* the report, para. 5.6.

[45] *Cf.* the report, para. 5.20; it is consequently unclear whether the Act's reference to 'war crimes' would permit prosecution for all the murderous atrocities alleged to have been committed by U.K. residents; *cf.* Lord Carver, 519 H.L. Deb. (June 4, 1990), col. 1137; Lord Monson, *ibid.*, col. 1162; Lord Campbell of Alloway, *ibid.*, col. 1086-1087; Mr Merlyn Rees, 163 H.C. Deb. (December 12, 1989), col. 884-885.

[46] Art. 2, quoted by the report at paras. 5.18-5.19; *cf.* also Finnie, *op. cit.*, p. 65.

events during the war. The Government accepted the report's recommendation in this regard.[47]

The Nuremburg Tribunal did not, however, consider itself barred from prosecuting atrocities (committed under a peaceful occupation, or by a state against its own citizens) to which the contemporary international law did not apply. These were distinguished from war crimes as 'crimes against humanity'. The report noted that the legal justification for those prosecutions was 'not entirely clear'; the sole basis appears to have been that 'at the time of their commission the various crimes against humanity existed in the penal code of every civilised country', though not enacted by treaty as international law.[48] This is reminiscent of the wording of art. 7(2) of the European Convention, but the authors of the report concluded that it was at best unclear whether international law prohibited such acts, and that therefore 'to legislate now for offences of genocide (*i.e.,* as distinct from war crimes) committed during the Second World War would, in our view, constitute retrospective legislation'.[49] That is surely the correct view; it cannot be just to punish someone purely because his actions would have been a crime in many other countries.

To return to war crimes, the relevant customary international law has been defined as 'the principles of the law of nations, derived from the usages established among civilised peoples, from the laws of humanity, and from the dictates of public conscience'.[50] To say the least, the content of customary international law in 1939 was

---

[47]See, *e.g.*, the Home Secretary's (Mr Kenneth Baker) remarks when moving the re-introduced Bill's Second Reading: 188 H.C. Deb. (March 18, 1991), col. 27.

[48]The report, para. 6.39; *cf.* paras. 5.21-5.25, para. 5.43; *cf.* also Lord Mackie of Benshie, 519 H.L. Deb. (June 4, 1990), col. 1133.

[49]The report, para. 6.44; *cf.* Earl Ferrers, 519 H.L. Deb. (June 4, 1990), col. 1084; Lord Campbell of Alloway, *ibid.*, col. 1086-1087, also 513 H.L. Deb. (December 4, 1989), col. 621; *cf.* also Finnie, *op. cit.* pp. 65-67.

[50]The 4th Hague Convention, quoted by the report at paras. 5.2-5.3.

regrettably vague. However, in Parliament, a further argument was deployed which had been eschewed by the authors of the report.[51] This was that, regardless of the position under municipal or international law, the acts in question were criminal by their wickedness alone:[52] 'murder is murder in any language and in any country'.[53]

The relevance of these arguments in defence of the Act rests on the point that the *true* objection to retrospection is that it is unjust to punish someone for something which, at the time, he had no reason to believe to be wrong. That is the reason for the principle *nullem crimen sine lege*. The principle is a corollary of the rule *ignorantia iuris neminem excusat*;[54] for ignorance of the law *would* be a valid excuse in the case of a law which had not yet been written.

Simply to cite the principle of *nullum crimen* is an insufficient argument against the Act, for it deals with circumstances which call the principle into question. This was anticipated by Sheriff Gordon long before the present debate: 'the weakness, and indeed the danger, of the principle of *nullum crimen* can be seen when it is used, as it has been, to attack the propriety of the conviction of Nazi leaders for acts condemned as utterly evil by all civilised societies'.[55] However, for Sheriff Gordon's proposed exception to be properly evaluated, it requires to be formulated in more general terms.

The reason why it is thought unfair to punish someone retrospectively is because we cannot exclude reasonable doubt that, had he known that his act was illegal, he might not have done it. The

---

[51]The report's position was based very squarely on *law*, and it was implicitly careful to avoid advocating jurisdiction purely on the basis of evil.

[52]*E.g.*, the Home Secretary (Mr David Waddington) 163 H.C. Deb. (December 12, 1989), col. 889; Mr Ivan Lawrence, *ibid.*, col. 908.

[53]Earl Ferrers, 519 H.L. Deb. (June 4, 1990), col. 1082.

[54]*Cf.* Gordon, *op. cit.*, para. 1-16.

[55]*Op. cit.*, para. 1-16. Doubt is also cast on the status of the principle in Scots law by the existence of the declaratory power of the High Court; see Macdonald, *op. cit.*, p. 193; Gordon, *op. cit.*, paras. 1-15ff.

counter-argument (implicit in Gordon's comment) is that we *can* exclude any doubt, and so be certain that ignorance is not an excuse, in the case of conduct whose wickedness no one could ever doubt;[56] in turn, because in such a case the offender cannot have been ignorant, and must therefore be culpable. Assuredly, if that reasoning applies to any offences, it applies to Nazi atrocities.

The problem with this is how to define exactly the exception which is thus to be created to the rule against retrospective punishment. It requires that a distinction to be drawn between ordinary crimes and those crimes of such wickedness that they may be prosecuted even retrospectively. Such a distinction would be close to that which has often been attempted between *mala prohibita* and *mala in se*. That distinction is between crimes which are merely 'public welfare' or 'regulatory' offences and crimes wicked in themselves. It is of particular relevance here that in support of this distinction it is typically averred that *mala in se* are the same in all civilized nations, whereas *mala prohibita* exhibit no such uniformity.[57] We would, for example, regard a country which did not punish parking offences as unusual, but hardly barbarous; similarly, the argument for retrospective legislation against murders committed in the last war deserves a consideration which would be withheld from a plea for retrospective laws against parking offenders of that era.

However, the distinction between *mala in se* and *mala prohibita* is 'so vague as to be unusable'.[58] An exception to the *nullum crimen* principle based on a distinction between what is wicked and what is merely antisocial would be indefinite and controversial to such a

---

[56] *Cf.*Earl Ferrers, 519 H.L. Deb. (June 4, 1990), col. 1082.

[57] *Cf.* the major premise in the old Scottish form of indictment: 'Albeit by the laws of this *and every other*well-governed realm [murder] is an heinous crime and severely punishable, yet true it is and of verity that you A.B. did . . .'. The authors are indebted to Professor Black for this comparison.

[58]Gordon, *op. cit.*, para. 1-09.

degree that it would give no security against the exception swallowing the rule. This is not a question of the status of moral canons; it is simply a fact that on such issues people notoriously and enduringly disagree.[59] In any event, such a formulation goes beyond what is permitted by art. 7 of the European Convention, which is the obvious place to seek guidance, particularly in the references there to international law and 'the general principles of law recognised by civilised nations'.

But international law in the context of the Act means an amorphous customary international law. 'The general principles of law recognised by civilised nations' (a definition of dubious utility in view of its latent circularity) is an equally vague concept.[60] It is not suggested that the atrocities in issue did not clearly breach those 'general principles', but it has to be questioned whether they constitute an adequately clear and distinct substitute for the unqualified principle of *nullum crimen sine lege*. It is appropriate to compare these standards with the standards used to define 'crimes against humanity'. We have seen that the authors of the report advised against legislating retrospectively to prosecute for such offences, apparently because, at the relevant time, the 'law of humanity' had not been codified.[61] It is unclear whether the heart of their objection was that the absence of international codification meant that such law did not technically apply in (for instance) Germany, or instead that it was too vague to justify derivative legislation today. However, in either case, there is an inconsistency in the report inasmuch as the former objection applies equally to the 'general principles of law', and the latter equally to customary international law. The report rejected legislation to enact the law of humanity as objectionably retrospective, but the European Con-

---

[59] *Cf.* the American objections, which were upheld, against prosecuting for breaches of the law of humanity after the First World War; the report, para. 5.22.
[60] *Cf.* Green, *op. cit.*, at pp. 225-226, 231-232.
[61] The report, paras. 6.39-6.44.

vention would permit such legislation where it adhered to these 'general principles', and both the convention and the report would do so where it adhered to customary international law. Yet all three were and are equally vague concepts. In the absence of a perspicuous reformulation of the principle of *nullum crimen* on lines which would permit the Act and yet would forbid the extension of retrospection into other departments of the criminal law,[62] it must reluctantly be concluded that the Act is a dangerous precedent.

The central question is whether in legislating retrospectively to punish conduct which cannot be doubted to be immensely evil, the legislature should be influenced by the possibility that future legislators with different views of right and wrong might cite their decision as a precedent for legislating retrospectively to punish people guilty of lesser wrongs, or guilty of none at all. In the absence of a written constitution, the underlying tenets of our law have to be inferred from the statute book. The Act risks obscuring one of the most basic of those tenets, and leaving it open to distortion. Whatever else is uncertain, it is central to our law that vagueness is to be avoided with peculiar vigour in the criminal field. That applies not only to the substantive law but also to those principles, such as that of *nullum crimen sine lege* or any exception thereto, which have so far served us well in place of a Bill of Rights.

Selectivity

The most remarkable aspect of the Act which attracted comment in Parliament was its narrow scope: it applies only to offences in Germany or German-occupied territory'[63] between 1st September

---

[62] *Cf.* Lord Fraser of Kilmorack, 519 H.L. Deb. (June 4, 1990), col. 1135; Lord Rees, *ibid.*, col. 1158-1159.

[63] Doubts have been expressed about what this last expression might mean; Mr Robin Maxwell-Hyslop, 163 H.C. Deb. (December 12, 1989), col. 888. The question arises in particular in relation to areas occupied by Germany's allies, for example, Romania, on the Eastern Front.

1939 and 5th June 1945.[64] 'The bill,' as was said in the Lords, 'does not attempt to enunciate any general principle'.[65] Indeed, so narrow were its terms that, had it not been criminal legislation, it would almost have merited private Bill procedure; it was likened in the Commons to an act of impeachment or attainder.[66]

Furthermore, given the Geneva Conventions Act, the Act has left a curious *lacuna* in war crimes law for the years between 1945 and 1957,[67] not to mention the period before 1939. The territorial restriction also contrasts with the 1957 Act, whose application is not geographically limited. Ironically, it was parliamentary supporters of the Act who said, 'humanity does not recognise national boundaries', and 'murder is murder . . . in any country'.[68]

---

[64]See generally: Lord Campbell of Alloway, 513 H.L. Deb. (December 4, 1989), col. 621; Lord Hailsham of St Marylebone, ibid., col. 630-631; Sir Nicholas Fairbairn, 163 H.C. Deb. (December 12, 1989), col. 885, 888; Mr Quentin Davies, *ibid.*, col. 888; Mr Roy Hattersley, *ibid.*, col. 891; Mr Edward Heath, *ibid.*, col. 896; Mr Ivor Stanbrook, *ibid.*, col. 902; Mr Ivor Lawrence, *ibid.*, col. 908; Sir John Stokes, *ibid.*, col. 912; Mr Winston Churchill, *ibid.*, col. 915; *cf.* the Minister of State, for the Home Office (Mr John Patten), *ibid.*, col. 918; Lord Shawcross, 519 H.L. Deb. (June 4, 1990), col. 1098; Lord Fraser of Kilmarnock, *ibid.*, col. 1134; Lord Morton of Shuna, *ibid.*, col. 1150; Lord Shaughnessy, *ibid.*, col. 1165; Lord Thomas of Swynnerton, *ibid.*, col. 1171; Lord Gridley, *ibid.*, col. 1186-1187; the Earl of Onslow, *ibid.*, col. 1194; Sir Ian Gilmour, 188 H.C. Deb. (March 18, 1991), col. 53; Lord Houghton of Sowerby, 528 H.L. Deb. (April 30, 1991), col. 621; Lord Campbell of Alloway, *ibid.*, col. 628; Lord Ackner, *ibid.*, col. 672; Lord Wilberforce, *ibid.*, col. 678; Lord Kennet, *ibid.*, col. 702; Lord Monson, *ibid.*, cols. 728-729.

[65]Lord Rees, 519 H.L. Deb. (June 4, 1990), col. 1159.

[66]Mr Ivor Stanbrook, 163 H.C. Deb. (December 12, 1989), col. 902; *cf.* Lord Rees, 519 H.L. Deb. (June 4, 1990), col. 1159; however, limits to this comparison are suggested by the unusual reasoning to which its application can read; e.g., *McMullen, Petitioner,* International Enforcement Law Reporter, vol. 7, Spetember 1991, p. 352, applying art. 1, s. 9(3) of the U.S. constitution. The Authors are interested to Mr Wilson Finnie for drawing their attention to this case.

[67]*Cf.* the report, p. 96, para. 9.25; Lord Donaldson of Lymington, 519 H.L. Deb. (June 4, 1990), col. 1173; Lord Glenamara 528 H.L. Deb. (April 30, 1991), col. 702.

[68]Lord Fitt, 519 H.L. Deb. (June 4, 1990), col. 1194; Earl Ferrers, *ibid.*, col. 1082.

It is not unreasonable to presume that, if a rule is a good one, it should be applied without exceptions. The report did not address this issue at length as its authors were inhibited by the restricted terms of their commission.[69] On being challenged in Parliament, the government acknowledged that the restriction required to be defended. They put forward two main arguments in its favour. First, that there was no reason to believe that those guilty of war crimes in other times and places are now resident in Britain; secondly, that in any event, the Nazi crimes 'are regarded as so unique and so abhorrent'[70] that they should be accorded special treatment. Both of these arguments are frankly untenable; they are both irrelevant in the strict sense of the word.

To consider first the latter argument, it amounts to the suggestion that, because the Nazi crimes were so unique and abhorrent, *therefore* persons committing war crimes of murder and culpable homicide in less abhorrent ways should not be pursued. But it is wholly irrelevant to culpability for any one offence that it is more or less heinous than another. Even if that were not so, the government's argument is open to the further criticisms that it exhibits *either* an astounding ignorance of the history of the twentieth century, *or* a readiness to indulge in an inhuman process of grading the atrocities of the past into a nice scale of ascending obscenity.[71] Where, in other words, is there a clear and significant line to be drawn between the activities of the Nazis and those of the Japanese at the same time?; or of the Japanese in China and Manchuria before the Second World War?; or of the Italians in that war, or in

---

[69]They were asked to consider only allegations arising out of the war crimes in Germany or German occupied territory during the Second World War; the report, p. ii.

[70]The report, p. 64, para. 6.44; *cf.* the Home Secretary (Mr David Waddington) 163 H.C. Deb. (December 12, 1989), col. 890; Baroness Ryder of Warsaw, 519 H.L. Deb. (June 4, 1990), col. 1180-1181.

[71] *Cf.* Lord Fraser of Kilmorack, 519 H.L. Deb. (June 4, 1990), col. 1135; Lord Thomas of Swynnerton, *ibid.*, col. 1172.

Abyssinia in 1935-1936, or in Libya in 1911-1912?; or the genocide of Armenians by the Turks during the First World War?; or in
the internecine atrocities of the Serbs and the Croats during the last
war?; or the Soviet murders of Poles at Katyn in 1940?; or the war
crimes committed by the several nationalities in Spain in 1936-
1939?; or the 'ordinary', unremarkable killings in violation of the
laws of war undoubtedly committed in the course of almost any
hostilities prior to the 1957 Act which one cares to examine closely?
'One can go anywhere and find war crimes. They are littered about
the world and throughout history . . .'.[72] The point is that crimes,
albeit rarely committed by such calculated means as those of the
Nazis, yet assuredly equally deserving of punishment, have been
widely committed.

The best attempt at a distinction was made in the Commons by
Sir Bernard Braine, who argued that the Nazi crimes fell to be
singled out because they were not committed in the heat of battle,
but were the premeditated mass murder in cold blood of non-
combatants.[73] But his argument misses the point: the Act is in terms
directed at crimes committed in Germany or German occupied
territory, yet it is surely not the fact that they were committed there
which made them so evil. It is rather that they are premeditated
mass murders. If a distinction *has* to be drawn between different
wartime atrocities, then legislation should be framed not in terms
of the accidents of history, but in terms which go to the essence of
the crimes.

In this regard, it should be observed that, strictly, the Act's
reference to crimes committed 'in a place which at the time was part
of Germany or under German occupation' by 'a person in the
United Kingdom irrespective of his nationality at the time of the
alleged offence'[74] does not restrict its scope to Nazi war crimes;

---

[72]Lord Houghton of Sowerby, 528 H.L. Deb. (April 30, 1991), col. 625-626.
[73]163 H.C. Deb. (December 12, 1989), col. 882-883.
[74]War Crimes Act 1991, sec. 1 (1).

while, *ex hypothesi*, only Nazi agents could operate in *German-occupied* territory,[75] atrocities could be and were committed in *Germany* by non-Nazis; *e.g.*, the Soviet massacres of Germans in East Prussia in 1944-1945. This produces a curious anomaly, in that, for instance, a Soviet war crime committed during the Red Army's advance through Poland in 1944-1945 would fall outwith the scope of the legislation while exactly the same act would be punishable under the Act if it had been committed across the German border.

The government's other argument in this regard was made by the Home Secretary in answer to references to Soviet atrocities: 'there is not the slightest evidence that any foreigner resident in Britain could have been responsible for the Katyn massacre'.[76] Presumably in the event of such evidence coming to light, the government will be prepared to bring forward another equally selective piece of legislation! The possibility of such persons settling here in the future is also entirely ignored. Only six years ago there was, so far as Parliament was aware, 'not the slightest evidence that any foreigner resident in Britain' could have been responsible for Nazi atrocities.[77] There is evidence today because the government

---

[75]Soviet, French and other partisans also operated in German occupied areas of Europe. Neither the authors of the Report nor any speakers in Parliament appear to have considered that any war crimes which might have been committed by such partisans who now resided in the U.K. would fall within the ambit of the Act.

[76]163 H.C. Deb. (December 12, 1989), col. 888; *cf.* Lord Mishcon, 519 H.L. Deb. (June 4, 1990), col. 1199; Earl Ferrers, 513 H.L. Deb. (December 4, 1989), col. 679; the Home Secretary (Mr Kenneth Baker) 188 H.C. Deb. (March 18, 1991), col. 24. *Cf.* also Lord Waddington 528 H.L. Deb. (April 30, 1991), cols. 621 and 739.

[77] *Cf.* the report, para. 3.59. However, it appears that the British Cabinet was alive to the possibility of war criminals settling in Britain after the war. On 12th *March* 1945 the Cabinet discussed the handling of war criminals in Britain, especially in respect of the possibility of their extradition to ther nations; Lord Mayhew, 528 H.L. Deb. (April 30, 1991), col. 713.

commissioned a special investigation and placed advertisements in the press inviting the public to submit allegations. There could only be equal certainty about Soviet, Japanese, or Italian atrocities if the government committed equal resources to investigate them. In the absence of such certainty, there is not the slightest reason to legislate in such a selective manner.

This aspect is all the more objectionable because it is unnecessary for the purposes of the Act to aim it only at Germans and their allies; moreover, it is also in breach of the spirit of the Delhi Declaration on the content of the rule of law,[78] and of art. 14 of the European Convention, both of which strike at discrimination against national groups. It is ironic that a measure whose guiding principle according to the government, 'has been the need to avoid creating a special regime for war crimes trials',[79] and which was seen to be required in order to bring the suspects under the same law as all other British citizens,[80] should be so peculiarly selective in its scope; 'or do such laws apply only to the losers of world wars?'[81] In the words of Lord Morton of Shuna, 'it is vitally important, if we are to remain a democracy, that we retain . . . the concept of equality of all people before the law'.[82]

It is instructive in this regard to recall that it was once thought that, while English law was inductive (and therefore concerned with precedent), Scots law was a deductive system (and consequently able to accord greater authority to institutional writers). Insofar as that remains true, statute law should respect that ap-

---

[78] *Cf.* Wade and Bradley, *op. cit.*, p. 101.

[79] Earl Ferrers, 519 H.L. Deb. (June 4, 1990), col. 1083.

[80] *Cf.* Earl Ferrers, 519 H.L. Deb. (June 4, 1990), col. 1204; Viscount Tonypandy, *ibid.*, col. 1147; Sir Bernard Braine, 163 H.C. Deb. (December 12, 1989), col. 880; *cf.* also Mr John Morris, 188 H.C. Deb. (March 18, 1991), col. 44.

[81] Mr Winston Churchill, 163 H.C. Deb. (December 12, 1989), col. 915; *cf.* Finnie, *op. cit.*, p. 63. n. 10.

[82] 519 H.L. Deb. (June 4, 1990), col. 1151.

proach. A deductive system of law requires that statutes enunciate general rules, which the courts may then apply to particular circumstances. Such an approach should be preserved, if for no other reason, than because it is basic to the idea of law that it consists of general rules which may be applied in each and every materially similar case. That is also an element of the rule of law. These tenets are defied by the creation of a body of statute law which applies different rules to materially similar cases which are distinguished obtusely or quite arbitrarily; for example, the distinction between 'German' and 'non-German' war crimes. One of the merits of a deductive system of jurisprudence is that it should constitute a defence against such developments.

It is inappropriate here to draw any conclusions about the influence of English law or statute upon Scottish jurisprudence. It is sufficient to observe that the Act is a further step away from an admirable tradition. It is a further move towards the collapse of our *corpus* of law into an unsystematic kaleidoscope of arbitrarily narrow and selective rules which reveal no guiding philosophy other than the prostitution of the law to the demands of the most vocal lobbyists.[83]

It may appear undemocratic to resist that in favour of gnomic appeals to a deductive tradition. But such a criticism would ignore the conclusive argument for law to be expressed in rules of general application; and that is *clarity*. The collapse of law into a myriad of rules of narrow application increases its inaccessibility to the layman. The proliferation of statutory exceptions and qualifications requires an associated proliferation of lawyers to interpret them. On the other hand, to restrict the expression of the law to as few rules, all of as general application as is practical, is to facilitate its statement in a code or an institute which the lay reader can

---

[83] *Cf.* Lord Hailsham of St Marylebone 528 H.L. Deb. (April 30, 1991), col. 639.

understand. The law, and above all the criminal law, should strive for clarity: legal obscurity is at best a mild form of tyranny.

These remarks would be unnecessary if the Act did not exemplify the disregard in which such considerations are held. The rule of law is not a vague academic irrelevance; it is the set of standards against which every piece of proposed legislation should be judged.

Trials under the Act

This part of the paper addresses those criticisms which relate to procedural matters which would have to be considered by the courts if prosecutions are taken under the Act. It has been said that the 'central theme of Scots criminal procedure is the need for fairness'.[84] In the House of Lords it was said that, 'in its 108 packed pages there is no mention in the report of the fact that the central tenet of our system of criminal justice is that every accused, at all levels, must be guaranteed a fair trial. Nowhere among the difficulties listed are those which will inevitably confront the defence of an accused person. . . . The only consideration in the report was: will there be a realistic prospect of a conviction?'[85] Despite government assurances in Parliament that trials under the legislation would be fair,[86] this was widely doubted.[87]

In particular, the following procedural matters are considered in this part of the paper; first, the possibility of oppression arising from delay in bringing the prosecutors; secondly, the possible effect on a trial of prejudicial publicity; thirdly, the methods, both those

---

[84]G. H. Gordon, *The Criminal Justice (Scotland) Act 1980* (Edinburgh, 1981), p. xiii.

[85]Lord Hutchison of Lullington, 519 H.L. Deb. (June 4, 1990), col. 1111; *cf.* Mr Roy Hattersley, 163 H.C. Deb. (December 12, 1989), col. 893-894; Lord Ackner, 528 H.L. Deb. (April 30, 1991), col. 670.

[86]*E.g.* by Lord Waddington, 528 H.L. Deb. (April 30, 1991), col. 621.

[87]*E.g.*, Lord Hailsham, 528 H.L. Deb. (April 30, 1991), col. 638; Lord Bridge of Harwich, *ibid.*, col. 658; Lord Ackner, *ibid.*, col. 670; Lord Wilberforce, *ibid.*, col. 679.

already available and those recommended by the report, of obtaining evidence, and the problems arising therefrom.

Delay

First, there is the question of the passage of time. While common law crimes do not prescribe,[88] the court nevertheless retains the power to dismiss a prosecution where the Crown has acted oppressively in view of the passage of time since the discovery of the offence. A prosecution may be dismissed where there has been delay which has resulted in grave prejudice to the accused.[89]

In *H.M. Advocate* v. *Stewart*[90] a plea in bar of trial based on undue delay in relation to the bringing of charges of receiving bribes was sustained where the alleged offences took place some 14 years before the accused was brought to trial. The ground of the plea in bar of trial could be from a trial under the War Crimes Act: 'the long, unexplained and unjustified delay in bringing him to trial has caused, or may have caused, gross prejudice to him in his defence, due to the death of potentially helpful witnesses, the destruction of important documents and the dimming of the recollection of witnesses, which delay is contrary to normal justice and a violation of the right to a fair trial within a reasonable time.'[91] Lord Kincraig

---

[88] *Sugden v. H.M. Advocate* 1934 J.C. 103, *per* Lord Justice-Clerk Aitchison at pp. 111-112; *cf. H.M. Advocate* v. *Macgregor* (1773) M. 11146; Macdonald, *op. cit.*, p. 211; Renton and Brown, *op. cit.*, 13-04; Finnie, *op. cit.*, p. 61.

[89] The test appears in the case of *McFadyn* v. *Annan* 1992 S.L.T. 163 overruling the earlier formulation in *Tudhope* v. *McCarthy* 1985 S.C.C.R. 76 (cf. *H.M. Advocate* v. *Leslie,* Edinburgh High Court, 31st January 1984 (unreported, but see 1985 S.C.C.R. 81); *cf. R.* v. *Bow Street Stipendiary Magistrate, ex parte D.P.P.; R.* v. *Bow Street Stipendiary Magistrate ex parte Cherry* (1990) 91 Cr. App. 283, D.C.; *cf.* also *Buchan* v. *H.M. Advocate* 1990 S.C.C.R. 549, where it was held that a delay of some five years between the date of offence and charging during which time the destruction of certain documentary evidence and pauses in the preparation of the Crown case had taken place was not such an exceptional case as to warrant allowing a plea in bar of trial.

[90] 1980 J.C. 84.

[91] *Ibid. per* Lord Kincraig at p. 87.

accepted that the degree of prejudice arising from the destruction of documents and the loss of witnesses could only be adequately assessed in the light of all the evidence bearing on the charge, and that it was preferable to leave it to the jury to decide, under appropriate direction, whether the accused had been prejudiced thereby to such a degree as to make it unfair that he should be convicted. Nevertheless, he decided 'that the delay by itself is sufficient to constitute prejudice to the accused, and that it would be unfair to him to go to trial on this charge. While it may not be possible to assess the degree of prejudice caused by the dimming of the recollection of witnesses after such a long delay between events and the giving of evidence in relation to them, it is possible in my judgment to affirm that some prejudice will be caused to the accused through these circumstances. In my judgment it is unfair to the accused, if not oppressive, to compel him to answer allegations of corruptly receiving bribes between 1960 and 1964 some 14 or so years later.'[92] In contrast, however, in England it was recently held in the Blake escape trial that even a delay of 23 years may not necessarily constitute an abuse of process.[93] Therefore, if a prosecution were to be brought in Scotland under the Act there would appear to be a *prima facie* basis for a successful plea in bar of trial, on the ground of delay resulting in grave prejudice to the accused.[94]

There is, however, a counter-argument. It is that the effect of the Act has been to repeal by implication any judicial discretion in respect of dismissing a prosecution on the basis of delay. This argument was developed by Lord Bridge of Harwich in the House

---

[92] *Ibid.*, at 88f.

[93] *R.* v. *Central Criminal Court, ex parte Randle and Pottle, The Guardian,* 16th November 1990; John Wadham, 'Abuse of process through delay in the criminal courts', *Legal Action,* February 1991, p. 15 at pp. 16 and 17, n. 16 and 25.

[94] *Cf.* Lord Shawcross 519 H.L. Deb. (June 4, 1990), col. 1185; Lord Goodman, *ibid.*, col. 1107; Lord Donaldson of Kingsbridge, *ibid.*, col. 1155; *cf.* also Green, *op. cit.*, pp. 227-228.

of Lords.[98] The passing of the Act means that Parliament, or at least the House of Commons, clearly wishes to prosecute certain alleged war criminals living in the United Kingdom. However, doing so, is it Parliament's intention to deprive such suspects of the possible plea of delay? The Act does not expressly provide an answer to this question. While the government indicated that this is not their intention,[99] in trials under the legislation it will nevertheless depend on statutory interpretation. In construing statutes there is a presumption against interference with existing common law rights.[100] The silence of the Act on this matter cannot be taken to imply the repeal of such an important aspect of an accused's right to a fair trial. Such a serious interference with an accused's rights could only be made by express provision.

If the Act was read as Lord Bridge suggested, we would be witnessing the erosion of the rights of a particular class of accused. The effect would be to deny to suspected war criminals a plea which would potentially remain open to any other accused. That would be a move towards the 'special régime' which the government claimed to wish to avoid.[101] However, if such a plea remained open, the weight of authority would appear to suggest that it may well succeed. In view of this, it can be seen that the Act may lead either to every war crimes prosecution falling at this hurdle, or to the courts re-writing the general law on oppression to the benefit of the prosecution. Neither alternative seems satisfactory.

Lastly, in this section, it is appropriate to consider, as the report's authors recognised, the relevant provisions of the European Con-

---

[98]519 H.L. Deb. (June 4, 1990), col. 1186; *cf.* 528 H.L. Deb. (April 30, 1991), col. 658.

[99]*Cf.* Lord Waddington, 528 H.L. Deb. (April 30, 1991), col. 621.

[100]*Cf.* D. M. Walker, *The Scottish Legal System* (5th edn., Edinburgh, 1981), p. 360; Maxwell, *The Interpretation of Statutes* (12th edn., London, 1969), p. 116; Sir Rupert Cross, *Statutory Interpretation* (2nd edn., London, 1987), p. 169 *cf.* also *H.M. Advocate* v. *R.M.* 1969 J.C. 52.

[101]Earl Ferrers, 519 H.L. Deb. (June 4, 1990), col. 1083.

vention.[102] These include art. 6 (1) which provides: 'In the determination . . . of any criminal charge against him, everyone is entitled to a fair and public hearing *within a reasonable time* by an independent and impartial tribunal established by law' (emphasis added). The object of this provision is to protect a suspect or accused person from living under the threat of criminal proceedings for too long.[103] It is arguable that the undue delay in the prosecution of alleged war criminals living in Scotland would constitute a violation of art. 6 (1)'s requirement of holding a hearing within a reasonable time, notwithstanding the conclusion of the report's authors that: 'we would normally expect procedures in British courts not to fall foul of the European Convention on Human Rights in this respect'.[104] A ten-year period in the determination of a criminal charge has been held to violate art. 6(1)'s requirement of holding a hearing within a reasonable time.[105] This may not, however, be conclusive for trials under the Act. It is not clear when the clock starts running for the purposes of a violation of art. 6(1); it does not necessarily start with arrest or charge. A substantial alteration in the applicant's situation as a result of, for example, at least suspicion against him is necessary to start the clock running. This view is supported by the *Milasi* case where the violation of the 'reasonable time' requirement occurred in the

---

[102]Report, para. 9.32.

[103]Francis G. Jacobs, *The European Convention on Human Rights* (Oxford, 1975), p. 108; *cf.* Green, *op. cit.*, p. 228 on the equivalent provision in the Canadian 'Charter of Rights and Freedoms'.

[104]Report, para. 9.32. This sentence is taken to refer both to art. 6 (1) and (3) which are both considered therein.

[105]The *Milasi* case, E.H.R.R. 14/1986/112/160. The period which was held by the European Court of Human Rights to violate art. 6 (1) was the period between the date on which the Italian declaration recognising the right of individual petition to the European Convention took effect on 1st August 1973 (the applicant had been informed that proceedings were being instituted against him on 18th June 1973) and the date on which the Reggio Calabria District Court gave judgment, 10th December 1982.

period after proceedings had been instituted against the applicant.[106] On this view, an alleged war criminal could not rely on this article until after the suspicion of the authorities had been aroused in his particular case.

Thus, while a fair trial may not be possible because of grave prejudice to the accused on the ground of delay at common law, it is doubtful whether proceedings would contravene art. 6(1) of the European Convention.

Prejudicial publicity

Secondly, there is also the possibility that pre-trial publicity may prejudice the trial of the accused to the extent that it would be oppressive to proceed with the prosecution. Prejudicial publicity has already occurred in relation to certain individuals.[107] As was noted above a list of 17 alleged war criminals said to be living in Britain was sent to the Prime Minister in October 1986. That list was leaked and published in a number of national newspapers. Furthermore, Scottish Television made a programme about one of those named. When Scottish Television approached the Embassy of the Soviet Union they were given a further list of 34 names which was also published in the press. It was this publicity which lay behind the decision to commission the report. This publicity has certainly been prejudicial to the potential suspects named in it.[108]

---

[106]See also Jacobs, *op. cit.*, p. 108; John Wadham, *op. cit.*, at p. 16.

[107]See, *e.g.*, *The Times*, 4th December 1987, which named an individual living in Scotland and stated that he was an alleged Nazi war criminal.

[108]*E.g.* Lord Monson, 513 H.L. Deb. (December 4, 1989), col. 652-653: 'the impression that these people were guilty of conspiracy to commit large scale genocide will have been etched indelibly upon the subconscious minds of television viewers and hence potential jurors all over Britain'. Lord Monson's argument was not weakened by the apparent readiness of some speakers in Parliament to disregard the presumption of innocence: Baroness Phillips, 519 H.L. Deb. (June 4, 1990), col. 1139-1140; Lord Harmar-Nicholls, *ibid.*, col. 1182.

The present approach to the likely prejudicial effect of pre-trial publicity on the prospects of a fair trial may be found in the leading cases of *Stuurman* v. *H.M. Advocate*[109] and *X* v. *Sweeney*.[110] The test is whether the risk of prejudice is so grave that no direction of the trial judge, however careful, could reasonably be expected to remove it. On the facts, in both *Stuurman* and *Sweeney* this test was held not to have been satisfied. In the former case the publications had occurred some four months before the trial diet. On appeal it was held by the court that, given that the public memory for publications and broadcasts was notoriously short, any residual risk of prejudice to the prospects of a fair trial for the appellants could reasonably be expected to be removed by careful directions such as those given by the trial judge.[111]

This approach was followed in *Sweeney* (which became known as 'the Glasgow Rape Case'). There were some 160 newspaper articles and many radio and TV programmes devoted to the case, including publication by a national newspaper of an alleged confession by one of the respondents. Lord Justice-General Emslie held that,

> 'In considering what answer should be given I have not forgotten that while the public interest in securing fair trial of accused persons is of the highest importance, so too is the public interest in the fair administration of justice and the detection and trial of alleged perpetrators of crime. Great weight must be given to this latter aspect of the public interest in this case, for the crimes alleged are of a particularly serious and horrible nature. . . . The *risk* of prejudice will undoubtedly be present. I find myself unable to hold, however, that a trial judge will be unable, when all the admissible evidence has been led, to secure, by careful directions, that the members of the jury will reach their verdicts upon an unprejudiced consideration of that evidence, and that evidence alone.'[112]

---

[109] 1980 J.C. 111.
[110] 1982 J.C. 70.
[111] 1980 J.C. 111, at p. 123.
[112] *Ibid.*, at pp. 85 et seq.

It appears that the test may only be satisfied where there is pre-trial publicity immediately preceding the trial diet. This may have been the reason why the Crown abandoned the case against a nurse, Atkins, following the broadcast of material highly prejudicial to her prospects of a fair trial on the day before the trial diet.[113] However, in *Stuurman* Lord Avonside, one of the two judges consulted by the trial judge, cast doubt on whether such a plea would have succeeded even in the *Atkins* case.[114]

In *Stuurman* Lord Emslie did, however, make clear that each case would depend on its own merits. It would appear then that, following *Stuurman* and *Sweeney*, it is unlikely that the test would be satisfied in a trial under the Act of one of those whose names have already been broadcast or published, as the prejudicial material was published or broadcast many months ago. Given the public interest in such trials there may, of course, be additional publicity immediately preceding the trial diet which may prejudice the accused's prospects of a fair trial. Moreover, in the case of war crimes, there has been a vast amount of publicity since the war, which might be prejudicial to any suspect. War crimes have been kept in the public eye; and therefore Lord Emslie's comments regarding the public's 'notoriously short' memory in relation to news items in *Stuurman* cannot apply without qualification in the case of war crimes.[115]

General difficulties of gathering and admitting evidence

Given that most, if not all, the alleged war crimes which may be tried under the Act were committed in what was until recently the Soviet Union,[116] there are certain to be difficulties in gathering

---

[113]See the contempt action: *Atkins* v. *London Weekend Television* 1978 J.C. 48.

[114]1980 J.C. 111, at p. 117; the implication appears to be that, in Atkins' case, the prosecution was abandoned as a tactical step to strengthen the Crown's case for contempt; *cf.* Alistair Bonnington, 'Contempt of Court: A Practitioner's View', 1988 S.L.T. (News) 33.

[115]1980 J.C. 111, at p. 123.

[116]This article was written in November 1991.

evidence. Many of the witnesses will have died, while those that are living are likely to be hard to find and, if found, will be of advanced age with possibly dimmed recollections of the war years.[117] Moreover, assuming that witnesses are located, they may be unable to travel to Scotland by reason of advanced age or ill-health, even if they are willing to do so.[118] It is also difficult, given recent political events, to predict the readiness of the various competent authorities in what was formerly the Soviet Union to provide such assistance to either the prosecution or to the defence in, for example, locating witnesses, as was provided to the authors of the report in 1988-1989. In itself the recent appearance of a multitude of more or less sovereign states together with the doubts surrounding the subsistence of the central Soviet authorities and the consequent jurisdictional uncertainties may pose additional problems in obtaining evidence through official channels.

Assuming witnesses are located, there are several methods of obtaining evidence from them in what was formerly the Soviet Union, without requiring them to attend a trial in Scotland. Some of these methods are presently available and some which are, at the time of writing unavailable, were recommended by the report. The former include the use of letters of request and the latter the use of live television links and the taking of evidence on commission. These methods of obtaining evidence are not without difficulty or indeed controversy.

---

[117] *E.g.*, charges against a Canadian in relation to alleged war crimes were dropped by the Crown Prosecutor in the Ontario Court General Division in 1990 *inter alia* because of the death of a key witness; Lord Shaughnessy, 528 H.L. Deb. (April 30, 1991), col. 721.

[118] *E.g.*, in another Canadian case ten out of twenty witnesses interviewed by the Canadian authorities in the Soviet Union in 1990 refused to testify; Lord Shaughnessy, *ibid.*

Letters of request [119]

To obtain evidence from witnesses resident in another country, a court in Scotland may issue letters of request. These are in effect a request to a foreign magistrate to take statements from the witnesses for use in the Scottish proceedings. There are, however, significant problems with the use of letters of request.

First, the judge must be satisfied before he grants an application for a letter of request that 'there would be no unfairness to either party'.[120] It may happen that the defence will not be given an opportunity to cross-examine prosecution witnesses. If the defence were not to be permitted to cross-examine prosecution witnesses fully, there would obviously be unfairness to the defence. In the words of Lord Cameron in *Muirhead* v. *H.M. Advocate*,[121] 'it would be difficult to be satisfied in the case of a witness, whose evidence is other than formal, that there could be no unfairness to the opposite party, be he prosecutor or accused, if he is deprived of the opportunity of oral cross-examination before the jury or the judge, and particularly so in a case in which examination and cross-examination were to be conducted not *viva voce* before a commissioner but in the much less satisfactory form of administration of interrogatories and cross-interrogatories'.[122] There may also be a violation of art. 6 (3) of the European Convention, which provides: 'Everyone charged with a criminal offence has the following minimum rights; . . . (d) to examine or have examined witnesses against him and to obtain the attendance and examination of witnesses on his behalf under the same conditions as witnesses against him; . . .'.[123] Thus as the report accepted, this procedure should be confined to formal evidence only.

---

[119]As provided for by the Criminal Justice (Scotland) Act 1980 sec. 32(1)(a), (2).

[120]Sec. 32(2)(b).

[121]1983 S.C.C.R. 133.

[122]*Ibid.*, at p. 142.

[123]However, the European Court of Human Rights has held in relation to art. 6(3): 'In principle, all the evidence must be produced in the presence of the accused

Secondly, even if an application were granted, there would be enormous expense involved. Letters of request may require to be issued to several courts even within what was formerly the Soviet Union, if it is alleged that an accused committed crimes in the territory of more than one present or former Soviet Republic; each Soviet Republic has until recently been responsible for the prosecution of war crimes committed on its territory. Whether the defence will be given the resources to cover such expense is a question which must be borne in mind. If the defence is not given adequate resources a violation of art. 6 (3) of the European Convention could result. That article provides, *inter alia*, that 'Everyone charged with a criminal offence has the following minimum rights; ... (b) to have adequate time and facilities for the preparation of his defence'.

Giving of evidence by live television link

The report recommended amending the law in Scotland to enable evidence to be given over a live television link. This method of obtaining evidence is already available in England.[124] Amending legislation which would have extended this reform to Scotland was introduced into Parliament in 1990.[125] However, the House of Lords rejected its use in war crimes trials.[126] The government has

---

at a public hearing with a view to adversarial argument. This does not mean, however, that in order to be used as evidence statements of witnesses should always be made at a public hearing in court: to use as evidence such statements obtained at the pre-trial stage is not in itself inconsistent with paragraphs (3) (d) and (1) of Article 6, provided the rights of the defence have been respected.' *Kostovski* v. *Netherlands* (20-11-1989) Series A no. 166 E.H.R.R. 1990 Vol. 12 p. 434; *cf.* Steiner, *op. cit.*, at p. 183 n. 20.

[124]Criminal Justice Act, 1988, sec. 32(1)(a).

[125]Law Reform (Miscellaneous Provisions) (Scotland) Bill (subsequently Act) 1990, cl. 56.

[126]The House of Lords amended the clause so as to exclude the possibility of using live television links for giving evidence in war crimes trials only. However, that amended clause was subsequently withdrawn from the much modified Law Reform (Miscellaneous Provisions (Scotland) Act 1990.

indicated that it is committed to re-introducing this reform.[127] However, a number of points may still be made. Although, this method would enable cross-examination of witnesses by the defence, it would not permit evidence to be given in the actual presence of the accused. Safeguards may also be required to ensure that witnesses are not 'coached' by persons off-camera when responding to questions.

Evidence on commission

In Scots law it is competent to take evidence on commission in a criminal trial in certain circumstances, but the commissioner can only examine witnesses in the United Kingdom, the Channel Islands or the Isle of Man.[128] The report recommended that this be extended to permit evidence to be taken on commission from witnesses abroad.[129] This would enable examination and cross-examination of a witness resident abroad to take place before the commissioner without the witness being required to travel to Scotland, although as the report concedes, the accused will almost certainly not be present when evidence is taken in this manner.[130] At the time of writing no legislation had been introduced into Parliament to make this recommendation available in war crimes trials. Such a development, if confined to war crimes trials alone, would, however, be open to the criticism that it would not be available in other criminal trials, and would thus constitute another move towards a 'special régime' for war crimes.

These are some of the difficulties in obtaining evidence from living witnesses. Other difficulties present themselves in respect of the credibility and reliability of the witnesses and the consequent

---

[127]Minister of State for the Home Office (Mr John Patten) 188 H.C. Deb. (March 18, 1991), col. 109.
[128]Criminal Justice (Scotland) Act 1980, sec. 32(1)(b).
[129]Report, para. 9. 38.
[130]*Ibid.*

quality of their evidence. For instance, should identification of the accused be an issue, the trial judge will be faced with the problem of how much credibility to attribute to the evidence of witnesses identifying the accused at least 45 years after the alleged crime. This was a crucial issue in the *Demjanjuk* case in Israel.

Use of statements from witnesses now deceased and other documentary evidence

If the witnesses are now dead, as will often be the case,[131] much reliance will have to be placed by the prosecution on statements by deceased persons. Statements made before the trial diet by persons who, by that time, were dead are generally admissible. This is a recognised exception to the rule excluding hearsay evidence.[132] However, statements made by persons now deceased which are precognitions or in the nature of precognitions are inadmissible.[133] Many of these statements are likely to come from Soviet archives. An Extraordinary Comission was formed by the Soviet Union in 1942 to investigate war crimes.[134] This commission interviewed many witnesses, some of whom are now dead. The statements of these witnesses have been used in trials since the war. It seems likely that the prosecution would have to rely on the statements of deceased witnesses which were taken by this commission. In the words of the report, 'It would undoubtedly be helpful if such statements taken from witnesses who have subsequently died, could be admissible in the British Courts'.[135] However, little

---

[131]See note 114 above.

[132]Walker and Walker, *op. cit.*, p. 394-395; D. Field, *The Law of Evidence in Scotland* (Edinburgh, 1988), pp. 325-328; A. B. Wilkinson, *The Scottish Law of Evidence* (Edinburgh, 1986), pp. 49-51; Dickson *Evidence,* paras. 266-273; *H.M. Advocate* v. *Monson* (1893) 1 Adam 114, (1893) 21 R.(J.) 5.

[133]*Hall* v. *Edinburgh Corpn.* 1974 S.L.T. (Notes) 14; *Young* v. *National Coal Board* (O.H.) 1960 S.C. 6.

[134]Report, para. 7.10.

[135]Para. 9.39; *cf.* Green, *op. cit.*, pp. 223-224.

consideration seems to have been given to the problems likely to be encountered by the defence in confronting such evidence. These difficulties are outlined below.

First, there is the possibility that these testimonies are in the nature of precognitions. We may readily approve of Lord Cameron's view expressed in *Irving* v. *H.M. Advocate*[136] that 'the function of the police . . . in pursuing these inquiries is not a search for support of a partisan view of an issue to be litigated between adversaries in a private litigation but is the vindication of public justice'.[137] However, questions about the impartiality of the Soviet investigators working for the Extraordinary Commission must be raised, as the report recognises.[138] The statements taken may support a partisan view.

Secondly, the circumstances in which such statements were made may not be ascertainable. This point was made by Lord Hailsham of St Marylebone when he quoted a letter he had received from the Baltic Council on the proposal 'to use recorded statements of persons now deceased (without any apparent regard for the possible duress under which the statements may have been made) . . . '.[139]

Thirdly, there may well be no way of verifying the identity of the purported source of such a statement.

Finally, the defence will obviously have no opportunity to cross-examine a witness in relation to such evidence. Also, on a practical point, it has to be questioned whether the defence will be afforded the resources necessary to research statements of potential defence witnesses. While the report rightly recognises that 'it would be for the trial judge to comment on the weight to be attached to such evidence where the accused has not had the opportunity to cross

---

[136]1978 J.C. 28.
[137]*Ibid.*, at p. 34.
[138]Para. 9.41; *cf.* Green, *op. cit.*, p. 227.
[139]513 H.L. Deb. (December 4, 1989), col. 630.

examine the witness',[140] a conviction on the basis of such evidence alone might be unsafe.

The report also recommended that wartime archives should be admissible if they were authenticated by the archivist.[141] This recommendation shows little consideration of safeguards for the defence and its enactment would be unfortunate. Much of the criticism above applies equally to such archive evidence. Moreover, there must be an opportunity for the independent authentication of archives as forgeries are by no means unknown. The credibility of the archivist should also be tested. Furthermore, to sift through this evidence, an army of archivists and translators will probably be needed. That will inevitably stretch the resources of the defence. Once again the possibility of a violation of the provisions of art. 6 (3)(b) and (d) of the European Convention should be borne in mind.

Conclusions

The Act strikes at a real evil, and the onus is on its critics to show that it will do more harm than good. In the light of the foregoing remarks, it is submitted that that has indeed been shown. The fact that it was extraterritorial in effect is merely remarkable, but on the issue of retrospection it risks damaging a principle of law previously thought to be beyond question. While it cannot be denied that what is involved is a real moral dilemma in which there are persuasive arguments on both sides, nevertheless it is unfortunate to exchange the clear and time-honoured principle of *nullum crimen sine lege* for a novel exception of indefinite scope.

However, the selective scope of the Act is quite unjustifiable. Any such legislation should enunciate a general rule and strike at murder and culpable homicide in violation of the laws and customs of war in all times and places prior to the enactment of the Geneva Conventions Act 1957.

---

[140]Para. 9.41.
[141]Para. 9.42.

On the question of trials, it has been shown that one of three equally unfortunate results may be produced: either the Act will be found to have created a special régime favouring the prosecution by impliedly repealing the law on delay, or every prosecution will founder on that objection, or the plea of delay will become untenable in all criminal cases involving a delay of less than 50 years.

A special régime may also result in as much as acceptance of the report's recommendations would involve making available methods of obtaining evidence in war crimes trials which would not be available in other criminal proceedings.

While the precedents suggest pre-trial publicity would not prejudice an accused to the extent that a trial would have to be abandoned, the success of a plea in bar of trial on this ground could not be ruled out.

If trials proceed, underlying the difficulties and expense is the problem of whether, in relation to these events, a jury could now reach firm conclusions. If not, no prosecution could succeed; on the other hand, the authors of the report concluded that in certain cases the verdicts would be beyond reasonable doubt. Whichever is the case, the courts will need to bear in mind the peculiar evidential difficulties inherent in these cases.

Even if there may be two views on the merits of the Act, it has to be questioned whether such reforms to our system of criminal justice should be enacted in pursuit of particular suspects who have been identified beforehand. That is not the way to secure objective and dispassionate debate. Suspects and principles must be considered independently. Parliament must ask itself whether such reforms are generally desirable in all cases and, if not, how it can justify a special regime for war crimes. The presumption of innocence and the equality of all citizens before the law are at issue. "Our standards of justice should not be a further casualty of these awful events."[142]

---

[142]Lord Irvine of Lairg, 519 H.L. Deg. (June 4, 1990), col. 1088.

11

IN DEFENCE OF THE ACCUSED: ASPECTS OF CRIMINAL PRACTICE DURING THE EMSLIE YEARS

Charles N. Stoddart

Introduction

On 29th November 1958 James Little killed his father by striking him with an axe and stabbing him with a knife in their home at Locharbriggs, Dumfries. A few days later he walked into Carlisle Police Station. According to the police, he said he wanted to be arrested for murder. The police duly obliged after finding the body of the deceased in the bathroom of the house; they also found that the sum of £37 was missing. James was charged with capital murder, for in those days murder done in the furtherance of theft carried the death penalty. So began the case of *H.M. Advocate* v. *Little*, unreported in the law reports but noteworthy in the present context for quite a different reason.

The accused stood trial at a sitting of the High Court at Dumfries in March 1959. The judge was Lord Cameron, presiding over his second capital case within the year; his last experience of that awesome duty had been in Glasgow, where the notorious multiple murderer Peter Manuel had occupied so much of his judicial time. Little's case was to be much shorter, less arduous and destined to end in a different result.

In evidence, Little admitted the killing, which had followed a period of domestic disharmony. The real issue was his state of mind at the time, for there was evidence that he had a mental age of ten. Two distinguished psychiatrists were called for the defence; one of them, Sir David Henderson, then Emeritus Professor of Psychiatry at Edinburgh University, told the jury that the accused had a psychopathic personality, that he was backward both intellectually and emotionally, that he was of less than normal responsibility and 'verging on insanity'. This vital evidence caused the spectre of the supreme penalty to recede from the case; it disappeared completely when Lord Cameron directed the jury that there was, in fact, no evidence that the killing had occurred in the course, or in further-ance, of any theft. Thus, the jury were left to ponder the choice of conviction for murder or culpable homicide on the grounds of diminished responsibility. Like so many previous juries faced with the same problem, they brought in the latter verdict. Little was sentenced to fifteen years imprisonment.

Throughout the whole proceedings, his legal advisers repre-sented him gratuitously, for like most persons on serious criminal charges, Little could not afford to pay the cost of his defence. The fees of his experts were met by the Crown, as the then usual arrangements had been made for their names to be added to the Crown list of witnesses for payment. In addition, some contribu-tion to defence outlays was made from central funds. Those were the days before criminal legal aid had been introduced; Little was on the Poor's Roll.[1] Senior and junior counsel, along with Little's solicitor, thus assumed the burden of defending a man on a capital charge for no fee. That may seem strange from today's standpoint; then, it was (and had been for centuries) the norm.

The reader will have guessed by this time that Little's defence was led by George Carlyle Emslie, Q.C. Like him, the other members of the defence team were later to rise to judicial office: Peter McNeill, junior counsel at the trial, later became sheriff at Glasgow and is now at Edinburgh; while Little's solicitor, Robert Hay, having been instructed by the accused while carrying out his first

---

[1] The Poor's Roll was of great antiquity, having its roots in the act 1424 c. 45; A.P.S. 1424 c. 24.

spell of duty as agent for the poor in Dumfries Sheriff Court, now holds the office of sheriff principal in the sheriffdom of North Strathclyde.

The nature of criminal defence work has changed radically since James Little had the benefit of their combined skills. In this essay, some of those changes which span Lord Emslie's professional life are examined, with particular emphasis on how criminal legal aid came to be introduced, the struggle thereafter by the profession to obtain proper payment for work done and the risks for future accused persons if present proposals to change the rules on legal representation are carried through.

The years before 1951

When Lord Emslie was called to the bar in 1948 the representation of persons accused of crime, particularly in summary cases, was characterised by a general lack of professionalism. By comparison with today's pressured caseload the work of the criminal courts was light. In the High Court of Justiciary the number of cases both on circuit and in Edinburgh was minimal; in many sheriff courts a jury trial was a rare event: while in the sheriff summary criminal court there was nothing approaching the frenetic litigation so familiar to modern practitioners. As for the district court, it had not yet been invented: minor criminal cases were tried in the burgh or police courts throughout Scotland.[2] Lack of numbers meant lack of interest from the profession; and that lack of interest permeated through the work of the courts to the study of criminal law, as well as its practice. Few bothered to research, write upon or stimulate discussion in one of the most intrinsically Scottish parts of our legal system, with the result that it was in danger of atrophy. Additionally, there appears to have been a great degree of professional

---

[2]These inferior summary criminal courts were abolished with the passing of the District Courts (Scotland) Act 1975.

disdain in many quarters towards criminal practice, arising not just from the likely lack of reward usually implicit in accepting instructions in a case, but also from the view that accused persons were not 'worthy of the lawyer's efforts'. Representation in criminal cases was also patchy in a geographical sense, again particularly in summary cases which were often the most time consuming.[3]

The problems evident at the beginning of Lord Emslie's legal career had their roots in history, but were particularly acute just as he entered the profession. Then, there was great uncertainty as to the statutory basis on which legal representation was to be provided to accused persons. For almost four centuries the only provisions governing this matter had been two Acts of the Scots Parliament passed in 1587. By the Act 1587 c. 38 (A.P.S. 1587 c. 16) it was provided

> 'That na Advocate, nor Praeloquutour, be nawaies stopped, to compeir, defend and reason for onie person accused in Parliament for treason, or utherwaies: Bot that quhatsumever partie accused sall have full libertie to provide himselfe of Advocates and Praeloquutoures, in competent number to defend his life, honour and land, against quhatsumever accusation; Seing the intending thereof, suld not prejudge the parties of all lauchfull defences: as gif it were *pro confesso*, that the accusation were trew . . .'

Further, the Act 1587, c. 91 (A.P.S. 1587, c. 57) appeared to confirm the competency of legal representation thus:

> 'And that all and quhatsumever lieges of this Realme, accused of treason, or for quhatsumever crime, sall have their Advocates and Procuratoures, to use all the lauchfull defences quhom the Judge sall compell to procure for thame in case of their refusal; that the sute of the accuser be not tane pro confesso and the party accused prejudged in ony sute before he be convicted of lauchfull trial.'

---

[3]For a description of the prevailing practice, see the Guthrie Report on Legal Aid in Criminal Proceedings (1960) Cmnd. 1015, Chap. III.

Alison commented on the latter statute thus:

'In terms of this excellent enactment which has ever since been and still is *in viridi observantia* every prisoner whether charged with the highest or the lowest offence is equally entitled to the benefit of legal assistance; and it is invariably afforded to him insomuch that if the prisoner has not previously applied for Counsel or solicitor, the Court will assign them to him as soon as the diet is called.'[4]

Alison's view provided the bedrock for the assumption by the profession of the burden of criminal defence work as if a right to representation existed under the Act. What gradually evolved over the centuries was a system whereby the agents for the poor appointed for civil cases would also undertake the defence of accused persons in the sheriff court, whether on indictment or on summary complaint. If the accused was to appear in the High Court, the local agent would instruct one of the counsel for the poor appointed annually by the Faculty of Advocates at its anniversary meeting. In very serious cases such as murder, senior counsel would accept instructions as a matter of professional duty, in conformity with the long tradition of such representation carried on by the Faculty.

Throughout the nineteenth century at least, there was little uniformity of practice and often little preparation for the defence, particularly in cases before the High Court on circuit. One commentator writing in 1891 bemoaned the absence of remuneration as the prime cause for the unsatisfactory state of affairs. As he put it:

'At present about 225 persons are acquitted by juries annually. A sum equal to the salary of one Advocate-Depute would pay for their defence; but while the state provides a Lord Advocate, a Solicitor-General, four ordinary and one or two extra Advocates-Depute, and

---

[4]Alison, *Principles and Practice of the Criminal Law of Scotland* (1833) vol. ii, pp. 370-371.

an army of Procurators-Fiscal at the public expense for their prosecution, and appoints Agents for the defence and Counsel also in the High Court, it leaves the poor agents to bear the whole expenses, except those of the witnesses. In other words, the cost of punishing the guilty is borne by the nation; that of defending the innocent poor by about a hundred young men.'[5]

I pause to observe that the numbers of advocates-depute has doubled in the century since those words were written; like the cases they process, their numbers reflect the troubles of the time. But the Crown Office of those days did not have to staff many circuits simultaneously in different parts of Scotland, nor deal with a huge volume of paperwork from the lower courts which is its modern daily chore.

By the early and mid-twentieth century, reform (so far as concerned the defence) was in the air. The Morton Committee recommended[6] the setting up of a legal aid system, which the existing arrangements palpably were not; and eventually the Legal Aid and Solicitors (Scotland) Act 1949 was passed, providing a new statutory base for legal aid in criminal causes. But only those sections of the Act dealing with civil cases were brought into force immediately; criminal legal aid as we know it today was still fifteen years away.

Another major difficulty emerged in 1951. In a famous judgment Lord Justice-General Cooper torpedoed Alison's notion that the Act of 1587 c.91 granted every accused person, rich or poor, a statutory right to be provided by the court with gratuitous legal assistance for the conduct of his defence.[7] This judgment, and its

---

[5] J. M. Lees 'The Defence of the Poor' (1891) 7 *Scottish Law Review* 209 at pp. 212-213. The reference to 'young men' indicates that the poor's agency, at least in the cities, was generally the province of the newly-admitted (and inexperienced) practitioner.

[6] *Report of the Poor Persons' Representation (Scotland) Committee* (1937) Cmnd. 5435.

[7] *Graham* v. *Cuthbert* 1951 J.C. 25.

implications, require more than just cursory examination, for it was vital in changing practice and shaping attitudes in the succeeding years.

The impact of Graham v. Cuthbert

The case concerned five men who were charged on summary complaint before the sheriff court at Fort William. At their first appearance they were represented by a local solicitor who was prepared to act for them on a fee-paying basis. But no fee was forthcoming from the accused, who then approached the poor's agent in Dumbarton for assistance. The agent took some precognitions and sent them to Fort William to be dealt with by the poor's agent there. But the only poor's agent in Fort William was the same solicitor who had originally appeared. At the trial diet he asked for and was granted leave to withdraw from the case. The accused then elected to conduct their own defences, were convicted and appealed against their convictions on the ground that the sheriff had failed to appoint a solicitor to act for them, as it was allegedly his duty to do in terms of the Act of 1587 c.91, and that his failure to do so had resulted in a miscarriage of justice. Their appeal was rejected by the High Court on three grounds.

Firstly, the court rejected the argument that the Act of 1587 c.91 granted every accused person, *rich* or *poor* a statutory right to be provided by the court with gratuitous legal assistance for the conduct of his defence. Lord Justice-General Cooper doubted:

'... whether the Act of 1587 had anything whatever to do with the provision by the Court of counsel for the defence, either to poor or to rich. The problem in 1587 was an entirely different one, *viz:* to remove some of the scandals which then disgraced the criminal administration of the time, and habitually led to the accused being condemned (and often executed) unheard ('tane *pro confesso*'); ...'[8]

---

[8] *Ibid.*, at p. 29.

According to Lord Cooper, all that the Act of 1587 c.91 did was to authorise the presentation of the defence case by an advocate whom the accused had *himself* already retained under the Act of 1587 c.38. The accepted practice of the High Court in requiring the presence of counsel to defend 'poor' prisoners, said Lord Cooper, was not so much forced upon the legal profession by the court as accepted by the profession as a *munus publicum* and had nothing at all to do with the Act of 1587 c.91.

> 'But it was only afterwards, when distance had lent enchantment to the view of sixteenth century criminal 'justice' that Alison by a patriotic anachronism ascribed the . . . practice . . . to the Act 1587 c.91, and for the first time invested that statute with something of the glamour which once attached in England (and with no greater justification) to Magna Carta.'[9]

The second ground for the rejection of the appeal was much simpler; none of the accused claimed to be even *prima facie* poor persons. Whatever may have been the statutory justification (if any) for the practice of providing of gratuitous legal services, those services were owed by the Act of 1587 c.91 only to poor persons.

Finally, Lord Cooper startled the twentieth century legal profession by saying that, in his view, the Act of 1587 c.91 did not and never had applied to the sheriff court. Since the criminal jurisdiction of that court was extremely limited in the sixteenth century and long after, there was very little opportunity for legal assistance, most criminal trials at that time being taken by the Justice-General or by one of the many holders of special Commissions of Justiciary, or by Barony, Regality or burgh courts.

This decision completely undercut any basis for current practice. With this additional burden the profession began seriously to call in question the *munus publicum* referred to by Lord Cooper. In the early years of civil legal aid it had been confidently expected that the

---

[9] *Ibid.*, at p. 30.

provisions of the 1949 Act relating to criminal legal aid would be introduced quickly. But by the mid 1950s it was clear that this was not so. Firstly, the prospective cost was spiralling: based on the number of criminal cases for 1952, 1953 and 1954, one estimate put the annual cost at £429,000 taking into account both fees payable to the profession and administrative costs. Secondly, the experience of the working of civil legal aid cast doubt on whether the 1949 Act provisions were apt to deal with criminal cases, particularly in relation to checking financial eligibility if a case went to trial. The solution to these difficulties was inevitably the reference of the whole matter to a new inquiry.

The Guthrie Committee

In December, 1957 a committee under the chairmanship of the late Lord Guthrie was appointed with the following terms of reference:

> 'To review the provisions of the Legal Aid (Scotland) Act 1949 so far as they relate to criminal proceedings and to consider whether, and if so to what extent, they should be varied in the light of the experience gained of the operation of that Act in relation to civil proceedings and any other relevant circumstances.'

Its report appeared in May 1960 and, after a review of the historical background to date, contained a detailed survey of the then-existing arrangements for the legal assistance of poor persons facing criminal charges.[10]

As far as the sheriff court was concerned, the committee noted the informality of the practice whereby the agents for the poor appointed under Rules 152-158 of Schedule 1 to the Sheriff Courts (Scotland) Act 1907 acted for accused persons and the fact that the arrangements varied from area to area. Whereas in Glasgow each agent for the poor did a 'duty week' once every six months, in

---

[10] *Legal Aid in Criminal Proceedings (the Guthrie Report)* (1960) Cmnd. 1015.

Dumfries the duty period was for three months at a time. Variations were also noted in different parts of Scotland regarding the point at which legal assistance for the accused was provided before the accused's production to the court, the financial eligibility for representation as a poor person and the type of case in which representation was afforded. Apparently the only matter in which the practice throughout Scotland was consistent was that once an accused person had been accepted as a client by an agent for the poor, the agent carried out for him all the functions carried out by a solicitor on behalf of a client in criminal proceedings, whether the trial was summary or on indictment. The committee noted that in the High Court of Justiciary formal arrangements existed for counsel to appear on behalf of poor persons in sittings of the court in Edinburgh and on the Glasgow circuit, but that at circuit sittings in other towns no such formality existed, local agents often drawing upon the services of counsel eligible for the Glasgow circuit. The services of a solicitor in High Court cases were always available: either the local agent for the poor or a member of the W.S. or S.S.C. Societies if the trial was in Edinburgh High Court. Appeals to the High Court under the Criminal Appeal (Scotland) Act 1926 were similarly covered, but this did not extend to representation of poor persons in the Justiciary Appeal Court.

The committee then went on to consider the main criticisms of the existing arrangements in the High Court and the sheriff court. It was satisfied that it was no longer reasonable for the legal profession to continue to act for accused persons without adequate remuneration. Nor was the quality of service all that it might be, due to the absence in some cases of a satisfactory relationship between solicitor and client based on mutual trust and understanding. Further, the absence of any uniform standard of financial eligibility was a regular source of abuse: the assessment of the accused person's means was frequently rough and ready. In the inferior summary courts, the absence of legal assistance for the accused, especially where the court was presided over by lay magistrates, meant that there were risks of miscarriages of justice.

The future form of criminal legal aid was thereafter discussed in detail against the background of the skeletal provisions of the 1949 Act and the experience gained in civil cases. In particular, it was noted that the same financial conditions applied in criminal cases as in civil, if legal aid was required for a trial or appeal, and that an accused person might be required to make a contribution to the cost of the proceedings.[11]

A number of criticisms were expressed to the committee by witnesses concerned with possible abuses by accused persons and solicitors, and the high demands which would be placed on the legal profession if criminal legal aid were introduced in a similar form as for civil cases under the 1949 Act. Some of these criticisms had more validity than others, but it was on the question of financial eligibility and its determination that most witnesses agreed that the civil provisions were impracticable. For instance, how could one accurately project an applicant's income for the next twelve months if he were to be found guilty and sent to jail? The 'irregular lives' of criminals would in any event make it difficult to ascertain their resources; if they were obligated to make contributions to the cost of their defence, those contributions would be difficult to collect.

These criticisms led the committee to review what it considered were the only two alternative methods of providing legal aid in criminal cases. The first, supported by the majority of the professional bodies, was that the 1949 Act provisions should be introduced, although with modifications. The second alternative, also with its supporters, was that the existing system should continue, again with some improvements, on the view that to introduce the 1949 Act provisions would be costly and inconvenient. When comparing these proposals the committee emphasised its conclusion that it was unreasonable to expect the legal profession to

---

[11] *Ibid.*, paras. 81 *et seq.*

continue to carry the financial burden of representation. Since the state would have to assume this, it would be inappropriate for any sum distributable to the profession to be simply provided without the introduction of proper accounting for work done. The administrative cost would thus be incurred in any event and it was perhaps this consideration above all which impelled the committee to conclude that the state should take over the financial burden which rested on the profession and that proper payments should be made from state funds to the profession based on records of work done. The balance of advantage thus lay with the discontinuance of the existing system.

The main recommendation of the committee were generally that legal aid should be available as a right in all cases before courts of solemn jurisdiction; in sheriff summary proceedings where the offence was punishable with imprisonment without the option of a fine; and in all other sheriff court and other summary court proceedings only where a legal aid certificate had been granted in the discretion of the court.[12] Financial eligibility was to be determined by the court on the basis of a written declaration by the applicant; no contribution would be payable by a successful applicant. Prior to the determination of financial eligibility, any arrested accused (irrespective of his means) would be entitled to legal aid in solemn proceedings until admitted to bail or fully committed; in summary proceedings until the conclusion of the first diet at which he was called upon to plead; and for proceedings relating to any application for bail following that diet. Legal aid for the purposes of an appeal would be granted only if there were substantial grounds for the appeal; financial eligibility would be determined by the court. Recommendations were also made as to the extent of the service to be provided by the profession, in particular regarding the employment of counsel and the setting up of local duty rotas. The

---

[12] *Ibid.*, paras. 118, 120.

Law Society of Scotland would prescribe the services which a legal aid solicitor conducting a trial was authorised to provide without specific sanction.

After the Guthrie Report

Although the committee recommended total implementation of their proposals, as opposed to partial introduction of legal aid in criminal cases in the High Court and sheriff court, there was in fact further delay. The Law Society formulated a list of observations on the Guthrie Report and in general found themselves in agreement with the report's proposals. The society was however opposed to the extension of criminal legal aid to the inferior summary courts, mainly on the ground of economy; it also had some reservations on the proposal that the 'certifying authority' in first instance cases was to be the court, due to the lack of uniformity in decision-making which it (correctly) foresaw. Reservations were also expressed on the absence of statutory guidelines on financial eligibility and in appeal cases of the proposed dual determination on eligibility. The society also regretted the rejection of their proposal that payment of fees should be on the principle of 'fair remuneration according to work actually and reasonably done'.

A year later, in June 1961, a parliamentary question produced the response that the government was still considering the report, but it was clear that the existing system was reaching breaking point. In July 1961 the Law Society of Scotland presented a memorial for the opinion of counsel[13] in which it expressed its concern at the increasing burden which was being borne by the profession in representing without adequate remuneration accused persons in the High Court and the sheriff court and commenting on the absence of legislation to follow the recommendations of the Guthrie Committee. The memorial drew attention to proposals

---

[13]The Law Society instructed the then Dean of Faculty W. I. R. Fraser Q.C. (later Lord Fraser of Tullybelton) for this opinion.

which had been made in May 1961 by the Ayr Faculty of Solicitors to restrict their services to the genuine poor, and sought counsel's opinion as to the extent of the service which it was by law incumbent upon solicitors to provide in criminal causes. The five particular questions for his opinion were:

(1) Was a solicitor for the poor in the sheriff court under obligation to act gratuitously for any accused who requested his services no matter what might be the means of the accused person; or

(2) Was he under obligation to act only for accused who were 'poor persons'?

(3) If the answer to question two was in the affirmative, how did the question whether or not an accused was a 'poor person' fall to be determined?;

(4) If the answer to question one or two was in the affirmative:

  (a) did the duty extend to summary proceedings?
  (b) how far did the duty of the solicitor originally instructed extend

    (i)   in the Sheriff Court and
    (ii)   in the High Court?

(5) Was there a legal duty on solicitors to appear in the High Court; and if so what was its extent?

In his opinion of 28th July 1961, counsel agreed with the view taken by Lord Cooper in *Graham* v. *Cuthbert* that Alison was wrong in construing the Act of 1587 c.91 to the effect that *any* accused was entitled to the services of the agent for the poor; question one was thus answered in the negative. Counsel did however take the view that whatever was Lord Cooper's opinion as to the non-applicability of the Act 1587 c.91 to the sheriff court, Rule 159 of the rules in Schedule 1 to the Sheriff Courts (Scotland) Act 1907 was sufficient statutory authority for the proposition that a solicitor for the poor in the sheriff court was obliged to act gratuitously as procurator for accused persons who were 'poor'. Question two was therefore to be answered affirmatively. As regards Question three, counsel's opinion was that the 'poor' persons for whom a solicitor for the poor was bound to act were persons who had been admitted to the benefit of the Poor's roll. Rules 152-169 provided the machinery for admission which, although not operated in practice in criminal cases, was strictly speaking appropriate. Counsel went on to confirm that the duty to act extended to summary cases. In the sheriff court it covered the conduct of all proceedings except where counsel was instructed; in the High Court when on circuit, the solicitor was obliged to attend personally on behalf of his 'poor' client or arrange for another solicitor in the circuit town to attend on his behalf. There was, said counsel, no obligation imposed in Rule 159 on the solicitor to act for his 'poor' client in an appeal to the High Court in Edinburgh, but it would be contrary to established practice for him to decline to act. This was the limit of a solicitor's legal duty; there was no legal obligation on the W.S. and S.S.C. societies to appoint agents for persons tried in the High Court in Edinburgh. Finally counsel's opinion was that the custom of acting for poor persons on criminal charges could not be transformed into a legal duty merely because of its longevity.

Meanwhile, the Poor's Roll solicitors in Glasgow and Dumbartonshire became impatient. Before the opinion was issued, they decided to work-to-rule by requiring applicants to produce affidavits setting forth their circumstances, as was required in civil cases. So far as Glasgow was concerned, the insistence on the affidavit was to be confined in the first instance to court appearances after the first diet, but the agents subsequently intimated that from 4th September 1961 they would require affidavits for all appearances. The Law Society deprecated such action due to the potential hardship and dislocation which would be inevitable, and the solicitors reconsidered their position in the light of the opinion of counsel which was then available. In the result, the date for operating the full affidavit procedure was postponed to 31st December 1961. Two weeks before this deadline, the Secretary of State for Scotland announced that the government accepted in principle the Guthrie Committee's recommendation that there should be statutory legal aid in criminal cases on the lines of the 1949 Act. That Act would however require amendment and the details remained to be finalised. The Glasgow agents were not mollified by this statement and from 1st March 1962 commenced their work-to-rule. Further parliamentary questions were asked; it appeared that during the first week of the disruption 157 persons appearing from custody at Glasgow Sheriff Court were not legally represented. On 12th March, the Lord Advocate refused to direct procurators-fiscal at Glasgow Sheriff Court to advise accused persons on completing the affidavits of means supplied by the agents.

Eventually after an assurance that the government was considering legal aid legislation for 1962-1963, the agents in Glasgow called off their action. In October 1962 the Criminal Justice (Scotland) Bill was introduced; included therein was a clause amending the 1949 Act. The main effect of this proposed amendment was fourfold:

(1) the provisions of the 1949 Act relating to the ascertainment of means in civil cases would *not* apply to criminal cases. Under s. 2(2) of the Act as amended, there would be no means test initially in either solemn or summary proceedings where the accused was in custody. In all other cases, means would be considered in summary fashion by *the Court,* the criterion being whether the accused was unable without undue hardship to himself or his dependents to meet the expenses of the case;

(2) legal aid would be granted or refused (except in appeals) by order of the court and *not* by local Legal Aid Committees or the Supreme Court Committee;

(3) in summary cases, except where the proceedings were being concluded by a plea of guilty tendered at the first diet, the court would also have to consider whether it was in the interests of justice that legal aid should be given; and

(4) the assisted person would *not* be required to pay any contribution if he was admitted to legal aid, and the reference to *probabilis causa* in sec. 1 (6) of the 1949 Act, which was inappropriate for criminal cases, was deleted.

The differences in these provisions from what was proposed in the Guthrie report will be evident: summary cases were to be included whether or not the offence was punishable with imprisonment without the option of a fine. It also became clear that legal aid was not to be available in the inferior courts of summary jurisdiction; the relevant commencement order on this matter was not to be made until 1975 with the passing of the District Courts (Scotland) Act.[14] The reason for this non-introduction was the feeling that initially there was no widespread public demand for such an extension and the Law Society's view that it would involve an unwarrantable expenditure of public money.

Criticism of these provisions was confined to two matters: firstly, the sheriffs did not approve of the system whereby they would determine applications for legal aid for criminal trials. They were given little guidance on what constituted 'undue hardship' or what constituted 'the interests of justice' in summary cases. Their fears on this point appear to have been amply justified, for the practice which subsequently arose varied widely from sheriff to sheriff and court to court.[15] Secondly, the inclusion of all summary cases in the scheme caused many to believe that the number of persons pleading

---

[14]District Courts (Scotland) Act 1975, sec. 21.

[15]If anything, the position was even worse when legal aid became available in the District Court after 1975.

not guilty and going to trial would increase dramatically. This proved rather more difficult to assess accurately, although it was clear that the criminal case load of the courts did increase.

Even after the Criminal Justice (Scotland) Act 1963 was passed, criminal legal aid was not introduced until October 1964 because of the necessity of preparing the relative scheme, regulations and Acts of Adjournal prescribing rules of procedure and fees. These were to bring their own problems of interpretation and application, one of which was entirely predictable; as the years passed there emerged increasing difficulty with the test that legal aid for summary cases had to be 'in the interests of justice'. In some courts a liberal attitude was displayed by the bench and the rate of granting legal aid was high. In other courts it was sometimes extremely hard to convince the sheriff that he should grant an application; in Glasgow there arose a practice of holding a 'legal aid court' each afternoon at which an applicant was required to appear and state his defence, usually with an anxious solicitor-to-be hovering on the sidelines.[16]

Another major problem was fees, and in particular fees for cases of exceptional length, complexity or difficulty. This running sore festered for over a quarter of a century; it is gone now but it remains etched in the memories of all those who practised criminal law during the period. Its story should be briefly re-told here, if only to rejoice in the fact that it is concluded.

13(2) and all that

Ever since the beginning of criminal legal aid the Scottish Home and Health Department has always been concerned about increases in the cost of proceedings. It has little control over expenditure from the standpoint of the number of cases in the system: the more prosecutions, the more defence costs will be incurred. But long

---

[16]See Act of Adjournal (Rules for Legal Aid in Criminal Proceedings) 1964, sec. 4 (1).

before the Secretary of State first assumed the right to fix legal aid fees, the department was apprehensive as to abuse of the provisions and mindful of the perceived need to keep the cost within manageable limits. Meanwhile, the profession has always sought proper remuneration for work done. From 1964 onwards, there were prescribed maximum fees for trial work, but there was also a provision to cover exceptional cases. The provision quickly became known as '13(2)', being a reference to sec. 13(2) of the Act of Adjournal (Criminal Legal Aid Fees) 1964 as subsequently amended.

At the inception of criminal legal aid in 1964, the form of words used in the original Act of Adjournal gave no hint of the difficult years ahead. By the original sec. 13(1) it was provided that the determination of the sum to be allowed to a solicitor should take into account all the relevant circumstances, including the nature, importance, complexity or difficulty or the work and the time involved (including waiting days) and should include such amount as appeared to represent fair remuneration for the work actually and reasonably done. The original sec. 13(2) was in these terms:

> 'If it appears at any time after the final disposal of the case that for *any* reason, *including* the exceptional length, complexity or difficulty of the case, the sums payable by virtue of the foregoing paragraphs or any of them would not provide fair remuneration according to the work actually and reasonably done by the solicitor, then any limitation contained in these provisions on the amount of any fee payable shall not apply and such fees shall be allowed, after taking into account all the relevant circumstances of the case, in respect of the work done as appear to represent fair remuneration according to the work actually and reasonably done.'

Accordingly, the guiding principle was 'fair remuneration for work actually and reasonably done'. The statutory maxmimum fees would not apply not only in cases of exceptional length, complexity or difficulty, but also if for any other reason the fees chargeable would not represent fair remuneration. If the solicitor could justify his charges to the Central Committee or, in a disputed case to the auditor, he would be paid from the Fund. Most striking of all was the absence of any reference to a scale of charging or to any means by which there could be certified that the case met the criteria of 'exceptional'. Certification by the court was, at that time, not necessary.

By 1967 the adjustment of solicitor's accounts, especially in exceptional cases, was causing the Legal Aid Central Committee much difficulty. Section 13(2) was being increasingly invoked. A 13(2) certificate became a prize almost as important as an acquittal; without it, many criminal trials were hopelessly uneconomic. But the Central Committee was unable to obtain any guidance on the proper approach to the section, as auditors of court were reluctant to consider its applicability. The Scottish Home and Health Department became perturbed at the rising cost of legal aid in criminal causes and initially proposed that sec. 13(2) should be repealed. Although this was successfully opposed, the department insisted that certification of the applicability of this section should be dealt with otherwise than by the Law Society or the auditors of court; it should be put into the hands of the trial judge who had observed the conduct of the case.

Protracted negotiations were carried on between the Law Society and the department towards the end of 1968. The department maintained its insistence that certification should be placed in the hands of the court; the Law Society drew the department's attention to the fact that in England the government appeared prepared to accept that the adjudication of fees should be carried out by the Law Society of England. In December 1968 a new Act of Adjournal was prepared providing for certification by the court, which brought matters to a head. The Glasgow Legal Aid Committee received a letter from the Glasgow Bar Association intimating that the association held over 100 letters of resignation signed by solicitors on the Glasgow criminal legal aid lists and that these were to be lodged with the committee to take effect on 2nd January 1969 if the new Act of Adjournal in its present terms came into operation on that date. In spite of disapproval from the Law Society's Council, the Act was introduced on the due date and 102 solicitors in Glasgow resigned from the list.

This 'strike' was criticised on many sides as not being in accordance with the standards of conduct which the profession should seek to uphold. Eventually the emotional atmosphere lessened and many solicitors returned to the lists, but the Council expressed its great regret that an Act of Adjournal had been passed to which strong exception had been taken by the solicitors' governing body.

The main point of difference between the department and the Society related of course to the particular authority (*i.e.* the judge) on whom was conferred the exclusive right to determine whether or not sec. 13(2) was to apply. The Society maintained that the right should have remained with them in order to achieve uniformity and to avoid the undignified procedure of a solicitor having (in effect) to grovel for his fees. The Society correctly foresaw that some of its members would regard this as a highly demeaning experience.[17]

The new sec. 13(2) provided for an application to the trial judge for a certificate that the case had necessarily been one of exceptional length, complexity or difficulty. If such a certificate was granted then limitations on the statutory fees would not apply '. . . and such fees shall be allowed, after taking into account all the relevant circumstances of the case, in respect of the work done as appears to represent fair remuneration according to the work actually and reasonably done due regard being had to economy'. The contrast with the original provisions was stark. Under them, fair remuneration was to be paid in all cases, the exceptional length, complexity or difficulty of the case being merely *one* factor in the assessment. Now the 1968 provisions excluded fair remuneration in all cases of exceptional length, complexity or difficulty where the trial judge

---

[17]In civil cases, no maximum fees then applied and there was no question of a solicitor having to seek certification once his fees had passed a prescribed level.

was not disposed to grant a certificate. In the result, representing an accused in such proceedings became a gamble for the legal advisers; they might spend many hours preparing and conducting the case, but at the end of it receive totally inadequate remuneration if a certificate was refused.

Sadly, judicial attitudes differed. Just as obtaining legal aid for a summary case was fraught with difficulty, an application for a 13(2) certificate often required a thick skin. Some judges would grant certificates in almost all cases which lasted more than a day or two; some would refuse certificates where on any reasonable view the issues were grave and complex, apparently with no recognition of the work done. Few cases appear in the law reports, but the difference in judicial approach is even more striking with the passage of time. In *H.M. Advocate* v. *Gray* 1969 J.C. 35, the accused was found by the police in possession of firearms and explosives. He commented 'You've hit the jackpot.' His advisers prepared for a trial, but at the trial diet the accused pleaded guilty. A certificate under section 13(2) was refused by Lord Wheatley, who held that while a certificate could be justified by the presence of any one of the qualifications of exceptional length, complexity or difficulty, such an application could only be granted if, in the opinion of the presiding judge, the case, *as presented in court*, had necessarily been one of exceptional length, complexity or difficulty, the judge not being called upon to inquire into what happened in the course of preparing the case. In particular, he rejected a submission that 'length' referred to the length of preparation time. Lord Wheatley was of the clear opinion that a certificate could only be granted if there was some special feature present which differentiated the case from a normal case in respect of one or other of the factors mentioned, and this was to be decided from the trial judge's experience of the case as presented in court.

'He is not an inquisitor at large, going, if need by, beyond the confines of the court to check on whether the submissions about the length or complexity or difficulty of the preparation work are justified.'[18]

While no doubt a plea of guilty might have been regarded as inevitable in this case, the point was that some pleas of guilty are appropriate only after full investigation, which can be costly; Lord Wheatley appeared to shut the door on even meritorious cases.

H.M. Advocate v. *Gray* was decided on 8th January 1969, and was the first case in which the new Act of Adjournal was interpreted. In February 1969 in the unreported case of *H.M. Advocate* v. *Flynn,* an application under sec. 13(2) was made to Lord Justice-Clerk Grant. Written grounds were submitted; the application was refused on the ground of 'length' but granted on the ground that the preparation of the case had been one of exceptional complexity or difficulty. In court the matter was disposed of on a plea of guilty, but the submissions concerning the application related to matters which had not emerged in court and would have been most unlikely to emerge even if the case had gone to trial, including difficulties which had arisen in the course of preparing the defence as a result of the accused being an alcoholic and of a very low mental calibre.

In *H.M. Advocate* v. *Kennedy* 1973 S.L.T. (Notes) 57, a change was apparent. Lord Cameron granted a certificate on the ground of exceptional length, holding that 'length' included length of preparation. In that case he adjourned the hearing of the application from open court to chambers and there considered written submissions, counsel's file of precognitions and a rough draft account of expenses, before concluding that there had been a full and proper preparation of the defence. He considered the wording of section 13(1), from which it was clear that 'time' included time spent on preparation, and stated:

'It would be a strange result if that time is to be taken into account in assessing what I may call a 'normal fee' but is to be disregarded

---

[18]1969 J.C. 35, at p. 39.

when considering the 'length of the case' — not the trial — when the issue of a solicitor's right to claim on a written basis is raised. In addition it is the exceptional complexity or difficulty of the *case*, not of the trial, to which attention is to be directed in section 13(2). It would be strange that when considering exceptional complexity or difficulty the case as a whole has to be considered, but upon the issue of exceptional length only the time taken by the trial can be regarded.'[19]

Lord Cameron's view that 'length' included length of preparation was given legislative effect in 1973 in a further amendment of the Act of Adjournal of 1964 when provision was also made for certificates in summary cases. In that rather uneasy state the matter rested until 1976.

At that point in the saga, the Central Committee came under criticism from the Scottish Home and Health Department. It was said that too generous a rate of payment was being made on criminal legal aid accounts and that unscrupulous agents were 'padding' their entries. Conflict between the profession and the department was avoided by the passing of a further Act of Adjournal linking the charges for work done in criminal cases to the then-existing civil scales. Additionally, sec. 13(2) was amended; henceforth the intention was that certification on length would be granted relatively freely, but more sparingly on grounds of complexity or difficulty. The profession adhered to its frequently-expressed view that certification should be removed from the court, but the Act of Adjournal was passed on 2nd March 1976. The result in practice was that certificates on 'length' were granted frequently in the High Court, but certificates on 'complexity' or 'difficulty' became uncommon. The position thus eased, but blips remained. One of these was the absence of a prescribed right of appeal against refusal of certification. In *Heslin, Petitioner* 1973 S.L.T. (Notes) 56

---

[19] 1973 S.L.T. (Notes) 57, at p. 59.

it had been held incompetent to use the mechanism of a petition to the *nobile officium* of the High Court to bring under review such a refusal; but in *Rae, Petitioner* 1982 S.L.T. 233 the High Court (presided over by Lord Emslie) granted such a petition and sustained an argument that one particular refusal had been oppressive.

The assumption in 1983 by the Secretary of State of the responsibility for fixing legal aid fees made no difference to the terms of the provisions dealing with certification. The next staging post was the reform of the legal aid system in 1986. It might have been hoped that this would bring abolition, for the principle of fair remuneration for legal aid work was one of the major planks of the campaign run by the Law Society of Scotland when the detailed proposals became known. But the power to fix fees by regulation remained with the Secretary of State under sec. 33 of the Legal Aid (Scotland) Act 1986, and the setting up of the Scottish Legal Aid Board made no difference to the legal position in respect of fees chargeable. Indeed, the original regulations on criminal legal aid fees promulgated under the 1986 Act were a mirror image of those which had previously applied, except that "13(2)" became "12(1)".[20]

For two further years, matters remained unchanged. Eventually, however, the efforts of the Law Society bore fruit when the Scottish Home and Health Department agreed in 1989, as part of an ongoing review designed to achieve simplicity and standardisation, that 12(1) could go. This was achieved on 31st August 1989 (coincidentally about a month before Lord Emslie retired from the bench) when new fees regulations came into force.[21] Simplified rates were therein prescribed, with no mention of maximum fees

---

[20]Section 13(2) of the Act of Adjournal became sec. 12(1) of the Criminal Legal Aid (Scotland) (Fees) Regulations 1987.

[21]The fees chargeable in criminal cases are now governed by the Criminal Legal Aid (Scotland) (Fees) Regulations 1989 (SI. 1989 No. 1491), as amended.

for trials or appeals and no provision for certification: for a change, the regulations were exceptionally short, simple and easy to understand. Unmourned, certification passed away.

Criminal defence work —present trends and future prospects

With a proper statutory base and proper (if very modest) remuneration, the criminal legal aid system has come a long way during the Emslie years. The same can be said for the practice of criminal law, which has now acquired a far more distinctive niche in our legal life. For a start, criminal law and procedure is taught far more comprehensively and on the basis of far more extensive material than in earlier times. In 1948, the only modern textbook was the 5th edition of Macdonald which, although valuable, was not a discursive or thought-provoking text. Not many criminal cases were reported and few intending specialists entered the area of practice. Today, all that has changed. The student and the practitioner have a variety of texts, some general, some particular, from which to choose; there is now published a specialised series of Scottish Criminal Case Reports;[22] and the periodical literature regularly includes articles and information of current interest to the criminal lawyer. Many solicitors specialise only in criminal work, and a regular band of unofficial specialist counsel are regular attenders at the High Court, both at first instance and on appeal.

None of this has come easily, but it has been an essential feature of the struggle to preserve the unique status of Scots law as a distinctive system. Further, as Lord McCluskey observed in his address to the Annual Conference of the Law Society of Scotland at Gleneagles in 1990, 'Criminal justice is after all almost invariably a better index to a country's civilisation than is civil justice.'

---

[22]This series has proved absolutely invaluable to the practitioner; every criminal case of any importance, including those simply concerned with sentence, appears to be included.

If criminal law is better known, taught and practised now, then Scotland is all the better for it; an area of law and practice which is allowed to wither through disinterest will surely die.

I turn finally to the Law Reform (Miscellaneous Provisions) (Scotland) Act 1990, which continues to generate great controversy. Much has been written and spoken about the risks to our system by the enactment of its provisions, not least of all by Lord Emslie himself in a notable contribution to the debates in the House of Lords.[23] Of particular relevance to this essay are those sections of the Act dealing with rights of audience. For the purposes of the present discussion, the relative sections deal with (a) the extension of the rights of audience in the High Court to solicitors; and (b) the possible extension of rights of audience to other, non legally-qualified persons.[24]

I would venture to suggest that there are some risks to the proper practice of criminal law in the former provisions, but they are as nothing to the risks inherent in the latter.

As to the former, I have never been able to accept the argument that properly qualified and experienced solicitors should not, if they wish, be entitled to exercise advocacy rights in the High Court and that the standard of pleading would drop if they were allowed to do so. Dealing firstly with criminal trials, it has to be remembered that solicitors regularly conduct jury trials before the sheriff in cases which, only a short time ago, would have automatically been indicted into the High Court. Of necessity, Crown counsel mark more and more cases to the sheriff court because of the pressure in obtaining High Court diets. The sheriff can now impose up to three years' imprisonment in indictment cases, and many say that this is not enough. Accordingly, more and more serious cases are coming

---

[23]See H. L. Debates, 5th series, vol. 525, cols. 183-185 (30th January 1990).
[24]Law Reform (Miscellaneous Provisions) (Scotland) Act 1990, sections 24, 25.

into the sheriff court where inevitably more solicitors are gaining greater experience. Just like counsel, some are better at conducting trials than others. In any event counsel do not frequently appear in sheriff and jury trials because of the reluctance of the Scottish Legal Aid Board to sanction their employment. Those solicitors who do conduct jury trials are usually older and more experienced than those who appear in summary cases and have a track record of criminal work.

It is no doubt true that they do not practice advocacy to the exclusion of all else. They have offices to run, staff to pay, overheads to meet and all the hundred and one distractions which counsel can avoid. But they have one advantage: they have been with the case since it started and they are able to use that knowledge to best effect. Unlike counsel who usually come into the case not long before the trial, the solicitor has had contact with the client and has an awareness of the background that are invaluable assets when it comes to conducting the trial.

Proponents of the present system deny these advantages. Counsel's independence is his prime asset, they say: it is precisely because he is one step removed from the hurly burly of the developing case that his skills are of benefit. This however fails to recognise that the lack of so-called independence displayed by the solicitor conducting a trial before sheriff and jury does not, in my experience, prevent him from doing an adequate job in most cases. To prevent a solicitor from appearing in a High Court trial just because of his prior involvement in preparing the case seems to me a flimsy basis for maintaining the status quo. I do however recognise that there would have to be some means of checking the experience of those solicitors who wish to acquire advocacy rights in High Court trials and that a free-for-all is undesirable.

There is however a much stronger argument for not interfering with the present system when we come to consider criminal appeals. Quite apart from all the logistical arguments (to some of which I will return), appeal court pleading is a clear speciality.

Having had a number of years experience as a solicitor instructing counsel both in appeals under the Criminal Procedure (Scotland) Act and in the Justiciary Appeal Court, it is clear to me that a specialist body of pleaders brings considerable benefit both to appellants and to the court itself. The appeal court is at present overwhelmed with work and this is likely to continue. The pressure on the bench to assimilate a large amount of information in a very short time is intense. In that state of affairs, an appellant's legal representative needs to bring to bear on an appeal a peculiar set of skills: he must be able to advise on the grounds of appeal; identify the points quickly; separate the non-essential from the essential, apply to the grounds a considerable knowledge of the law on miscarriages of justice; and above all, have a 'feel' for how the court is reacting or is likely to react when particular points are raised. None of these can be acquired easily, quickly or on the basis of an occasional foray to Edinburgh. I used to instruct counsel drawn from a very small group of regular attenders, as did most Edinburgh agents in the circumstances. It was (and still is) very much a case of 'horses for courses'.

Now it may be that solicitors would be able to acquire such skills: in theory at least. But the way the profession operates at present militates against this, and simply to pass a law allowing solicitors to appear in criminal appeals is unlikely to promote the maintenance of current standards. While some solicitors are accustomed to pleading in serious trials before sheriff and jury, no solicitors are accustomed to pleading in the appeal court.

Quite apart from the lack of experience, there are a host of practical reasons why solicitors are unlikely to exercise any advocacy rights which they may be given. Take a typical day in the Justiciary Appeal Court. About thirty cases may be listed including the usual mixed batch of notes of appeal against sentence and appeals by stated case, with perhaps an occasional bill of suspension or advocation thrown in. The published list may be cut down a bit by abandonments before hearing. The court sits at 10.30 a.m. and starts the list from the top. Thereafter the waiting begins. Solicitor X from Kilmarnock or Y from Wick may have to hang about all day waiting for his one appeal to call. Even then it may not be reached or completed; it might be continued to the next day. For all this he would receive (under the present system) a paltry sum from the Scottish Legal Aid Board for his advocacy and waiting time and have lost much more than the equivalent remuneration by his absence from Kilmarnock or Wick. This assumes the present rules on criminal legal aid fees remain unchanged and that his attendance in Edinburgh is sanctioned. By contrast, the present system whereby a small number of Edinburgh agents on behalf of local solicitors instruct a small group of counsel is efficient and relatively inexpensive, since both those agents and counsel are likely to be in Parliament House all day for other reasons anyway and can quite easily arrange their respective schedules round appeal court sittings. I cannot think that improvements to justice will flow from abandoning this well-tried system.

Turning lastly to the provisions under which non-legally qualified persons may be able to practice in the courts under a scheme whereby their qualifications, expertise and organisation are approved, the less said about this the better. A criminal trial is not like a small claim with no rules, where the judge can (if he chooses) be an arbiter. It is a serious judicial proceeding where the liberty of the subject is often involved; both sides require to be represented by properly qualified lawyers to ensure that justice in its widest sense is done.

It is thought that extended rights of audience for solicitors will be a reality by the end of 1992. How the system will operate in practice remains to be seen. But whatever the outcome, the public have much for which to thank criminal lawyers; as we stand at a crossroads, we should heed Lord Emslie's reminders that those contributions should not be forgotten.

12

GEORGE CARLYLE EMSLIE: A PERSONAL APPRECIATION

The Hon. Lord Grieve

In the months of January, February, and March, 1946, an observant pedestrian, who happened to be at Nithsdale Cross, in the Pollokshields district of Glasgow, at the unearthly hour of 7.30am, might have noticed two young men, with books under their arms, boarding a number 3 tram for the University. No matter how observant he was however, he would not have realised that one of them, the one with the blue greatcoat, was to become The Lord Justice-General of Scotland and the Lord President of the Court of Session. The other young man was myself. It was the start of a long and enduring friendship.

George and I had known each other in our pre-teenage youth, and indeed had been members of a football team called the Darnley Rovers which played their matches on vacant ground near Maxwell Park. Alas no records exist of that team's achievements, so George's earliest flirtation with the Association code must remain a mystery. Later on however, while at Glasgow University George's experience with the Darnley Rovers resulted in his playing for the University. He retained an interest in football which he shared with his boys, and from time to time, with me and my son. Many a happy Saturday was spent at Easter Road or Tynecastle, or when in the west, at Hampden or Cathkin Park. (Those were the days when football teams not only tried to score goals but often succeeded in doing so!)

His athletic prowess was not limited to football. He was no mean cricketer, playing for Glasgow High School, and their F.P.'s, the

University and later, after the war, for Grange, until the demands of his practice became too exacting. Happily he was able to resume his cricketing career when the annual match between the Faculty of Advocates and a Parliament House XI was started. Many a run did he score over the years. I had the privilege of opening the innings for the Faculty side with George, and, as time went on, we became known as "the two elderly professionals". It was a term of endearment rather than a recognition of ability!

George's interests outwith the law were not limited to sporting ones. He is quite an informed ornithologist, and, there was a time when he was something of an expert on edible fungi. For all I know he may still be. I can confirm his expertise in that sphere because my wife and I were the recipients on occasion of chanterelles which we ate with great enjoyment, and no ill effects.' So there emerges a man of many parts.

So far I have not mentioned what has been for some times George's recreational love, namely golf, now his only form of recreation listed in Debrett. George takes his golf seriously. In all he does he tends to be something of a perfectionist, and his approach to his golf is no exception. He gets very irritated with himself if his game as a whole, or in parts, does not come up to the standard he sets himself. Do not for a moment imagine that he is self centered in his approach; far from it; he gets just as irritated with me if I fail to reach the standard he thinks I should attain! It is all great fun, and despite his serious approach George treats it as such. I have played golf with "the Colonel" as I affectionately dubbed him many years ago, for nearly half a century, with and against, and we are still speaking to each other!

I've been told that some people find George a rather formidable person, difficult to approach. I cannot comment on that except to say that there is a streak of shyness in George's nature, which is perhaps not readily recognised. That illustrates his innate modesty, which is a praiseworthy trait in a person of such distinction.

An interesting insight into the effect George's qualities as a man can have on other people is very well illustrated by what I am now going to tell you.

I sat for a year or two in the First Division with George, Jock Cameron and Gordon Stott. When the day dawned for Gordon to retire, we had, along with a few others, a little party in the Conference Room at lunch time. We drank Gordon's health and wished him well. In reply Gordon said something like this, "I never really wanted to come into the Division, and I never thought I would enjoy it if I did. But I have enjoyed it; much to my surprise it has been great fun." These remarks from a someone who, as his Diaries demonstrate, liked to be, in the jargon of the day, "his own man" was a striking tribute to George as a man. It was not George's judicial qualities which had made the division 'fun', but his personal ones.

George and I have been such close fiends for so many years it has been very difficult for me to stand aside as it were and try to set out some of his many qualities other than his professional ones. I hope I've given a fair picture of George outside Parliament House as it were. But no such picture would be complete without adding this. Behind what may appear to be a formidable exterior there beats a very warm heart, and an ebullient sense of humour, both of which combine to make him not only a good friend, but a very entertaining companion.

INDEX